PURPOSEFUL
PERFORMANCE

CONTENT WARNING:

This book is for mature audiences.

Mental Health
Suicide

PURPOSEFUL PERFORMANCE

The **Secret Mix** of **Connecting, Leading,** and **Succeeding**

JONATHAN STANLEY

EARTHYPILOT PUBLISHING

533 E Girard Ave, Unit #560
Philadelphia, PA 19125

ISBN: 979-8-9906357-0-8 (paperback)
ISBN: 979-8-9906357-1-5 (ebook)
ISBN: 979-8-9906357-2-2 (hardcover)
ISBN: 979-8-9906357-3-9 (audiobook)

Library of Congress Control Number: 2024908932

Ordering Information:
Special discounts are available on quantity purchases by corporations, associations, and others. For details, contact: www.simplestrategicplans.com/contact

Publisher's Cataloging-in-Publication Data
Names: Stanley, Jonathan, 1969- .
Title: Purposeful performance : the secret mix of connecting, leading, and succeeding / by Jonathan Stanley.
Description: Philadelphia, PA : EarthyPilot Publishing, 2024. | Includes bibliographic references. | Includes 1 chart and 4 diagrams. | Summary: Unveils hidden business value by highlighting empathy and meaning for employees, customers, and the community. It emphasizes a crucial yet overlooked element for success, guiding towards a higher purpose. Through aligned actions and values, the framework presented fosters enduring prosperity and positive social impact.
Identifiers: LCCN 2024908932 | ISBN 9798990635722 (hardcover) | ISBN 9798990635708 (pbk.) | ISBN 9798990635715 (ebook)
Subjects: LCSH: Leadership. | Strategic planning. | Business ethics. | Employee morale. | Social responsibility of business. | BISAC: BUSINESS & ECONOMICS / Leadership. | BUSINESS & ECONOMICS / Motivational. | SELF-HELP / Personal Growth / Success.

To the brave and fearless leaders who dare to bring positive change, your relentless pursuit is an inspiration. Your courage in the face of obstacles and determination to break barriers show us the way toward a better future for all.

FOREWORD

The greatest gift we have to offer as leaders is helping others instill purpose and meaning in their lives. It is a gift to those prepared to seize the opportunity and embrace the teaching. It is a reward and obligation for the teacher or mentor. This obligation must be accompanied by a commitment and willingness to challenge existing thought while expanding the barriers of the possible.

Purposeful Performance is a book about obligation and reward. It is a book about personal renewal. It is a book that invokes individual responsibility and evokes collective achievement.

As an author and professional speaker, I am daily engaged with people who create, lead, manage, or work in companies across the United States. My message challenges the audience to be driven by purpose, fueled by passion, and defined by pride. I have learned that the speaker's effectiveness is not found in the immediate applause of the audience (although it is always appreciated) but is measured in the sustained implementation of the lessons relayed in the message. For a message to be of value, it must be applicable and sustainable.

Jonathan Stanley has created an applicable and sustainable guide for those desiring to improve their station in life. *Purposeful Performance* is a learning platform, a springboard to future possibility for those willing to see, seize, and create opportunity. The hardest step, as in most things, is the first.

Are you ready to learn the secret mix of connecting, leading, and succeeding—an endeavor that will influence your life? Then read this book from cover to cover. In doing so, you will grasp the function of cultivating meaning, adding value, and finding purpose. The direction—the ways, means, and methods—is here. The implementation is up to you.

Purposeful Performance is that rare, indispensable resource for those determined to make the best of their lives today. As you start every day, *aim for excellence, lead through influence, be authentic*, and *find the fun* in the process that will become the path to your success.

There will be leaders driven purely by profits who will be offended by Jonathan's honest approach, and there will be apathetic people who prefer not to make waves or rock the boat. This book isn't for those who think they know it all or for those unwilling to do the work. It provides both a thorough process and a planned approach. It is a step-by-step guide that will become an integral part of the determined achiever's tool kit when implemented with personal stamina and clarity of vision.

Purposeful Performance will challenge you to create value and determine your success by embracing personal responsibility. It will show you how to lead your life and not cede the responsibilities to the whims of others. You must choose influence over power, show transparency between thought and action, and remain aware of the emotional bandwidth that sets the tone for those in your wake.

Curious learners find the courage to apply what is of value in furthering their careers. They express gratitude and appreciation for the chance to change today with what they learned from yesterday. Most importantly, they understand that individual achievement depends on all cooperation in an organization. *Purposeful Performance* is a recession-proof formula for enduring value—life is a process of construction, adaptation, and assimilation. This process requires authentic, humble, and hungry leadership.

If a company is to survive, leadership can't be a luxury—it's a requisite. Leadership is the lived embodiment of thought through action. If your company is to thrive, leaders must engage, challenge, and encourage their people to grow through intelligent risks. *Purposeful Performance* outlines the strategies of engagement that are tried, accurate, and tested from the crucible of Jonathan's personal experience. Through hard-won lessons, he shares with the goal of advancement for those willing to step forward and become vital contributors to their success.

We can stumble forward mindlessly, blaming circumstance, condition, and fate as tangible factors in our professional and personal pursuits. Or we can become aware, regain our accountability, and move beyond the excuses of past conditions that must not define us.

Growth comes from meeting a new challenge; confident competence ensues from exceeding the challenge's demands. You will find that life may support those who coast and select "easy," but it rewards those who overcome the difficulty. Difficulty can be temporary—the chronic discomfort of accepting average or less than average in your life can become permanent. Take the *Purposeful Performance* challenge—accept the temporary pain to achieve the gain—develop a mindset that reflects empathy, accountability, authenticity, and intention.

Companies are composed of and led by people who exhibit positive energy, live with integrity, exemplify authentic self-belief, and build irrefutable reputations from these qualities. Reputation precedes personality and establishes the baseline for performance expectations. Today is when you take on a personal challenge and become the best "you" possible.

Purposeful Performance is your guide on the path forward to your future. Take ownership of that future today!

All the best,

Steve Gilliland

Bestselling author and Speaker Hall of Fame member, SteveGilliland.com

TABLE OF CONTENTS

INTRODUCTION

I spent so long building a company that I believed in, one that was involved in social impact and volunteer work. But in an instant, everything changed.

In spring 2020, we were in the early stages of the coronavirus outbreak. The U.S. border shut down, and overnight, our markets collapsed. Within 60 days, I had laid off half of my team.

Rationally, I understood that the business could only support people's salaries if we had customers, but I was disheartened to be letting go of the people who had given their hearts and minds to make the business a success. It was hard to see my employees and their families left without the futures I had promised them.

I was one of the so-called lucky ones. I sat at the executive table for the company that had acquired us the previous year, contributing to a fast and immediate pivot, positioning the company and our message to help organizations overcome communication barriers caused by social distancing. Our strategic pivot was an extension of our existing capabilities, which enabled us to preserve and enhance the value of our solutions.

Against this success, I was tasked with negotiating exits, breaking agreements, and signing settlements. It was heart-wrenching work. I was conflicted about my role of leading the ramp-down of operations of my old company while leading the ramp-up of marketing and communications for the new company. The darkness starts when you begin to think about what could have been.

During this tumultuous time, I felt anger, guilt, and profound sadness. I wept in my home office after delivering more layoffs on Zoom. I felt guilty for having a seat at the table. Before the first summer of the pandemic, I laid off almost everyone. These were my people. These were people I cared for and loved. Each of them, with their unique talents, abilities, gifts, and skills, was never coming back.

The company's focus on profits over people was all wrong. In executive meetings, I would talk about fulfilling our purpose and gaining alignment across the organization, but everything was all about hitting our EBITDA targets.

That focus didn't sit right with me, and I found myself becoming detached from my identity—as if I no longer had purpose and meaning and had no value to offer. The waves of self-loathing and depression came crashing down.

When I was enduring those feelings, I felt so alone.

I shared my frustrations with my wife, and she reminded me about gratitude. Early in our relationship, we had read *The Last Lecture* by Randy Pausch in bed every night before we went to sleep. Pausch shares his wisdom and life lessons in the book, the final legacy he wanted to leave behind for his children after he was diagnosed with terminal cancer. We laughed, cried, and talked about Pausch's words, going through the experience of his book with gratitude for the small moments we often overlook.

In *The Last Lecture*, Pausch writes, "Showing gratitude is one of the simplest yet most powerful things humans can do for each other."[1] So, at my wife's request, I began practicing gratitude to move past the stagnation of emotional dissonance.

I focused on expressing gratitude for my family, friends, and colleagues. Every day, I would think about the good things I've received while acknowledging the people who have brought goodness into my life. I made it a personal goal to share kindness with strangers whenever possible (while still under lockdown). I became mindful of my passion for helping others instill purpose and meaning in their lives—and day by day, I became reengaged at work. I encouraged the executive team to change their thinking, shift from a product-centric mindset to a customer-centric one, and lead purposefully. The CEO got behind me and empowered me to begin the purpose journey. I became reinvigorated in my quest to create meaning at work, albeit at a new company, and I was grateful.

I learned from this experience that developing a gratitude mindset is not complicated—it just requires some practice. As you intentionally direct your focus toward things that evoke gratitude, you will notice even more things to be grateful for. When you choose to be mindful of gratitude, it changes your emotional landscape. I learned appreciation is an art. It transforms and lives beneath the folds of every experience, lifting us when we allow ourselves to grow. I got past the resentment to do what I love: to support people and help them reach their full potential.

This is a lesson that lots of others need to hear as employee disengagement keeps climbing ever higher. It was measured at 18% in the United States in 2023.[2] If current trends continue, the number of engaged and disengaged people in their jobs is soon going to even out.

We tie so much of our identity to our jobs. But as people are evaluating purpose and meaning and looking within themselves, they are discovering giant gaps between what they need to feel fulfilled and what they are receiving at work.

I wrote this book for business leaders who want to create more meaningful relationships inside and outside their companies. Profit is nice, but it's only one metric by which to measure business growth, and I would argue it's an incomplete and short-sighted one.

Instead of being profit-driven, companies should be purpose driven. I know it sounds cliché, but employees of purpose-driven companies are more engaged and more passionate about their roles.

According to a study published by Deloitte in 2019, "purpose is a core differentiator."[3]

"Much like what a foundation is to a house, a conductor is to an orchestra, and a canvas is to an artist's masterpiece—a clear purpose is everything to an organization. It is an organization's soul and identity, providing both a platform to build upon and a mirror to reflect its existence in the world," the authors wrote.

Later in the article, they sought to quantify the impact of purpose.

"Purpose-oriented companies have higher productivity and growth rates, along with a more satisfied workforce who stay longer with them. Our research shows that such companies report 30 percent higher levels of innovation and 40 percent higher levels of workforce retention than their competitors," the authors wrote.

The impact of purpose is especially clear for millennials and Gen-Zers, whose purchasing decisions are greatly influenced by the way their purchases make them feel, preferring "to buy from ethical brands that truly care about people and the planet."[4] In order for your company to survive and thrive in today's business climate, meaning needs to be a fulcrum to creating prosperity.

I get the urge to prioritize profit! Early in my career, I also found myself chasing profit and going after every shiny new object that came along. I wasn't motivated to make a difference in the world—I was motivated by money. In one case, my company wasted six months going after an opportunity we had no business considering. Such missteps are costly!

Along the way, I came to realize that a lack of focus, clarity, and direction was leading to a great deal of wasted time and effort. And it made me feel better inside to know that we were making an impact. When we applied the framework I outline in this book and reoriented our company based on meaning, our Net Promoter Score, a metric that measures customer loyalty, went from a 20 to a 58.

Over the course of a few years, as we shifted to a purpose-driven approach, we went from industry average to world class.

I focused on making our values and our purpose a part of everything we did. One of my strategies for doing so was to implement a gratitude platform, where everyone could share their gratitude with a coworker, both in their departments and cross-functionally, so this concept of reward and recognition and gratitude took off. It was a way to create a more inclusive world.

I wrote this book with my career experiences in mind. The first half of the book deals with the elements of being a purpose-driven company, while the second half details how to ensure, through strategic planning, that purpose is maintained and infused throughout your entire company.

My goal with this book is to help you recognize the value of pursuing purpose within your company and to put purpose into practice. Being a purpose-driven company will help you better engage your employees, stay aligned with customers, and make the biggest impact.

It will fill you with so much pride and satisfaction—you're thinking big and helping the world and doing something bigger than yourself. And with purpose as your North Star, you'll never feel disengaged from your work again.

INSPIRED TO MAKE A DIFFERENCE

Focusing on purpose makes me think about the time I was invited to participate in a panel at a business conference in Miami. The topic was "Why your story matters," and as one of the panelists, I shared my views on the power of storytelling with CEOs and business owners. Toward the end of the discussion, we had the chance to pose questions to the audience. When it was my turn, I asked, "What motivated you to start your business? Was it a desire to innovate and improve products and services, or did you see an opportunity to create something meaningful?"

The audience chimed in with their thoughts, mostly centered around financial gains. As I listened attentively to their responses, a common theme emerged—it wasn't about building meaningful connections with their customers but increasing profits.

I couldn't help but feel these entrepreneurs were missing out on a significant opportunity. While making money is crucial for any successful business, it shouldn't be the only goal. Research has shown that companies prioritizing customer engagement and connection are more likely to see long-term financial success.

At that moment, I chose to emphasize that storytelling goes beyond simply marketing—it evokes emotions and establishes a deep emotional connection with your audience. So I asked, "What drove you to risk jeopardizing your well-being to start your own company? What was the driving force behind that decision, and what obstacles did you have to overcome? These are the narratives that, when retold time and time again, form the essence of your organization's identity. Your stories serve as a source of inspiration, reminding everyone of their role in positively impacting people's lives." As I scanned the audience's reactions, it was clear that my words had little impact.

After the conversation finished, I reflected on how to shift people's focus away from solely making money through launching new ventures. For my next speaking engagement, I decided to take a different approach. Rather than simply discussing the advantages of storytelling in business, I would share my journey of discovering purpose through entrepreneurship.

Initially, my main goal had been to make as much money as possible. As a result, I needed help staying focused and spent all my time chasing sales. However, I soon realized that this approach left me feeling unfulfilled and disconnected from my work and customers. I felt a true sense of purpose when incorporating values and beliefs into my business. By partnering with local causes and organizations that aligned with our beliefs, we gave back to the community and established our brand as one that values more than just making money.

I encouraged the crowd to reflect on their values and consider how they could integrate them into their business practices. I talked about how stories can captivate, evoke emotions, and motivate us to action and how storytelling is about sharing narratives that resonate with people and leave a lasting impact. Many top brands and influential leaders use storytelling in their sales, marketing, and leadership strategies—well-known corporations like Apple, Nike, and Chobani. Influential individuals such as Martin Luther King, Jr., John F. Kennedy, and Maya Angelou, and accomplished entrepreneurs like Richard Branson and Sheryl Sandberg all share a common thread: an engaging narrative.

As I addressed the audience, they nodded in understanding, some wiping away tears as I shared a personal story. It was about my brother's suicide and how it influenced me to prioritize purpose and meaning in both my personal and professional life.

This is an excerpt from that talk:

Let me share a story about my brother, Peter. He's in his early 30s and has been struggling with depression for some time now.

During a phone call one evening, we conversed in a way we never had before. He opened up about his passion for cars and the satisfaction he took from repairing them. He confided in me about his marital struggles and the rift between him and his closest friend. Despite these challenges, he remained optimistic and uplifted. I took pleasure in basking in Peter's joy.

While listening to him, I could feel the strong emotional bond between us. His words were unapologetic yet raw and beautiful. As our call came to an end, I finally felt the closeness with Peter that I had been longing for.

At the time, I had no idea that the call that evening would be my last conversation with Peter. A week passed before my dad called and told me that Peter was no longer with us.

"What do you mean, he's gone?" I asked, already knowing the answer.

"Peter's not here anymore," my dad replied, his words heavy with grief and finality.

I fell to the ground, my legs giving out beneath me. The fear of losing Peter overwhelmed and paralyzed my mind. After Peter died, I learned that no matter how hard you try to remember the positive aspects of a person's life—their kindness, their humor, their ability to inspire and teach—suicide has a way of casting a shadow over everything. It becomes the focal point of your thoughts, overshadowing all the good memories and lessons they left behind. So I am here to honor Peter's life. Before my brother left for good, he made sure to leave a message for me to find—and also something for you.

Never doubt your potential to accomplish anything, become anyone, conquer any challenge, and inspire everyone around you.

After my talk, as I was packing up my things, a man approached me. He had tears in his eyes as he thanked me for sharing my story. He told me that he had lost someone close to him in a similar way and that my words had given him hope and inspiration.

In that moment, I knew that all the struggles and hardships I'd faced meant something. Because if I could make even one person feel a little less alone, a little more connected, then I had accomplished something truly meaningful.

I left the event feeling inspired and fulfilled, knowing that I had helped to spark a small movement toward more meaningful entrepreneurship. As I walked back to my hotel room, I couldn't help but smile at the thought of all the stories yet to be written—stories of businesses that weren't just a means to an end but a way to make a difference in the world. Stories like yours.

PART 1:

PURPOSE OVER PROFIT: FOSTERING MEANING AND VALUES AT WORK

Chapter 1

BEYOND THE BOTTOM LINE: CULTIVATING A THRIVING WORKPLACE CULTURE

Create meaning, clarity, focus, and clear direction…

    or…

f@&# it up, stagnate—or worse, fail!

Every entrepreneur and small-business owner faces the same four problems: **creating meaning, clarity, focus, and a clear path forward.**

Many businesses operate without a plan for the long-term future, let alone for the upcoming year. This lack of direction and purpose can lead to confusion and inefficiency within teams. With a clear understanding of why the business exists and what values it stands for, employees can prioritize tasks that will make a real impact. I have seen well-intentioned executives leading their companies without holding their teams accountable for achieving challenging goals and displaying strong leadership behavior. When no unified vision or defined outcomes exist, time is wasted and progress is hindered. Everyone in the company needs to be on the same page and working toward common goals to see true success.

PRIORITIZING CONNECTION WITH EMPLOYEES, CUSTOMERS, AND COMMUNITY

More and more companies are recognizing the impact of building people-focused organizations, prioritizing employee well-being as much as financial success. These companies approach interactions with employees and customers with genuine curiosity, attentiveness, and empathy rather than emphasizing rank, authority, or control. Prioritizing your employees' well-being will increase productivity and loyalty, making them valuable brand representatives to your customers. As Richard Branson famously said, "Train people well enough so that they can leave, treat them well enough so that they don't want to."[5] Incorporating community engagement into a company's culture creates a more joyful and harmonious workplace. Employees experience a boost in overall job fulfillment when volunteerism and social responsibility are emphasized.

ATTRACTING AND KEEPING THE RIGHT PEOPLE

Finding the right individuals to join a company is a challenging task, and there are no guaranteed methods to ensure that candidates will fulfill the expectations they presented during interviews and assessments once they are in a role. As a result, companies are increasingly focusing on recruiting based on shared values and beliefs. They seek out candidates who are motivated by more than just a paycheck and are aligned with their purpose and core values. Integrating this approach into overall recruitment processes can not only improve diversity, inclusion, and belonging but also lead to successful long-term hires. If a company chooses to ignore purpose and values, they are disregarding the desires of the 86% of the workforce who are seeking employment with companies that share their values.[6]

CREATING DIFFERENTIATED STRATEGIES TO GAIN AN ADVANTAGE

Many companies neglect to create strategic plans, putting themselves at risk of falling behind in their industries. This can force them to be reactive instead of proactive, potentially leading to negative consequences if they don't respond effectively. A business can stay ahead of challenges and adapt to changing market trends by implementing a strong strategic plan. Proactivity is vital to achieving success and setting yourself apart from competitors. However, despite the importance of strategic planning, many organizations need to allocate more time or resources toward strategy. Studies show that most leadership teams spend less than one hour per month on strategy, with 50% of leaders not paying attention to it.[7] Unfortunately, many strategic-planning teams create plans without any real strategy.

DRIVING EFFECTIVE EXECUTION

For a plan to be effective, it is vital to establish clear and meaningful goals. This requires strong, effective leadership that values open communication, transparency, empowerment, and accountability. However, not all companies prioritize setting quarterly objectives. Even when they do, these goals are often too vague to have a meaningful impact. Sadly, I have witnessed numerous businesses struggle due to wasted time and decreased productivity as their teams were focused on the wrong goals. While most companies can set revenue targets for each quarter and year, they often need to establish other important objectives. As a result, companies lack direction and struggle to make progress toward their overall goals. Without well-defined objectives, there is no clear vision for their future. CEOs who rely solely on past performance and wishful thinking operate ignorantly in dark rooms, searching for something that may not even exist.

Amid the challenges faced by business owners, CEOs, and entrepreneurs, a surge of individuals is launching new ventures in the United States. In

2022, more than five million new ventures were started, a 42% increase from pre-pandemic levels,[8] with an upswing of new entrepreneurs putting their ideas into action each day.

While you may be encouraged by the entrepreneurial spirit thriving, the harsh truth is that most small businesses fail. Despite the ingenuity and enthusiasm of each new venture, an abysmal 20% of businesses fail within their first year, 30% end up shutting down by the end of year two, half (50%) don't make it past five years, and a staggering 70% won't survive 10 years.[9]

Small businesses have been an immense success in America—a story of triumph despite the odds. And with the next great wave of innovations being in deep learning, which is "artificial intelligence (AI), synthetic biology, nanotechnologies, and quantum computing, among other advanced technologies,"[10] all areas where complex issues are solved that were previously beyond our human capabilities, it's hard to dispute that many entrepreneurs are paving the way to a brighter future for all of us.

No matter if you are launching a new business or growing an existing one, as long as you have the willpower and creative solutions to address real customer needs, success is within reach. What you need is a clear value proposition (why people should choose you) and talented people who will tirelessly work to achieve your vision.

Many business owners continue to operate their businesses with no clear plan or strategy and struggle with execution. According to a study conducted by Timothy Devinney and colleagues at the University of Technology in Sydney, 71% of employees cannot recognize their own company's strategy in a multiple-choice question.[11] This isn't surprising when you consider:

- Nearly 90% of executives believe a strong sense of collective purpose within their organization drives employee satisfaction,[12] but only a small fraction of small businesses has one.
- Two-thirds of small businesses don't have a business plan.[13]
- Most businesses don't have a strategy.
- Of those that do, 90% of organizations fail to execute their strategies successfully.[14]

The other top reasons businesses fail include not having any plan, not putting customers first, hiring the wrong people, and trying to do it all alone.[15] But what if there was a simpler way to create a clear path forward?

If you want to build a company that truly means something to the people you serve, I am offering you the opportunity to cut through the confusion and chaos of your daily operations by harnessing the power of a simple strategic-planning framework so you can get on the path toward fulfillment and purposeful growth.

It doesn't matter what you sell. If you are leading your business with a greater purpose, if you're creating meaning for the people you serve, and if you have a clear, simple plan backed by people who believe in your cause, you're going to grow faster. If you want to survive and thrive, you need to stop wasting time on the things that don't matter, and you need to focus your energy on the customers who are driven by how you treat your employees, the environment, and your community. By connecting purpose with doing good, your business can build deeper connections with your customers and be more relevant in their lives.

A simple strategic plan is a way to guide your business and team, create a connection with employees and customers on an emotional level, and create clarity, focus, direction, and meaning for the people you serve. Strategy informs your plan, and your plan serves as the foundation for execution—crafting your intention around the difference you want to make in people's lives.

Despite the research, the evidence, and the top-performing businesses that are making a social impact and creating loyal customers, much of this success is ignored. While there are shining examples of how doing good in the world pays (purpose-driven organizations are growing three times faster on average than their competitors[16]), few business owners are paying attention to a reason to care. But you can create a story that can change people—and reimagine what it means to make an impact.

Your strategic plan can be the difference between failing and succeeding. Every business owner and entrepreneur must know strategy and how it can help their business gain advantage—but few spend time on strategy or planning. There is more to running a business than selling more stuff to more people for more money. Money is the fuel that drives your cause forward, but it isn't your primary goal. Your primary goal should be difference thinking, taking the time to reflect on how your products and services are meaningful to the people who use them and how you can make small shifts in attitude and perception by standing for something people can believe in.

You can continue to run your business without purpose and a plan and make the same mistakes I did, wasting thousands of hours of time, or you can use this book as a guide to create a higher cause and a strategic road map to assist your company in making a difference for the greater good.

Your purpose and values, backed by a simple strategic plan that every employee can understand, give clarity, focus, and direction for your culture and your brand—so everyone is aligned, unified, and motivated to make a difference.

Each chapter in this book will give you strategies, tips, and step-by-step processes to create and communicate a simple plan that will eliminate confusion and propel your business forward. This book is all about making your leadership easier, creating a clear direction forward for your business, so you can lead with meaning and impact, engaging your employees and inspiring and motivating your people to win. Most importantly, this book will help you get the right things done by focusing on the key activities that will move your business forward.

So many businesses fail at execution because they believe execution means working harder to get sales, pulling every lever they can to close more deals, or spending hundreds of hours trying to find micro-savings in expenses across departments, sticking to a plan that was created by enormous effort and supported by staunch discipline. If you're so set in your ways that you can't adapt when faced with unexpected obstacles or opportunities, then you, too, will fail.

At simplestrategicplans.com, you can download a free paper framework that, along with this book, will save you time and help you and others get on the same page about what is most important in your business and how to create meaning for your employees and the people you serve.

If you haven't started strategic planning yet, this book will save you hundreds of hours in trying to find a system that works for you, while creating a workplace where people feel their work matters. You deserve the joy of leading a business where you're making a difference, and so do your employees and your customers.

DON'T WASTE YOUR TIME ON GOOGLE

If you haven't started your search for a strategic-planning framework on Google yet, don't waste your time and energy on the promised results. Many of those frameworks require long documents complete with objectives, goals, strategies, and spreadsheets forecasting costs and revenue well into the future. You may find good planning documents, but you'll come up short on strategy.

All those frameworks look pretty much the same. You'll state your vision and mission and set an aspirational goal, like doubling revenue in the next five years. Next, you'll lay out the annual goals you want to accomplish, such as opening a new office in Europe, launching a new product, or generating more qualified leads. This comfortable planning work will waste valuable time and resources as you review and approve others' work, stuck in meetings and discussions about the pivot tables in spreadsheets that show your business achievements as numerical bliss—increases in revenue and profit margins over the next 25 years.

You're now in the planning trap, devoid of customer meaning, strategy, or simplicity. Without meaning or strategy, your plan won't work. Without simplicity, you can't eliminate the unnecessary.

Over the years, I've seen a lot of business owners create unnecessary complexity—in their plans, messages, and offerings. I'm guilty, too, of not hacking away the inessentials. And while simple is harder than complex, we need to make simplicity the goal, not the starting point. Eliminate everything that limits cooperation, and work with others to create a simple plan everyone can believe in.

If you're a business owner, entrepreneur, or leader in your organization, this book will serve as your blueprint for creating something that matters.

You will use this framework to empathize with your customers and create meaningful bonds of connection and belonging, building your plan around shared goals and values.

THE INFINITE LOOP OF CONNECTION

There are countless online resources to help you understand what it means to be purposeful and how a higher cause can effectively enhance business performance over time. And if you don't have a purpose, I'm going to share a step-by-step process for unlocking your cause in chapter 2. But more than believing in your purpose is needed to make an impact at work and in your community. Knowing why your organization exists and how you contribute to the greater good is just part of the story. To truly maximize the potential of this purpose, it must be united with your capabilities so that you can have a real effect on those you serve—a union that will turn your intentions from ideas into actionable outcomes.

So what is the purpose of your purpose? The answer is simple: **to be meaningful** to the people you choose to serve.

Think of your purpose as the engine driving your organization, while the meaning you create is the fuel that keeps it running toward your objectives.

By understanding your customers and seeing the world through their eyes, you can create a unique bond with them that no one else can copy. This is your chance to redefine the way things are done—where both employees and customers feel valued and taken care of. In order to attract people to your business, you need to stay true to your purpose and values and express them genuinely.

To that end, I'd like to introduce a helpful tool that can help create an unrivaled path for your business. This framework serves as a model for uniting purpose and values with the tangible actions of meaning. It should point out the one-of-a-kind experiences that are exclusive to your business, connecting your aims to impact. The Purpose Pi, like the never-ending mathematical equation, is an endless loop of defining the meaning you are striving to create while holding your team accountable to your authentic truth.

The Purpose Pi, the Infinite Loop of Connection: Insights for Customer and Employee Connection and Social Community Impact

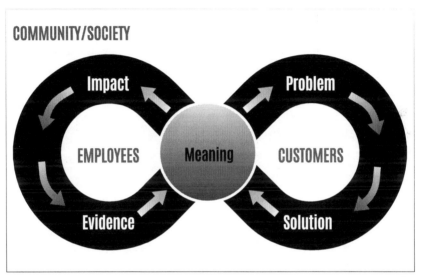

Figure 1

To use this tool, you'll begin, as any company begins, with a customer's problem to solve—the company's aim is to help solve customers' problems (pain) and demonstrate the potential benefits that their product or service can provide to improve their lives (gain).

Solving customers' problems engages workers, who carry a deep sense of purpose. Success is measured by evidence—the influence infused within your company and the effect of your efforts on your community and society.

This tool defines "meaning" as the emotional significance of what you do. In other words, your ability to empathize and be genuine with others can be the key to unlocking meaningful discoveries that set your ideas and aims apart from the rest.

To help unify your team around your purpose and values, you will clearly define the meaningful interactions, experiences, and contributions you want to make for the greater good—giving people reasons to care about you and answering the question of why they should belong.

The infinite loop is supported by an endless cycle of change and improvement. Making continual improvements means that you acknowledge the importance of creating positive experiences for both your customers and your employees. This isn't a competition to finish first. When you take the time to discover what your customers actually need, want, and believe, and you create a plan to get there, you are on a path to deeply connecting to the beliefs of the people you serve as well as the story you want to tell the world. Everything you do—specifically your strategic-planning efforts, which we'll cover in chapter 11—should uphold and strengthen the Purpose Pi.

Let's get started at the beginning of the cycle—with a customer's problem.

PURPOSE, VALUES, AND CONNECTION

The Purpose Pi is designed to invite people into a trusted relationship with your brand. Think of the infinite loop as a map, where you'll identify new opportunities to create emotional points of difference that forge meaningful human connections.

You will take the job of an empathic voyager—just like a cartographer who collects, measures, and studies geographic information to make maps and diagrams for use in planning and education. Instead of making charts of physical geography, you'll create representations of meaning and plot opportunities for building strong emotional bonds with your customers, employees, and community.

To make this map on your voyage, you'll first have to craft your authentic reason for being and clarify the deeply ingrained principles that guide your company's actions. Only with this knowledge can we recognize and respond to the feelings of others, building solid and genuine relationships and trust. If you want to inspire, change the way people feel instead of trying to change the way people think.

It wasn't that long ago that Simon Sinek presented his idea of the Golden Circle concept in his TED talk "How Great Leaders Inspire Action," which has since become the third most-viewed video in the website's history.[17] The Golden Circle is an easy yet profoundly effective model that explains why some companies and leaders are more successful than others. It involves three circles: the outermost is "What," the middle is "How," and the innermost is "Why." Most people concentrate on the "What"—their goods or services. Others also focus on the "How"—their unique process or strategy. But what sets organizations and influential leaders apart is their attention to the "Why"—the fundamental reason they exist over and above making a profit. Sinek proposes that individuals aren't just drawn to what you do or how you do it. They're inspired by *why* you do it.

Simon Sinek asks *what* motivates you to get out of bed every morning and *why* people should care about the work you do.[18]

To summarize Sinek's message, you can't create meaning for your customers and employees without first understanding what your business stands for. Purpose-driven companies exist to make a change—your purpose is your organization's aspirational reason for being beyond profits alone. It's why your business matters—and fits into your customers' worldview. To quote Salesforce CEO Marc Benioff, "Companies can do more than just make money, they can serve others…. The business of business is improving the state of the world."[19]

I am going to expand on Simon Sinek's model by offering you a blueprint that shows you how to unlock meaning and value in your business while revealing what many organizations unintentionally overlook as they explore a higher cause—the missing piece that successful companies instinctively recognize and live out through their good deeds and actions.

To create something meaningful, these companies invite people in by saying, "I see you. I exist for you." They look through the lens of empathy and apply the infinite loop of emotional connection—where customers, employees, and the community feel close, valued, and cared for.

In life and at work, we all desire to share an understanding with someone who recognizes us for who we are and what we can become. These companies understand the power of empathy. They understand and relate to the people they serve, sharing their feelings, experiences, and beliefs—being there when people need to be seen and heard. The measure of their successes isn't in what they make but in the difference they make in people's lives.

Organizations, whether companies in the fashion retail sector, crypto-based software as a service businesses, or consultant firms, all progress through three stages when building meaningful relationships with their brands. And you must take your time with these stages to authentically embody your core beliefs.

These are the three stages to create meaning at work:

1. Define Your Purpose
2. Identify Your Core Values
3. Follow the Infinite Loop of Connection

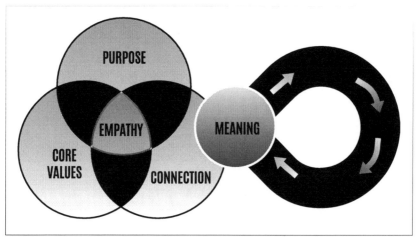

Figure 2

Building and shaping your business around a purpose inspires your employees, motivating them to contribute to building something better for your customers and for society at large. Your values guide behavior and inform decision-making, defining what your business believes and the daily behaviors it agrees to live by. When you align purpose and values and identify the emotional connections you're trying to build, these high-impact motivators become the primary drivers of customer, employee, and community value.

As you work on these three stages, consider how you want people to perceive your business. The best way to do this is by looking at the world through the eyes of those you wish to reach.

YOUR PURPOSE JOURNEY

Recently, I began rereading Seth Godin's book *This Is Marketing: You Can't Be Seen Until You Learn to See*. In the book, Godin expands upon what Theodore Levitt, a famous Harvard marketing professor, once said: "Sell the hole, not the drill."[20] Levitt was trying to emphasize that customers don't purchase products for the sake of the product—they want products to do a job for them. In other words, you should focus on the problem, not the solution.

Godin says:

The lesson is that the drill bit is merely a feature, a means to an end, but what people truly want is the hole it makes. But that doesn't go nearly far enough. No one wants a hole. What people want is the shelf that will go on the wall once they drill the hole. Actually, what they want is how they'll feel once they see how uncluttered everything is, when they put their stuff on the shelf that went on the wall, now that there's a quarter-inch hole. But wait…They also want the satisfaction of knowing they did it themselves. Or perhaps the increase in status they'll get when their spouse admires the work. Or the peace of mind that comes from knowing that the bedroom isn't a mess, and that it feels safe and clean. "People don't want to buy a quarter-inch drill bit. They want to feel safe and respected."[21]

Bingo.

As business leaders, we need to understand our customers' motivations before we can influence their actions. But all too often, we try to sell the drill, not the feelings. When you think about your purpose and the people you choose to serve, think about what your customers want, how you fit into their worldviews, and how you make them feel when they buy your products or services. Avoid making the mistakes of marketers who focus on features, not feelings.

What would it be like if you changed the way you thought about what gives businesses an edge and started to understand the advantages of being more human? Not only could you create a smarter company, truly connect with your customers, and become a better leader, but perhaps our world would improve too.

The story's moral here is that you can't change minds without winning hearts to create the future you want to see. The first stage of defining your purpose is to build your business around improving people's lives—to show people that their feelings matter.

If you want to stand out, focus on showing care. Establish a cause that goes beyond your business endeavors—whether that cause is climate change, promoting diversity and equality, assisting refugees, advocating for the underserved, fighting poverty, or working with underprivileged kids. As a leader, realize that part of your job is making the world better.

Taking care of people and being there for those in need is a conscious decision. Looking out for others isn't done for money or material gain, and it doesn't show up on your profit and loss statement. When we comprehend how our target audience feels and thinks, it helps us build a strong emotional connection that can generate unique customer value. You can bridge this gap through a continuous cycle of understanding and definition using the infinite loop to define the meaning you want to create for your employees, customers, and community.

As you work to reach your purpose goals, be aware of the struggles, pain, and fears of others as opportunities for problem-solving. This is the foundation of every good business model.

Chapter 2

WHICH COMES FIRST, PURPOSE OR PROFIT?

To begin, let's discuss your company's purpose. At its core, your statement of purpose should address the question of why you are here. It's the driving force behind your actions and explains the reason for everything you do. It is the essential element that sets your business apart, leading it toward genuine connections and powerful transformations and solidifying its presence in the hearts and minds of those it serves.

The reason you exist should be a motivating force to break free from limitations, make a positive difference in society, and leave behind a meaningful legacy.

As you search for meaning, a multitude of thoughts about your corporate identity and values will certainly come up. Take your time in sorting through them. By defining your purpose, you aim to motivate employees and boost engagement, enhance your reputation with customers, and make a positive impact on people's lives.

Your mindset should prioritize purpose over profit, meaning that the success of your company will become intertwined with the well-being of others—your employees, customers, suppliers, and the larger community. Remember, purpose is not a marketing tactic or short-term campaign. It requires a fundamental shift in thinking—your goal being to integrate purpose into every aspect of your operations.

To achieve success in fulfilling your purpose, incorporate empathy and compassion into the process. Discover how your company can make a difference first, and focus on growth later. Analyze current initiatives and determine the most influential approaches for your company to take from your customers' perspectives. Discuss the unique value that your company offers, and evaluate the resources needed to activate your purpose. Demonstrate openness and bravery by discussing your core beliefs and explaining their significance to the people you serve.

Based on my own experiences advocating for purpose in both my own company and others, you need to prepare for a deeply emotional process. If you can, don't go on the purpose journey alone. If you lead a small team, involve them. If you're the CEO of a larger company, involve your entire organization. Include individuals ranging from top executives to new employees. By seeking feedback from a diverse group, you can gain valuable insights into what truly drives and motivates your team. Objectively evaluate the strengths and weaknesses of your company. Release any preconceived ideas about what your company should be like, and dive into the creative process with an open mind. You may discover new opportunities in unexpected places.

After my business was acquired, I was presented with the opportunity to lead a purpose-driven effort at a new company. For several weeks, I engaged in deep philosophical conversations with fellow executives over Zoom, through email, and in Word documents. We delved into our core beliefs, defining our identity as a company and discussing the impact we wanted to have on the world.

For the founder of this company, undergoing this transformation was a deeply personal and life-changing experience. After 20 years of successful product-driven thinking, he had to shift his mindset toward a purpose-driven approach that would guide the company into the future. To craft our purpose statement, we conducted focus groups with every department and individual in the company. Their valuable feedback and perspectives helped us strengthen our statement and gain support along the way. During this process, we discovered that some employees were enthusiastic about leading with purpose, while others remained skeptical, seeing it as just another passing trend.

We took the time to gather feedback and use it to refine the overall purpose of the organization. However, something was missing. Through scheduling one-on-ones, I delved deeper into the founder's origin story and asked the main question: What had motivated him to create this company? As we talked, he gradually became more vulnerable, revealing his past experiences of feeling isolated, excluded, and misunderstood due to his hearing loss. This had ultimately driven him to create a community where individuals with hearing impairments could feel accepted and valued. Feeling as if he didn't belong in social settings due to his inability to hear clearly, he was driven to innovate and revolutionize an entire industry.

What I learned through this undertaking is that finding your purpose is more than a noble cause—it's a process that peels back the layers of our history until we reach our core beliefs. We may hesitate at first, dipping our toes in the water and avoiding facing ourselves and our past traumas. But as we open our minds and expand our experiences, we begin to realize that vulnerability is what truly connects us. The founder's heartfelt story resonated with everyone, sparking genuine emotions and fostering a sense of connection. Purpose became rooted in the strong belief that no one should be excluded due to their disabilities. This is a stance worth taking, standing up for those who may otherwise be left behind.

As you step into the unknown, remember that true courage is not the absence of fear, but the willingness to act despite it. According to Brené Brown in *Atlas of the Heart*, courage is rooted in our hearts. As leaders, we must be willing to embrace vulnerability and face our fears head-on. Change cannot happen unless we find the courage within ourselves to push through our fears. As you begin the process of defining your purpose, you can make a true impact by standing firm in your convictions.

In this road map, you will find examples to guide you in crafting a purpose statement that truly embodies the essence of your organization and guides your journey toward success.

As a leader, you must inspire imaginative and insightful ideas that will bring unique value to your customers, distinguishing your company from competitors. Then, communicate how this value ties into your organizational purpose and demonstrate how it addresses the unmet needs of your target audience.

When you keep your employees informed about what your customers value, your employees can become a valuable source of information. They will have a deeper understanding of industry trends and receive direct feedback from customers about their changing needs. This will help you identify gaps in your knowledge and prioritize the development of your products or services to meet your customers' most important needs. Ultimately, this allows you to improve your customers' lives and provide them with better experiences.

STEP 1: WHY YOU EXIST

What is our company's core reason for being, and what is the unique, positive impact we aspire to bring about in our community, in society?

Ask introspective questions to help shape a purpose that will guide you:

- Why do you exist beyond making money (or your other primary goal?)
- What would be missing in the world if your company were no longer around?
- How do you currently serve those who interact with your company—customers, employees, and members of the community?
- What kind of future do you want to help create?
- Does your company resonate with the values, concerns, and beliefs of your customers?
- Are these compatible with who you are and where you're headed?
- Are you willing to take a stand for something?

When your business adds meaning to the equation, you are looking for something far beyond just transactions. You seek to develop an emotional connection between your company's purpose and the purpose of those using its products and services. By doing so, you light a flame that can alter lives in positive ways.

STEP 2: EMBRACE ASPIRATION AND IMPACT

Infuse your purpose statement with aspirational language that speaks to the positive impact your business aims to make. Explore the societal change you aspire to create and express it in a way that resonates emotionally with stakeholders. Embrace a sense of ambition that compels action and inspires commitment.

Suppose you lead a tech startup with values emphasizing inclusivity, innovation, and accessibility. You have four values:

- **Inclusive design:** Your product development follows universal design principles, ensuring that technology is accessible to individuals with disabilities.
- **Innovation:** Your team constantly innovates to find new ways to improve accessibility.
- **Collaboration:** You collaborate with organizations advocating for accessibility rights, demonstrating your commitment to inclusivity.
- **User-centered approach:** User feedback drives your design and development process, reflecting your belief in empowering individuals through technology.

Your purpose statement is a commitment to your cause: "We are dedicated to creating innovative technology solutions that enhance accessibility and empower individuals of all abilities."

STEP 3: BE CONCISE AND CLEAR

Clarity is the linchpin of a compelling purpose statement. Aim for brevity while conveying a powerful message. Eliminate unnecessary jargon or complexity. A purpose statement should be easily understandable and memorable, making it accessible to everyone, from employees to customers.

Here are five tips to help you write with clarity:

1. **Organize your thoughts:** Before you start writing, work with your team to organize thoughts and ideas. Create an outline or a mind map to structure your content logically. I use Lucidchart's brainstorming software (www.lucidchart.com) for sharing ideas in the cloud, but there are many brainstorming and mind-mapping solutions to choose from.

2. **Use simple and concise language:** Choose straightforward language to convey your message.

3. **Edit and proofread:** After you've written your purpose statement, take the time to edit and proofread it carefully. Look for grammatical errors, awkward phrasing, or unclear sentences. Reading your work aloud can help you identify areas that need improvement.

4. **Hire a professional writer:** Hire a professional writer who can turn your writing into a compelling purpose statement. When writing copy and content for purpose, core values, website content, etc., I've always hired professional writers because I know content matters—and matters a lot—to customers and stakeholders. Bad writing is bad for brands—and for your business.

5. **Get feedback:** Seek feedback from employees and stakeholders, who can provide valuable insights into the clarity of your writing. Consider their suggestions and make necessary revisions.

If you want to learn about clear messages that work, check out Donald Miller's *Building a StoryBrand*. I use StoryBrand for my own work.

STEP 4: EVOKE EMOTION AND CONNECTION

Forge an emotional connection through your purpose statement. Use evocative language that tugs at heartstrings and kindles enthusiasm. Craft a narrative that captures the essence of your journey and invites stakeholders to join in your collective mission.

Creating an emotional connection with your audience in a purpose statement can make it more compelling and relatable.

- **Use evocative language:** Choose words and phrases that evoke emotions and resonate with your audience's values and aspirations. Instead of stating facts plainly, infuse your purpose statement with descriptive and emotionally charged language. For example, instead of saying, "We offer financial services to clients," you could say, "We empower individuals to achieve their financial dreams."

- **Tell a story:** Narratives have a powerful way of eliciting emotions. Share a brief story or anecdote that illustrates your organization's impact and how it has positively affected individuals or communities. Stories create empathy and help your audience connect on a personal level.

- **Highlight shared values:** Identify the values that your organization and your audience share. Your purpose statement should reflect these shared values, emphasizing your commitment to principles that matter to your audience. When people see their values mirrored in your statement, it fosters a sense of alignment and connection.

- **Appeal to aspirations:** Address the aspirations and dreams of your audience. Show them how your organization's purpose aligns with their desires for a better world. Use phrases that inspire hope and motivate action. Make your audience feel that by supporting your cause, they are contributing to something meaningful and fulfilling.

By tapping into your customers' aspirations, you can create an emotional connection that resonates deeply with your audience, motivating them to engage with your organization's purpose and values.

STEP 5: ADDRESS STAKEHOLDER IMPACT

Acknowledge the stakeholders who are central to your existence. Express how your purpose positively affects them, whether it's customers, employees, communities, or the environment. Highlight the transformative role your organization plays in society.

Reflect on what sets you apart from your competitors. What is your unique value proposition, the thing that makes your organization essential for your customers? This could be an innovative product, a personalized experience, or a commitment to social responsibility. Your purpose statement should showcase this unique value proposition, making it clear to your audience why they should choose you over your competitors.

STEP 6: TEST AND REFINE

Share your draft purpose statement with a diverse group of stakeholders. Seek their input and feedback to ensure that the statement resonates with various perspectives. Consider conducting surveys or focus groups to gauge how well the purpose statement aligns with their perceptions of your organization.

Testing and refining your purpose statement is a crucial step to ensure it truly captures the essence of your organization's cause.

STEP 7: SYNTHESIZE AND ITERATE

Synthesize the feedback and iteratively refine your purpose statement. Fine-tune the language, ensuring that every word contributes to the over-arching message. Strive for an outcome that reflects a consensus among stakeholders and captures the essence of your purpose.

Let's consider a tech startup with a social mission to bridge the digital divide. Their initial purpose statement might be "We aim to provide afford-able technology solutions to underserved communities." After consulting with their team and partners, they gain insights into the transformative power of education through technology.

They iterate their purpose to encompass this broader vision: "Our purpose is to empower underserved communities through affordable technology solutions, unlocking access to education and opportunities for a brighter future."

STEP 8: ALIGN WITH ACTION

A purpose statement is more than a proclamation—it's a call to action. Align your business's activities, strategies, and initiatives with your purpose statement. Let the purpose statement permeate every facet of your business, from decision-making to product development, fostering a cohesive and purpose-driven culture.

Imagine for a moment that you're the founder of a sustainable fashion brand with a purpose statement focused on environmental stewardship. Your purpose statement reads "We exist to revolutionize the fashion industry by creating eco-friendly, ethically sourced clothing." To embed this purpose in your operations, you might do the following:

- **Source:** You actively seek sustainable materials and partner with ethical suppliers, ensuring your products adhere to eco-friendly standards.
- **Design:** Your design team incorporates recyclable and biodegradable elements into clothing lines, emphasizing sustainability in every collection.
- **Manufacture:** Production processes prioritize minimal waste and fair labor practices, reflecting your commitment to ethical sourcing.
- **Market:** Your marketing campaigns highlight the brand's dedication to environmental sustainability and its social impact, making emotional connections with consumers who share your beliefs and values.

STEP 9: INSPIRE AND LEAD

Use your purpose statement as a source of inspiration and leadership. Incorporate the policies and processes into your business: the operational activities, incentives, and management protocols your business depends on to create value and fulfill its purpose. Let the purpose statement serve as a rallying point for your team, uniting them under a common cause and imbuing their work with deeper meaning.

The small businesses that follow are living their values and fulfilling their purpose, serving as examples that you can too!

Merit

Value: Empowering kids

Merit, a fashion business based in Grand River, Detroit, is challenging the way young people can access education. Their mission is to offer "high quality clothing that helps kids get to college." They create products that are both aesthetically pleasing and functional. In addition to producing T-shirts, sweaters, and accessories, Merit has established their FATE program to work with around 50 students in the local area so they can make the most of their education and become top-notch citizens.

By doing this, Merit aims to uproot the idea that "those companies that make a choice to strongly focus on bettering the communities in which they serve, cannot make and design products that are both functional and beautifully designed."[22]

A Dozen Cousins

Value: Healthy eating for everyone

A Dozen Cousins, located in Berkeley, California, is a family-run business driven by the purpose "to promote families of all backgrounds to eat healthier meals and lead longer, more dynamic lives." They offer seasoned beans, bone broth rice, and seasoning sauces made from natural ingredients while preserving their Caribbean, Creole, and Latin flavors. A Dozen Cousins makes nutritious, inexpensive, and convenient meal choices accessible to everyone regardless of income level while providing an annual grant (and volunteer support) to nonprofit organizations that are working to eliminate socioeconomic health disparities.[23]

Sightseer Coffee

Value: Empowering women

Sightseer Coffee is a queer-owned business that works exclusively with women-farmed coffees. This Austin, Texas, coffeehouse has set out to make the coffee industry more inclusive. The owners say that they are highly committed to bringing about gender equality in the coffee industry. Although women make up most of the manual labor force on coffee farms, they are excluded from having any power or authority. By purchasing only from female producers and cooperatives, the owners of Sightseer Coffee want to help women have a voice in the industry.[24] Sightseer focuses their roasts mainly on approachable coffees, with a new blend out now that benefits youth of all sexual orientations and gender identities.[25]

Helpsy

Value: Clothing sustainability

Helpsy, a socially conscious textile collection company based in the Northeast U.S., is dedicated to transforming how people view clothing recycling. Helpsy says that according to the EPA, the average U.S. citizen discards over 100 pounds of clothing per year, and 85% of that clothing ends up in landfills. Helpsy's purpose is to encourage upcycling and responsible handling of overstock. The organization affirms that 95% of all textiles can be reutilized with 50% being reused and 45% recycled.

In 2022, Helpsy, in partnership with cities, towns, brands, and retailers, installed over 2,200 collection containers, kept 29 million pounds of garments from going into landfills, saved 560 million pounds of CO_2, and conserved 14 billion gallons of water from being wasted. They've also donated more than $400,000 to charities and local governments for bin placement and donations. Moreover, the team at Helpsy facilitated 340 school and community clothing drives. All these efforts are helping brands and communities become more sustainable in their use of unwanted goods.[26]

Shades of Green Permaculture

Value: Sustainable landscaping

Shades of Green Permaculture has a mission to help people join in the restoration of the earth. They do this by transforming everyday landscapes into beneficial ecosystems. This small business in Avondale Estates, Georgia, specializes in "full-cycle edible and sustainable landscaping with an emphasis on chemical-free gardens." Shades of Green Permaculture creates outdoor spaces that protect biodiversity, providing landscape consultations and design and installation services. Connecting with their community, the company offers free education, resources, workshops, design courses, and volunteer opportunities. In 2018, Shades of Green Permaculture was a finalist for Best Small Business in America.[27]

These small businesses are shining examples of how brands that authentically lead with purpose are changing the nature of business today. By living their purposes, these progressive companies are reshaping what it means to bring meaning to their work and to their communities, demonstrating that purpose-driven leadership is attainable at any scale.

PURPOSE-DRIVEN STATEMENTS TO INSPIRE

The following purpose-driven statements come from both big and small companies, showing their dedication to making an impact and influencing real change in various industries.

- **Airbnb:** "Create a world where anyone can belong anywhere."[28]
- **Ben & Jerry's:** "We love making ice cream—but using our business to make the world a better place gives our work its meaning. Guided by our Core Values, we seek in all we do, at every level of our business, to advance human rights and dignity, support social and economic justice for historically marginalized communities, and protect and restore the Earth's natural systems. In other words: we use ice cream to change the world."[29]
- **Better World Books:** "To capitalize on the value of the book to fund literacy initiatives locally, nationally and around the world."[30]
- **Cardinal Health:** "To improve people's lives by merging innovation and technology with healthcare."[31]
- **Coca-Cola:** "To refresh the world, and make a difference."[32]
- **Kind:** "Creating a kinder and healthier world—one act, one snack at a time."[33]
- **Patagonia:** "We're in business to save our home planet."[34]
- **Philips:** "At Philips, our purpose is to improve people's health and well-being through meaningful innovation. We aim to improve 2.5 billion lives per year by 2030, including 400 million in underserved communities."[35]
- **Starbucks:** "With every cup, every conversation, every community—we nurture the limitless possibilities of human connection."[36]
- **Thistle Farms:** "To heal, empower, and employ women survivors of trafficking, prostitution, and addiction by providing safe housing, recovery support, and meaningful employment opportunities."[37]

Discovering your purpose statement can ignite profound change. It's a path where your unique passions, talents, and beliefs come together to create a powerful force for good. Remember that your purpose isn't merely a lofty ideal—it's a dynamic force that can ripple through your community, country, or even the world.

Embrace your true self, unfiltered and unapologetic. Your purpose statement blooms from the essence of who you are, and its authenticity resonates with others, inspiring them to stand alongside you in your quest for positive change.

So, take a moment to reflect on your passions, the causes that tug at your heartstrings, and the mark you wish to leave behind.

Chapter 3

WHAT RYAN SEACREST CAN TEACH US

Purpose is why we do what we do, and values are how we achieve that purpose. Purpose and values are the deeply ingrained beliefs and principles that guide our actions. These guiding principles have the power to set your business apart from the competition, clarify your identity, and serve as a rallying point for employees. The very bedrock of your organization is made up of values, your foundational beliefs and guiding principles, which form the collective product of how employees think and act so that everyone knows what is expected.

Your company culture is either deliberately established and cared for from the start or created chaotically as time passes due to your employees holding different opinions and experiences. Unfortunately, too many organizations choose to see a values initiative as another marketing campaign: It's all about getting attention when the initiative first launches, not about the integrity of the behaviors they want to see in their business. To avoid this trap, you must embody the core values you want your employees to live by.

When your employees see their personal beliefs mirrored in the core values of your workplace, a powerful resonance is established. This resonance fuels a sense of belonging, ownership, and emotional investment in what you do. Employees deeply connected to your organization's values are not mere bystanders but active contributors who pour their energy and enthusiasm into their roles. Values give your employees a foundation for adaptability and growth and provide a stable anchor during times of change, guiding strategic decisions as your business evolves. Simply put, your values give every member of your organization a sense of direction.

To create a great culture, provide the behavioral guidelines to amplify your employees' abilities and help them do their best work. By discussing how your values help your business succeed, you make your values mean something. Share your values everywhere: on the walls, in emails, in presentations, on dashboards, during staff meeting discussions, and even in everyday conversations. Talk about the values so often that they become as ubiquitous as air.

Remember, your core values shape the identity and culture of your organization. Whether you are figuring out what behaviors you want to live by or have already established your values, I have learned that less is more when leading an organization into the future.

WHAT MY CORE VALUES MISSTEPS TAUGHT ME AND CAN TEACH YOU

I knew what culture I wanted to foster when setting up my business—a culture where our employees felt accepted, understood, and appreciated for what they do and who they are. At the time, everyone talked about Tony Hsieh's 10 core values for Zappos and how they formed a compass to influence behavior. His book *Delivering Happiness: A Path to Profits, Passion, and Purpose* further demonstrated the power of happiness as a driver for organizational success. His message resonated with me, so I followed his example, created 10 core values to guide my team in the right direction, and proudly hung posters in the office.

Our weekly management meetings would start with discussions of how these values affected our decisions. When hiring new employees, we targeted people who shared our guiding principles. I wanted to create a culture that believed in the same things I did.

Over time, however, I realized that our company culture wasn't how I had envisioned it. Only some of our core values stuck with each person—the others didn't seem all that relevant. This wasn't just an issue at my company. Many businesses go through this same problem, drawing up a list of core values that don't align with who they really are.

I came to a crucial realization that I had created core values with myself in mind, rather than the company. I had failed where Hsieh had succeeded. So, I prompted my leadership team to think deeply about the core values that genuinely aligned with who we were and why we existed. Through this process, we identified four fundamental values. Suddenly, our core values became embedded in each of us and were clearly articulated. Our communication improved, clarity was higher, and decisions were made easily—all because we had a unified understanding of what we stood for. What had begun as a long list ended with four essential core values. Recruiting got simpler, productivity improved, and decision-making was easier. This taught me two things: First, it isn't quantity but quality regarding core values—and less equals more. And second, core values aren't about creating harmony—they're about introducing a strategic set of specific behaviors to guide employees in their work.

WHY ONE-WORD VALUES FALL SHORT IN SHAPING BEHAVIOR

Have you ever walked into an office where, behind the reception desk, you saw laser-cut core values displayed on a wall? Or have you ever, in researching a company, read the About Us page with an empty core values statement?

It might look something like this:

We believe in respect, integrity, trust, diversity, and safety.

You get the point.

How do these business owners guide decision-making and action? Sadly, these empty statements are often idle phrases reflecting the bare minimum of expected values. When I ask business owners or CEOs about core values, and I learn that the values exist on walls or paper but are rarely talked about or used to influence behaviors, I advise that they are putting their companies at cultural risk with unclear ethical standards.

For core values to be effective in driving culture and behavior, you must embody them at all levels of your organization. Your role as a leader is to hold yourself and others accountable for upholding values. Sometimes, this may lead you to make tough decisions, and if necessary, you must terminate the employees who ignore the values your company believes in.

If you want to inspire and motivate action, make your values active—and reward employees who demonstrate and uphold company values in their day-to-day work. Let's explore why values linked to action matters.

SEACRESTING YOUR VALUES

Ryan Seacrest works harder than anyone in Hollywood. His hustle is like no other, as he constantly goes from one job to another.[38]

His work ethic is legendary, not just because he's constantly on the go. It's because he lives out his values in everything he does. He's dedicated, focused, and always striving for excellence. These aren't just words—they're active principles that guide his behavior and drive his success.[39] So, how can you make your values more active? Start by asking yourself what behaviors you want to see in your business.

Do you value teamwork, collaboration, innovation? Think about how you can turn those values into actionable principles.

Teamwork could mean setting up brainstorming sessions regularly, encouraging employees to share their ideas, and rewarding those who work well in teams. Whatever it is, make sure that value is reflected in everything you do.

Don't just talk about collaboration—actively promote it by creating a culture that rewards teamwork and encourages open communication.

And don't just say you value innovation—actively pursue new ideas and approaches that can drive growth and success. If you want your values to be more than words on a page, you must implement them.

Just like "Seacresting" (a term I coined to describe a tireless approach to building a brand with guiding principles and actions), use active verbs to describe the behavior you want to see come to life in your employees.

These action-packed words aren't just there to sound good. They're the secret sauce that spells out the behaviors you're aiming to see in your company.

Let me show you what I mean. Imagine your company thriving on these core values:

- Innovate fearlessly
- Collaborate relentlessly
- Empower others first
- Deliver excellence

- Embrace change
- Inspire creativity
- Communicate openly
- Celebrate diversity

See how these verbs take your values from inaction to action? They're the driving force behind influencing the behavior you want to see—setting expectations for your employees and creating a culture you can be proud of. So, as you craft your core values, remember that active verbs are your trusty sidekicks in shaping the behaviors you want to champion.

Here are some examples of how to transform behavior in your workplace, jumping off from our earlier model of one-word core values:

"Respect" turns into *"Value* each voice": Actively listen, appreciate diverse perspectives, and treat every individual with kindness and consideration.

"Integrity" turns into *"Lead* with honesty": Demonstrate unwavering truthfulness in all actions. We hold ourselves accountable for maintaining the highest ethical standards.

"Trust" turns into *"Build* reliability": Cultivate relationships based on consistent delivery, open communication, and a commitment to fulfilling promises and fostering trust.

"Diversity" turns into *"Embrace* inclusion": Actively seek out and celebrate differences, creating an environment where everyone's unique backgrounds and perspectives are valued and respected.

"Safety" turns into *"Put* safety first": We take proactive measures to safeguard all individuals' physical and emotional security, ensuring a secure and nurturing environment for everyone.

By transforming these core values into actionable behaviors, you're laying the foundation for a workplace culture that tangibly embodies these principles.

The power of core values is evident in the growth and development of any organization. You attract top-tier talent in a crowded marketplace when purpose and values are aligned. Core values work like a magnet, attracting people who share your beliefs. Communicating, living, and tying your core values into decision-making creates an ongoing cycle of attraction and retention, which helps your business thrive and adapt.

Here are the six steps to identifying and crafting your core values.

Step 1: Reflect and Brainstorm

Take time to think about the qualities and behaviors that are important to you and your organization. Gather your leadership team and brainstorm together. What values do you want to guide your actions and decisions? Write down all ideas, even if they seem unrelated.

Step 2: Identify Key Behaviors

Look at your list of values and think about how they translate into actions. What specific behaviors reflect each value? For example, if "Value each voice" is a value, consider actions like active listening and embracing diverse opinions.

Step 3: Choose Your Values

Narrow down your list to the most meaningful and influential values. Aim for around three to five core values that truly represent your organization's beliefs and aspirations.

Step 4: Validate Purposeful Alignment

Your values should reinforce your purpose. Imagine you run a socially responsible coffee chain, and during step 1, you identified several values, but four values stood out, representing who you are and what you believe in: customer happiness, sustainability, fair trade, and community support. Your purpose statement reads:

> At our organic coffee chain, we ardently nurture joy by brewing happiness and kindness into every sip. Rooted in our purpose of providing exceptional coffee, we actively empower coffee-growing communities and champion environmental sustainability, ensuring that every cup makes a positive impact beyond the coffeehouse.
>
> Exceptional Quality and Service
>
> *Guiding principle:* Relentlessly pursuing excellence, we commit to delivering exceptional coffee that consistently surpasses expectations, providing customer experiences that reflect our belief that the warmth of our service should be as organic as our coffee beans.
>
> Fair-Trade Commitment
>
> *Guiding principle:* Fueled by a passion for equitable practices, we are dedicated to supporting fair trade in the coffee industry. Through transparent partnerships, we empower coffee-growing communities, ensuring fair wages and sustainable livelihoods, fostering a thriving and just global coffee community.
>
> Environmental Stewardship
>
> *Guiding principle:* As stewards of the earth, we are dedicated to promoting environmental sustainability at every stage of our coffee production, ensuring a harmonious relationship with nature.

Community Education and Inclusion

Guiding principle: Committed to fostering knowledge and inclusivity, we actively engage in community education initiatives and workshops. As a tangible expression of our commitment, we provide free coffee to homeless shelters, aiming to cultivate a shared sense of learning, understanding, and support within the communities we serve.

Look inward to ensure your purpose and values are in sync with one another—this harmony nurtures peak performance.

Step 5: Define Behaviors

For each chosen value, clearly define the behaviors that align with it. Be specific and actionable. Use active verbs to describe how these values should appear in daily interactions, providing everyone with a clear sense of direction.

Step 6: Communicate and Integrate

Share your core values with your team and integrate them into your organization's culture. Ensure everyone understands what each value means and how to apply it in their work. Use your values to guide decisions, recognize achievements, and shape your organization's identity. Here are five practical tips to help you get started:

1. **Lead by example:** There's a well-known saying that goes "Practice what you preach," and this holds true for leadership. Your leaders and managers must embody the core values they expect from their team. They serve as role models and inspire others to follow suit when employees see them living out those values in their daily actions.

2. **Integrate into everyday decisions:** When faced with decisions, reflect on how they align with your core values. Let your values

act as a compass to guide you. Whether it's choosing a new team member, taking on a project, or interacting with customers, let your values influence those choices.

3. **Celebrate values in action:** Take notice of and applaud employees who embody your core values. Show your appreciation with recognition during meetings and town halls, or even offer a quarterly award. By celebrating standout individuals, you can inspire others to elevate their own work and emulate the company's values.

4. **Include values in performance reviews:** Instead of just displaying your company's core values on a wall, incorporate them into real-time feedback and performance evaluations. Take these reviews as a chance to discuss how employees have embodied the values in their daily responsibilities. This helps employees see that living out the values is not just about words—it is a crucial part of their job descriptions.

5. **Foster open dialogue:** Motivate your team to openly communicate their perspectives on the core values and how they observe them being put into practice. Invite discussions during team meetings, company gatherings, or learning sessions. Give employees the opportunity to recognize and discuss how their colleagues exemplify a core value in their tasks. This fosters a mutual comprehension of your values and how they should be implemented in daily work.

By following the six steps to identifying and crafting your core values, you'll define core values that resonate with your team, guiding them to create a positive and purpose-driven workplace.

Chapter 4

MAPPING YOUR INFINITE LOOP OF CONNECTION

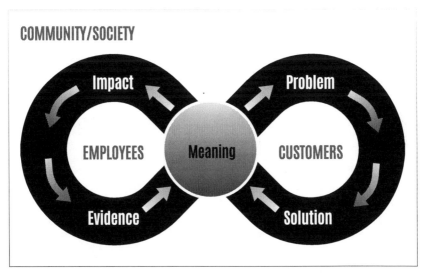

Figure 3

When we start or contemplate starting a business, we are consumed with finding solutions to potential customer problems. We frequently fixate on the issues we are working to solve and eagerly anticipate the overall goal and outcome. We think about how our efforts will revolutionize current practices, and some of us reflect on the potential impact on individuals' lives.

After thorough research, we identify a large market eagerly anticipating our arrival. Then we work on our business model, poring over spreadsheets and arriving at financial projections that show promising revenue growth in the operation's third, fourth, and fifth years. We may aim to overthrow a competitor, cater to an overlooked market segment, disrupt established practices, or generate enough profit to provide for our loved ones.

Whether you are a seasoned CEO leading a family business, an ambitious entrepreneur launching a new online venture, or a baker venturing into owning a cake shop, your goal is to alleviate pain and provide customer gain. These two perspectives are essential for understanding your customers' needs: how your product or service can solve their current problems (pain) and how it can enhance their lives (gain). To get ahead, you prioritize customer pain points, striving to comprehend their needs and determine if your products or services satisfy them. Then, by differentiating your business from competitors, you establish a position in the market, hoping to better fulfill the requirements of your customers.

More often than not, somewhere between your good intentions and how your business is promoted, your customer's wants, needs, and unspoken desires and the difference you want to make get lost in translation. Whether you or the marketing department are leading the way, your value proposition (a statement of what you offer and why you're the best choice) must be clear and compelling enough to convince customers to choose your business over competitors. In striving to create messages that will resonate with your customers, you focus inward, talking about all of the reasons why you're better. But here's a hard truth: You're not better. You don't get to decide what's better for your customers. They do.

When you need to buy deodorant, shampoo, or toothpaste, you have hundreds of options to choose from. When you want to buy a car, there are 129 brands, 7,110 models and 29,837 engine variations.[40] When you buy a car, it's not because it's the best car available—you buy a car because it's the best car for you.

The problem is, too many marketers want to put a spin on your customer's needs and how you solve them, selfishly shouting about how great you are—and how your best-in-class business offers the best solution. They try to steal attention away from your rivals by saying cringey things—you're "agile," "amazing," "world class," a "virtuoso," "integral," "seamless," "synergistic," and "state of the art."

When marketers focus too much on the technical aspects of their digital presence, such as website layout and design, they can lose sight of the ultimate goal: creating meaningful change and solving problems for their audience. Instead, they may get caught up in hustling and interrupting, losing the true purpose of their efforts. Whenever I search on Google, I see companies portraying themselves as heroes in their narratives. Rather than expressing, "I feel your pain, I am here for you, you matter to me, and I value you," these corporations boast, "Look at me. See how amazing I am."

The issue with communication like we see on these websites is that it damages trust. People are not interested in interacting with a business that doesn't prioritize their needs and interests. You probably don't have to go very far in your memory to recall a time when you met someone at a party or ran into an old friend who only talked about themselves, showing little curiosity about what you have to offer. Whether you proudly talk about your biggest accomplishment or confess your deepest fear, the conversation always leads back to them. It's like dealing with a conversational narcissist—they believe the world revolves around them, and no one can change their mind. How did this encounter make you feel? Anxious, uncomfortable, drained? I zone out whenever I find myself in these situations. I start thinking about politely excusing myself and using my time more productively. The same goes for your website. A tireless focus on "me me me" will simply drain your potential clients and cause them to click away.

ON CHANGING MINDS AND BEHAVIOR

Today's consumers have high expectations, and as per Salesforce research, 66% expect companies to understand their individual needs and preferences, while 52% always anticipate personalized offers.[41] This research highlights the importance of moving away from talking about how great your business is to decipher what the consumer truly desires and why and when they want it. Even with your greatest efforts, it is only possible to change someone's thoughts by first changing their emotions and sharing in their social identity. The way to do this is with empathy.

Empathy is the ability to acknowledge a customer's emotions and convey that you can understand their frustration and pain, and it's at the heart of every great innovation and customer experience. While your company may have brilliant founders and a team of top-notch talent, without empathy at the heart of your solution, you may be solving the wrong problems. I've seen this repeatedly. Back when I was enrolled in a boot camp led by Bob Cooper, the creator of Stage-Gate and author of *Winning at New Products: Accelerating the Process from Idea to Launch*, he posed a question to about 40 entrepreneurs. He inquired whether we collaborated directly with our customers during the product design process. To my surprise, not a single person raised their hand in response. Unfortunately, this is all too common, instead of listening to their customers' needs, wants, and desires, many companies persist in releasing new products and services they believe will be successful. Instead of prioritizing the needs and wants of their customers, the design and development approach caters to the egos of product managers and engineers on the team. This self-centered attitude results in a misuse of crucial resources such as time and money. All too frequently, these additions are incorporated into solutions that only hold value for some.

As you contemplate shifting from prioritizing profit to prioritizing your company's purpose, you must paint a clear picture of your business's positive impact on the world. To do this, you can use a powerful tool that many companies need to pay more attention to and make use of in their operations: emotional connection. By looking through the lens of empathy, you can sense and understand others' emotions and perspectives and envision how they might think or feel. When you show empathy toward your customers and employees, they will feel valued and understood, regardless of their circumstances.

People are waiting for you. You just don't know it yet. These are the people who share your worldview, who want to be a part of what you stand for, not for you but for themselves. A worldview is a collection of attitudes, values, stories, and expectations about the world around us. We each have a worldview that shapes our perception and interaction with the world. It influences our behavior and how we influence those around us.[42]

Your worldview invites people in and says, "We made this for you"— instead of saying, "Buy our stuff." Make the time to understand the worldview of the people you seek to change. Focus your energy on your people and ignore everything else. When you focus on the needs, wants, and unspoken desires of those you seek to serve, when you connect and align with who your customers are and what they want, you have the opportunity to help people become better versions of themselves.

Think about how Apple fits into the worldview of their customers. One of the most beloved instances of presenting a worldview in advertising is the iconic 1984 Apple commercial.[43] Its message is clear: embrace nonconformity. It's a worldview that celebrates individuality, originality, and ingenuity.

When Steve Jobs was forced out of Apple in 1985 due to a massive disagreement with the CEO and the board, Apple lost its way. When Jobs returned to Apple as interim CEO in 1997, he had the daunting task of restoring Apple's profitability. Through his remarkable efforts, the company went from a loss of $1.04 billion to a profit of $309 million in just one year. Thanks to Jobs's leadership, Apple transformed from a laughingstock in the tech industry into the most successful and valuable company in the world.[44]

But how did he do this? There were several factors at play, but the most important one is that Jobs knew Apple was no longer living its values. In a rare video of Jobs, he is shown speaking at an internal meeting, introducing the Think Different campaign. In the video, filmed on September 23, 1997, Jobs says:

> *The Apple brand has clearly suffered from neglect in this area in the last few years, and we need to bring it back. The way to do that is not to talk about speeds and feeds. It's not to talk about MIPs and megahertz. It's not to talk about why we're better than Windows....Our customers want to know, who is Apple and what is it that we stand*

for. Where do we fit in this world? And what we're about isn't making boxes for people to get their jobs done—although we do that well, we do that better than almost anybody in some cases—but Apple is about something more than that. Apple at the core, its core value, is that we believe that people with passion can change the world for the better.[45]

In fall 1997, Jobs executed this concept flawlessly with the Think Different campaign.

Here's to the crazy ones, the misfits, the rebels, the troublemakers, the round pegs in the square holes…the ones who see things differently— they're not fond of rules and they have no respect for the status quo. You can quote them, disagree with them, glorify or vilify them, but the only thing you can't do is ignore them because they change things. They push the human race forward. While some may see them as the crazy ones, we see genius, because the people who are crazy enough to think that they can change the world, are the ones who do.[46]

This brilliant campaign goes against traditional marketing principles. In the ad, there is no logo, no call to action. There's a worldview. The genius of the ad lies in its relatability: Don't most of us feel like we don't fit in? Don't most of us see ourselves as misfits?

The underlying message is that truly remarkable people do not conform to societal norms. They carve a unique path on their terms—and, oh, by the way, those people use Macs.

This was an effective approach that conveyed a powerful message. And it continues to resonate, even with the widespread availability of Apple products. Apple users still feel like rebels because our worldview is not about reality but how we perceive ourselves.

And the same holds true for you. Like the transformation of Apple so many years ago, your first step is to create something worth making, and the second step is to build something people will care about, not for yourself but for the change you want to make in their future. The third step is to move making a difference to action, to put what people value most at the core of what you do, to create meaningful bonds by envisioning the shape of things to come, and to create significance for the individuals who would reside in that world. The last step is to show people that you care, that the difference you aim to make is real, that the world they live in is getting better, and that they themselves are helping to contribute to it.

I call this the Purpose Pi, the infinite loop of connection, where instead of competing for the best solution, what if…

…we competed for meaning in the lives of those we choose to serve?

Let's take a step forward by putting ourselves in another person's shoes, setting aside our issues and perspectives and instead considering someone else's feelings, worries, and experiences. This is where we build connection and trust. This is where we develop a shared understanding of the world.

The infinite loop of connection starts with your customers and their problems, guiding you through a process of exploration to transform those problems into opportunities and solutions that can make an impact within and beyond your business. As you continue on, you'll develop methods to monitor and assess your progress in giving back, leading you to the heart of what it means to be meaningful—and to your unique emotional differentiators.

To illustrate how the loop can be used, within each stage of the cycle, you will discover examples of businesses that have navigated their own unique paths to uncover their emotional differentiators and achieve their desired impact on customers, employees, and the community.

Chapter 5

THE KEY TO UNSHAKABLE CUSTOMER LOYALTY

YOUR CUSTOMERS

In order to encourage customers to make a purchase, your business must meet the various needs, wants, and unspoken desires of your potential customers. These can include factors such as the functionality of products and services, price, and availability. To identify these things, your business has more than likely conducted market research or asked for feedback directly from your customers. By understanding and addressing a customer's specific problem, you can better cater to them, fulfill their needs, and ultimately, build stronger customer loyalty.

When you identify your customers' problems, immerse yourself in their stories. Your empathy shows that you genuinely understand your customers and their struggles. While you may be solving multiple problems, let's go back to the drill bit example. Your goal isn't just to assist me in making a hole in my wall. You also want me to achieve the satisfaction of decluttering a room by installing a shelf. I want to feel safe and respected within my living space. Use this opportunity to generate ideas for the problems you solve and the emotions your customers seek to resolve.

In this section of the loop, we are going to identify the bigger problem your business solves for your customers.

Problem

The problem is made up of the following components:

- Needs, wants, and unspoken desires
- Desired outcome
- Who benefits and why

Needs, Wants, and Unspoken Desires

To identify your ideal customer's pain, answer these two questions:

1. Which issue weighs heavily on their mind every day, potentially even disrupting their sleep and daily life?
2. What problem would they immediately pay to have resolved if given the opportunity?

Once you have determined your customer's pain, it's time to shift focus and uncover their greatest desires.

Desired Outcome

- What are your customers' greatest desires?
- What is their ultimate objective?

Who Benefits and Why?

- Who belongs to our shared worldview?
- Are we their kind of people? Do we care about the same things?
- Why should they care about us?

Let's examine a case study of how a business owner of a bakery, located in Ashburn, Virginia, with $735,000 in annual revenue, tackled these questions:

Bakery

Need

- **Need:** The constant worry about providing fresh, allergen-free, quality baked goods for family events or gatherings.
- **Immediate resolution:** Customers would pay for a reliable source of allergen-free specialty baked goods for celebrations.

Desired Outcome

- **Greatest desires:** Customers desire a gluten-free bakery that offers personalized and unique cake designs for special occasions.
- **Ultimate objective:** To create memorable moments through delightful and visually appealing baked goods for people with allergies, particularly celiac disease.

Who Belongs and Why

- **Shared worldview:** Individuals who appreciate the significance of celebrating life's moments with delicious, high-quality, allergen-free baked goods.
- **Our kind of people:** Those who value healthier food options, artisanship, creativity, and personalization in their baked goods.
- **Why care about us:** We share a passion for creating joy through exceptional baked goods, and our commitment to gluten-free quality aligns with customers' celebrated values.

Solution

The solution includes these key elements:

- Functional solution
- Social solution
- Emotional solution

As you move into the next section of the loop, solutions, think deeply about your customers' worldviews. Identify and propose a customer solution to meet a functional need, foster a social connection, and evoke positive emotions about what you stand for.

Functional Solution

Functional needs are the primary needs that come to your mind when solving a problem. These needs directly address what you are trying to achieve. Whether finding someone to mow a lawn, buying a new refrigerator, or ordering food delivery, customers expect businesses to solve their problems. Nowadays, these functional needs often go beyond just solving the initial issue. Companies like Amazon, Walmart, and Target offer a range of solutions and recommend related products and services to help customers identify and solve their problems.

Getting your lawn mowed meets the functional need of having grass that is short, neat, and clean. Your new refrigerator keeps food cold, and the DoorDash app on your phone lets you solve your taco cravings without leaving the office on a busy day.

There are several functional needs your customers have. For this exercise, brainstorm ideas about the various ways your business can meet these needs. If you are a restaurant owner with an online presence, you may recognize the functional need for a convenient ordering process. To meet this need, your solution is to invest in a user-friendly website and mobile app that allows customers to easily browse the menu, select items, and place orders with a few clicks. Implementing secure payment options and a straightforward checkout process means meeting your customers' functional needs for simplicity and efficiency.

If you own an electronics store, you recognize the need for personalized, convenient customer support. Your staff is well trained and knowledgeable about the products you sell. Your solution is to enhance the customer experience, offering multiple channels for customer inquiries, such as live chat, email, and a dedicated phone line, ensuring that your customers can quickly seek assistance when they have questions or encounter issues. Your responsiveness meets the functional need for reliable support and problem resolution.

TIP: In identifying ways to meet your customers' functional needs, talk to them and ask them what they truly value. Conduct surveys, focus groups, and a competitive analysis to understand your customers better.

Identify and write down how you can provide or improve a solution for a functional need your customers have. Remember, the infinite loop of connection isn't static—as improvements in your service continue to reset customer expectations, their needs and demands are evolving. It's important to recognize that the experiences customers have with any organization—whether it be yours or others in the same industry—greatly influence their perception of your business.

If this is your first time using the loop, avoid getting stuck on perfection. Brainstorm and look for ways to be unique—setting new customer expectations while you and your team work together to make your competition irrelevant.

Social Solution

Social needs refer to our inherent desire to be perceived by others in a specific way when using a product or service. These needs are intertwined with our fundamental need for social connection, recognition, and belonging.

In consumer behavior, social needs go beyond functionality and explore the emotional and psychological factors influencing how people want to portray themselves to their social circles. Satisfying social needs means creating opportunities for customers to align their identities and values with their products or services, creating a positive image among their peers.

For example, people feel better about themselves if they can buy more expensive things.[47] This gives them a sense of belonging and reinforces their sense of self in a way that isn't possible elsewhere.

Every decision you make about your purchases is influenced by your social identity, from where you get your daily coffee fix to the brands you choose to wear.[48] Psychologists theorize that Starbucks's popularity is partly due to people's desire to reward themselves.[49] After all, before a busy day at work, why not indulge in a luxurious Sugar Cookie Almondmilk Latte? It's a fairly affordable treat that many can enjoy daily.

Starbucks targets a diverse audience, ranging from 22 to 60 years old, primarily in urban and suburban areas. Their primary focus is on individuals with higher income levels, predominantly middle and upper class, who are well educated and socially conscious, leading busy and active lives.[50]

Every day, Starbucks works alongside their communities to improve and uplift the areas where their stores are located. Through events like open mic nights, service projects, and spreading messages of inspiration, the company affirms that they are dedicated to making communities stronger and more resilient. If you buy your morning coffee at Starbucks, you identify with your community and this group. You're saying, "I belong here—this is who I am." There are numerous brands that may resonate with you, that you may feel a sense of belonging to and want to patronize and differentiate yourself with.

If you are knowledgeable about the world of yoga and fitness apparel, then you are likely familiar with Lululemon. This company has established itself as a pioneer in the industry by creating a community centered around its brand. Lululemon has gained a devoted fan base by offering customers the resources and opportunities they need to reach their full potential.

Lululemon has always centered its branding efforts on the yoga community, starting with its roots in Vancouver, Canada. Unlike other companies that rely on celebrity endorsements and sports stars to promote their brands, Lululemon meets a social need by partnering with local yoga teachers and fitness experts to represent their values. In addition, Lululemon uses its physical stores as venues for hosting yoga classes, meditation sessions, and other related events.[51]

Lululemon creates clothing that encourages individuals to feel confident and at ease while practicing yoga or engaging in fitness activities. By wearing their apparel, you express a sense of belonging to a community, a group of people, that shares your values.

Think of how your business can create opportunities for people to identify and belong to your community. How can you help people connect? How can you make their lives better? Write down a new social solution your team can implement. You have everything you need to build something bigger than yourself. Help and lead your community by being social.

Ten Ideas to Be More Social

1. **Create community events:** Organize local events or workshops that unite customers, fostering a community around your brand.

2. **Leverage social media:** Actively engage on social media platforms to build a virtual community, sharing relevant content and encouraging conversations to help people become better versions of themselves.

3. **Design customer appreciation programs:** Implement loyalty programs or exclusive discounts to show appreciation for longtime customers and encourage repeat business.

4. **Facilitate networking opportunities:** Provide spaces or platforms where customers can connect, whether in online forums or in-store events.

5. **Encourage user-generated content:** Request and showcase customer content, such as reviews, testimonials, or photos, to strengthen a sense of belonging.

6. **Support local causes:** Align your business with local charities or causes to demonstrate social responsibility and connect with customers who share similar values.

7. **Host social challenges or contests:** Organize fun challenges or contests on social media to encourage participation and interaction among your customer base.

8. **Personalize communication:** Tailor your communication to acknowledge milestones or special occasions in your customers' lives, making them feel valued beyond just a transaction.

9. **Create a customer advisory board:** Establish a group of customers who provide feedback and insights, making them feel like valued contributors to your business decisions.

10. **Offer social spaces in physical stores:** If applicable, design areas where customers can gather, relax, or interact in your physical store, enhancing the overall shopping experience.

Emotional Solution

An emotional need is how your customer feels about an experience with your brand. When your customer interacts with your company, they may go through a range of emotions. Your objective is to offer the customer a positive and emotionally fulfilling experience. Understanding customers' emotional needs can be complex, but it's crucial in creating a lasting impression. Although the quality of your products or services may fade from memory, how you made them feel will stick with them.

When thinking about your customers' emotions, consider a few questions: Are they seeking thrills and awe? Joy and a sense of belonging? Security and trust? Confidence and pride? Do your customers want to stand out or feel a sense of freedom?

Whether it's the thrill of discovery, the comfort of familiarity, or the joy of a personalized experience at your favorite coffee shop, when you understand and cater to the emotional needs of your customers, you profoundly impact satisfaction and loyalty. Deloitte, a research and consulting firm, found that 60% of loyal customers use the same emotional language they'd use for family and friends when speaking about their favorite brands.[52]

Allow me to illustrate this point. Two years ago, we wanted to get our dog, Alvin, groomed for the Christmas holidays. We had anticipated that PetSmart would be busy, so I booked an appointment well in advance. When I arrived at the store, our dog, a Morkie who tends to get nervous around new people, was apprehensive about a new handler. Within seconds, the groomer looked at me and stated emphatically, "We're not grooming Alvin. He's not cooperating, and we're not taking him."

"But we've been here many times before," I said. "We've never had a problem."

The groomer looked at me sternly and said, "It's at our discretion. You're going to have to find somewhere else to go."

I immediately became frustrated. "But we made this appointment weeks ago," I replied. "For the Christmas holidays."

"I don't care—I'm not taking him."

Those three words—"I don't care"—turned my frustration into anger. "Thank you," I said. "I won't be back."

Within that two-minute exchange of words, I felt a range of emotions—annoyance, frustration, anger, and resentment. These are the opposite of the feelings a company wants to evoke. I took our dog, returned to my car, and called my wife—and I vented. We knew it was unlikely we'd be able to get an appointment before Christmas Eve, but I got on my phone and opened Google Maps, searching for pet groomers nearby.

After I called three pet-grooming services, which were all booked until January, it was my fourth call that changed my luck. "Who am I talking to?" I asked.

"Stacey," she replied.

"I'm desperately trying to get our dog groomed before Christmas," I said. Stacey said she was booked for the rest of the year.

I explained my situation and the humiliation of rejection, and I could hear the empathy in Stacey's voice. "That's not right," she said. "I'm booked all day, but if you bring Alvin in now, I'll fit him in so you can enjoy the holidays."

"Are you sure?" I replied.

"Yes," Stacey said. "I want you to come in. I don't want you and your family to worry about finding another groomer at this time of year."

I felt excitement, joy, appreciation, and gratitude. I called my wife and told her I was going to Shampoodles to meet Stacey.

When Alvin was dropped off, he immediately became nervous again.

"That's okay," Stacey said. "You can leave him with me."

"Are you sure?" I replied anxiously.

"Don't worry, he's in good hands," Stacey said. She needed two hours to clean him up and said she'd call me when Alvin was ready to be picked up.

When I arrived back at the pet-grooming salon, I was amazed by the care Stacey had taken with Alvin. He was so cute! I was elated. "He's all ready," Stacey said, smiling. "And he wasn't bad at all."

As I thanked Stacey repeatedly, paying for the service with a big tip, Stacey reached down with a big smile and handed me a Christmas ornament with Alvin's name hand-painted on it. Her face glowed. "Merry Christmas," she said. I felt unexpected joy, pride, and gratitude from her caring gesture.

Stacey had created a powerful emotional connection with me. Since that day, Stacey has been our groomer, running her business with the same empathy and caring that sets her apart. Our friends go to Stacey because she always cares—and is always smiling, drawing the same emotions from all of her customers—joy, pride, and appreciation. To this day, I haven't walked into another PetSmart. And every Christmas, we're reminded of Stacey's kindness when we hang Alvin's ornament on our tree.

How many times has a business elicited negative emotions in you? How did it make you feel?

Think about the emotions you want to evoke in your business. Brainstorm ways you and your team can influence ideas, attitudes, beliefs, and behaviors. Narrow down your list of emotions to two to three feelings your business can focus on to create meaningful bonds with your customers. Let's explore the identified functional, social, and emotional solutions in our bakery example.

Bakery

Functional Solution

Introduce a comprehensive allergen-free menu, ensuring the availability of high-quality specialty baked goods for various allergies, with a focus on gluten-free options.

Social Solution

Create a community platform for customers to share their celebration stories and experiences and even contribute ideas for new allergen-free designs, fostering a sense of belonging.

Emotional Solution

Craft visually appealing, personalized baked goods that meet dietary needs and contribute to the emotional significance of special occasions, creating joy and lasting memories.

Chapter 6

BRIDGING THE EMPATHY GAP

Throughout my professional journey, I have observed and consulted with various businesses, ranging from small startups to large corporations. Unfortunately, many of these organizations lacked clear purpose and values. This lack of direction was reflected in the attitudes and behaviors of their employees—going through the motions, conflicts among team members, low morale and productivity, and a focus on personal gain rather than team success. The leadership often seemed oblivious to the importance of building a strong team.

I have witnessed instances where individuals were promoted without the necessary skills or qualifications. And unfortunately, even one toxic employee can significantly affect a team and company. Even when a business is financially successful, a toxic employee can still have a noticeable effect on corporate culture. There is no denying the broken state of the American workplace. In far too many cases, organizations have no sense of purpose and no interest in creating meaning.

And yet the search for meaning and purpose is a fundamental aspect of being human that transcends geographical boundaries, eras, and societies. Throughout history, we have yearned to understand our existence and the significance of our actions in the world. This innate desire for meaning motivates us to seek fulfillment and connection beyond our daily routines. It compels us to delve into the mysteries of the universe, introspect on our thoughts and emotions, and contemplate existential questions about our purpose here on Earth.

In our professional lives, finding meaning and purpose becomes crucial. Our jobs are not just about completing tasks—they are where we strive to develop, express our identities, and fulfill our aspirations. We no longer want to be stuck in mundane routines that hold no significance. Instead, we seek roles that align with our values and allow us to make a meaningful impact.

As our work takes up a significant portion of our lives, we want to seek jobs that align with our desire for significance, allowing us to feel as if our contributions matter. This desire is felt by all—to be more than just a small part of a larger machine, to have our actions make a positive impact on humanity and leave a lasting impression.

The world came to a standstill when the COVID-19 pandemic struck, causing us to reevaluate our lives. We were forced to strip away all distractions and focus on what truly mattered. Our jobs, once just a means of earning a paycheck, now faced intense scrutiny. Were we making a meaningful impact? Was our work truly valued? This introspective pause caused a significant shift in perspective for many, with a majority of the American workforce considering a new direction for their careers.[53]

But that's not where the story ends. Many leaders overlook the untapped potential of their employees, failing to recognize their longing for validation and a sense of purpose in their work. Employees want to be part of something greater and make a meaningful contribution to the world, but many businesses fail to acknowledge this yearning within their workforce. Without meaning in the workplace, more and more employees are choosing to quietly quit,[54] and 58% of the hybrid workforce has resorted to "coffee-badging," a new term to describe employees who go to the office before quickly leaving to work remotely for the rest of the day.[55] As more and more employees simply go through the motions to maintain their jobs, a divide is growing between us—a disconnect between employers and employees.

As leaders, coaches, and mentors, we have lost our way. Our focus has shifted solely toward the bottom line, causing us to neglect the humanity within our businesses and work lives. We detach ourselves from what it truly means to be human—our faith, values, and souls. Society tells us to leave our personal lives at home and only show a fraction of ourselves at work—as if we are subhuman beings just trying to survive until we can clock out and finally live as real humans again. We must remember that work is not just about getting the job done. It is about connecting with others on a deeper level and honoring our own humanity in the process.

As a leader and entrepreneur, I always strove for growth and success in my business. However, I never forgot that my role was to guide and support others in reaching their full potential. In the equation of success, it is our responsibility to prioritize the well-being of others. This kindness and empathy fosters reciprocity and strengthens our capacity to care for those around us. When we neglect others, we contribute to the pain present in our world. Even small acts of kindness can have a ripple effect on the health and unity of our teams.

Despite this, many leaders and managers continue to neglect the impact they have on those responsible for achieving their desired success. In today's workplace, we have become too focused on being secular and detached, missing out on the opportunities to forge emotional connections with those we lead. We only have to look as far as *A Dictionary of Business and Management* to read the definition of "CEO," which is "the person with responsibility for ensuring an organization functions efficiently and generates profit acceptable to shareholders."[56] But I argue that this definition needs to change. The most successful CEOs are chief empathy officers. They embody empathy because they understand that creating an efficient organization requires motivating, uniting, and connecting people, customers, and organizations together through empathy. And yet, all around us, the empathy gap is widening.

THE VANISHING COMPASSION: A CONTEMPORARY CRISIS

Businessolver's 2023 state of workplace empathy report revealed that HR professionals have the lowest perception of empathy toward their CEOs since 2017 and that this lack of empathy is taking a toll on HR professionals' mental health. Interestingly, while 67% of CEOs believe they have become more empathetic since the pandemic began, both HR professionals and employees believe that CEO empathy levels are at an all-time low.[57] This stark contrast in experiences has led to a sense of cynicism and pessimism among HR professionals and employees, while CEOs remain optimistic and confident.[58]

So, what exactly is happening here? It's evident that there's a significant disconnect between the thoughts of CEOs and the actual state of the current workforce. If you're taking the time to read this book, I hope it's because you have a desire to bring about meaningful change. The main objective of the infinite loop of connection is to prioritize making a positive impact within your workplace, which will then extend beyond your business. To achieve this, we must look at the concerning trend of employee discontent and understand why it's occurring.

In one of the largest burnout studies ever conducted, Gallup found that the primary cause of burnout was unfair treatment in the workplace. This was closely followed by overwhelming workload, inadequate communication from managers, lack of support from superiors, and unrealistic time constraints.[59]

This situation might be occurring in your workplace right now. Michael, a talented engineer, had lost the spark that he'd once had. His eyes were red rimmed, and his face was unshaven after countless nights of sleepless frustration. He trudged into his supervisor's office, dreading the discussion about the project his team had been working on for months. Although Michael knew the sales team needed to be more helpful with their customer requests for new features, he wanted to let his manager know how demoralizing it was to continually receive changes and new demands without a vision for where the project should end up. But instead of offering him support or direction, Michael's boss, the head of engineering, shifted the blame to the sales department and refused to take any responsibility for the inefficient change-request process. Michael sat back down at his desk with a heavy heart and worked on his résumé, resigned to finding a new job outside the company. He longed to work on something meaningful again, something where his efforts made a difference. Michael is not the only one who is experiencing these feelings.

Like Michael, employees are putting employers on notice—and in the wake of a tidal wave of actual resignations, with more than 47 million people leaving their jobs in 2021 as part of the ongoing Great Resignation,[60] they are quietly quitting. Despite the misleading name, quiet quitting describes individuals who have given up on going above and beyond in their roles (sometimes referred to as soft quitting or silent resignation). These quiet quitters simply go through the motions and meet the basic expectations of their jobs to maintain employment. By putting in minimal effort, they show that they no longer feel valued or acknowledged.

This came to a head when, in 2022, career coach and YouTuber Bryan Creely coined the term "quiet quitting," and it quickly gained popularity after he posted a video about it on TikTok.[61] In the video, Creely narrates in front of a *Business Insider* headline stating, " 'My Company Is Not My Family': Fed Up with Long Hours, Many Employees Have Quietly Decided to Take It Easy at Work Rather Than Quit Their Jobs." He described the trend as employees relaxing and reducing their efforts at work and included the caption "More people are 'quiet quitting' instead of leaving." His terminology really caught on. His video received over 3.5 million views and nearly 500,000 likes.[62] The hashtag QuietQuitting has been viewed over 159 million times![63]

After a steady increase in past years, employee engagement in the United States experienced its first decrease in 10 years.[64] While silently leaving a job is not a new concept, it has become a coping mechanism for dealing with toxic work environments, inadequate pay, and lack of representation and inclusivity.[65] The key challenge for CEOs, entrepreneurs, and business owners is recognizing that disengaged workers often check out due to feelings of being overworked, underappreciated, and undervalued. The same factors that drive someone to resign from their job also contribute to quiet quitting. According to a 2023 Gallup poll, nearly half of the American workforce is contemplating quitting their jobs, and the number of disengaged workers has risen to 18%.[66] These figures are concerning, as they have a significant impact on productivity and growth. It's likely that your business is being affected by this lack of employee engagement.

Studies have shown that unmotivated employees are less likely to perform well, meet targets, or produce quality work. In fact, 73% of these disengaged workers are actively seeking new job opportunities. This problem results in low productivity and high employee turnover rates, causing businesses to suffer from substantial financial losses. Estimates show that these losses range from $450 billion to $550 billion annually. Currently, only 32% of employees are engaged in their work, while 18% are actively disengaged—the lowest ratio in a decade at 1.8 to 1.[67]

Chapter 7

STAYING IS A CHOICE YOU HELP THEM MAKE

When employee morale is low and the general attitude is negative, it's crucial to prioritize measures to boost engagement and to show genuine care for your employees. Having a cohesive team with clear communication, a shared focus on goals, and effective collaboration is essential for achieving success in any business. However, if you're dealing with issues like unfair treatment, overwhelming workloads, lack of communication, or little support from leadership, those are signs of a broken company culture.

The sense of being rejected, isolated, and not fitting in can have a negative impact on people's performance. These feelings may not be obvious in your workplace, but they exist in cubicles, on business trips, and even during board meetings. According to the EY Belonging Barometer, 75% of employees have felt excluded from work, while 56% believe that they cannot share certain aspects of their identity or are hesitant to share them while on the job due to concerns about it hindering their progress.[68] As we navigate through the lessons of the pandemic, many business owners still struggle with developing strategies for human connection, which only adds to the issue. People are feeling left out and disconnected. What if we shifted our focus from building better products or services to understanding and catering to the beliefs and needs of those we serve? How would our work environments change?

True leadership involves not just taking charge but also guiding others toward a sense of purpose and inspiration so that they can join us on the journey.

Just as empathy drives meaningful customer experiences on the right side of the connection loop, it is also essential for building strong relationships and trust within our companies. Great leaders cultivate emotional bonds with their employees through empathy and confidence. They harness the individual abilities, experiences, perspectives, and viewpoints of their team members to achieve their shared purpose. By genuinely caring about your employees' success and making them feel valued, you establish a solid foundation for a high-performing culture. This sense of support and direction boosts employee motivation, satisfaction, and even long-term loyalty, especially during challenging times.

Belonging is just as important for us humans as love is—it's a core aspect of our existence. The desire to fit in is ingrained in us. We all yearn to be recognized, acknowledged, and accepted at our jobs and in our personal lives. When we don't feel as if we belong, the world can seem like a cold and lonely place. This feeling can leave us feeling trapped, uneasy, and undeserving—these are incapacitating sensations. Most of us have experienced this at some point in our lives. One of my most painful memories from middle school involved being chosen close to last for team sports. When I look back now, I realize it wasn't a huge deal, but at the time it was heart wrenching. I can still hear the voice inside my head begging the team captains not to pick me last. All I wanted was to feel as if I belonged. Our need for belonging is a fundamental human need, yet many companies struggle to create a workplace culture where everyone feels included and valued.

People find fulfillment in serving their communities, caring for their loved ones, advocating for social and political change, practicing their faith, and pursuing careers that allow them to make a positive impact. However, we can sometimes lose sight of the fact that the purpose of hiring, training, and keeping employees is not just to meet performance goals but also to provide meaning and fulfillment for those who work for us. Our focus often becomes fixated on revenue, profits, products, and staying relevant.

We pour our efforts into reaching targets and making small improvements without fully grasping what truly matters to our employees and customers.

On the other side of the coin, leaders who prioritize caring and belonging at work are reaping the benefits: When employees feel a sense of belonging in their workplace, companies see significant positive effects on their bottom line. Studies have shown that high feelings of belonging are linked to a staggering 56% increase in job performance, a 50% decline in turnover risk, and a 75% decrease in the number of sick days taken. For a company with 10,000 workers, this could result in annual savings exceeding $52 million. Employees who reported higher levels of belonging also had a 167% increase in their employer Net Promoter Score, indicating a greater willingness to recommend their company to others. Additionally, they received double the salary raises and were promoted 18 times more often.[69]

It's important to remember that just having an HR department in your business doesn't necessarily mean you are taking care of your employees. Yes, HR workers handle important tasks like hiring and conducting interviews, managing pay and benefits, and enforcing company policies. However, these responsibilities do not necessarily contribute to creating a meaningful work environment. Many employees prioritize having a sense of purpose in their jobs, but often this is not something they find in their workplaces.

Creating an environment where employees genuinely feel they belong is about weaving the fabric of a workplace with threads of compassion and connection. It's not just a matter of productivity—it's about infusing the very soul of your organization with a sense of warmth and understanding. When individuals find themselves in a place that values their uniqueness and contributions, work transforms from a task into a shared journey. It's about creating a workplace where people don't just work side by side—they collaborate, inspire, and uplift each other.

Imagine a workplace where everyone feels wanted and like an integral part of a larger purpose. It's not just a job—it's a home where talents are cherished, ideas are celebrated, and everyone is embraced for who they are. It's about building a harmonious work environment where the melody of collaboration, understanding, and shared goals resonates in the hearts of every employee.

What if, before creating our business plans, we first thought about how we wanted our employees and customers to feel? And how could we shift the way our businesses operate by prioritizing meaning as our competitive advantage?

This is the power of the infinite loop. You can harness belonging in your workplace and use it to foster a culture of purpose. By promoting unity, support, and empathy, you can cultivate a workplace that values acceptance and recognizes its employees. This goes beyond simple engagement and allows for the creation of meaningful work. In doing so, you are creating value within and outside your company that your competitors can only envy.

To add more value and make a greater impact within the organization, let's begin by addressing these questions:

- Why do people join us?
- Why do people stay with us?
- What do our employees care about?
- What is our superpower?

WHY DO PEOPLE JOIN US?

As you make your way through the connection loop, the bakery case study at the end of this chapter will serve as an example of how your purpose and core values will guide you through this process. This is because, when individuals make decisions to leave a job, join a new organization, or stay in their current role, their sense of purpose greatly influences their choices. When you're growing and seeking new talent, research shows that over 90% of employees are willing to sacrifice a portion of their lifetime earnings in exchange for fulfilling work.[70] This holds true regardless of age or salary level, as workers value meaningful work so much that they are willing to pay for it with less compensation. That's not to say you should offer less compensation because your business is purpose driven. I'm making the point that people are actively seeking meaningful roles and can't find them!

As people search for new and fulfilling roles, they are checking two boxes: First, job seekers are ensuring that the job aligns with their skills and interests, and second, they often research your company's purpose and values. The talented people you're seeking want to make sure your culture and beliefs reflect what they believe. Even if the job description seems perfect, if your company doesn't align with their personal values or have a clear sense of purpose, they will likely continue their search for potential opportunities elsewhere.

According to a WeSpire survey,[71] Gen Z (born between 1997 and 2015) is the first generation to place purpose above salary when it comes to their career priorities.[72] And over half of millennials (born between 1981 and 1996) will not consider a job offer if your company does not have a strong corporate social responsibility policy. In today's world, your core beliefs and guiding principles are extremely important—they serve as your North Star. They not only define your company, but they also communicate to potential employees what is important to you, how they will be treated, and what kind of work environment they can expect. For example, the bakery we used in our earlier example prides itself on its artistic creations and fosters a welcoming and supportive environment. It values building a community that appreciates the little joys in life through indulging in delicious treats, while also taking into account various dietary restrictions. The bakery is dedicated to helping its employees grow professionally and has a strong commitment to giving back to the community by donating excess baked goods to those in need.

This company culture is appealing to job seekers who are looking for a sense of purpose and belonging in their work. They understand that their contributions will have a positive impact on people's well-being by creating allergen-free baked goods and promoting inclusivity and compassion within their community.

Take the time to consider why people choose to join your organization. Reflect on your own purpose and values, as well as what it means to truly make a difference for those seeking employment. Consider how you can establish trust and align with their social identity. Think about the kind of business you want to run and the type of work environment you wish to cultivate. How you approach this question shapes the culture you strive to create—or enhance.

WHY DO PEOPLE STAY WITH US?

Throughout history, people have sought to find meaning in their daily routines, seeking fulfillment beyond the necessities of survival. Today, the search for purpose has become even more pressing, as work takes up an increasing amount of our time and energy. Committed and motivated employees are the foundation of every successful business, and companies with a strong sense of purpose have mastered the art of nurturing a dedicated workforce. According to a global survey by PwC, employees in purpose-driven organizations report 1.7 times higher job satisfaction, leading to increased productivity and lower turnover costs.[73]

You can lead the way by implementing programs aimed at increasing employee engagement and satisfaction, such as volunteer opportunities, internal mentorship programs, and flexible work arrangements, as evidenced from the pandemic's necessity for work-from-home policies. By providing these options, you are not only helping your employees find meaning in their work, but you are also reaping the benefits of increased productivity and loyalty.

Providing these programs alone will not solve the problem of employees feeling unfulfilled. You must also take steps to ensure that the work being done aligns with your purpose and values and that employees feel valued and recognized for their contributions. Case in point—think back to the last time you poured your heart and soul into a project, crafting it into something you were truly proud of, and executed it flawlessly. That feeling of accomplishment is exhilarating, but it becomes even more powerful when others take notice.

The simple act of acknowledging achievement can have a tremendous impact on employee morale and performance. Acknowledging and appreciating employees' efforts can lead to increased engagement in the workplace. Research from Quantum Workplace found that employees who feel that their work will be recognized by management are 2.7 times more likely to have high levels of engagement.[74] And Gallup and Workhuman worked together on a study to gain insight into employees' views on recognition.[75] They delved into what recognition truly means to employees, whether they feel it is genuine, fair, and frequent enough, and how it affects their overall outlook on work and life. The study revealed that frequent recognition at work leads to the following improvements in employee morale:

- Fifty-six percent less likely to be looking for or watching for job opportunities
- Four times as likely to be engaged
- Three times as likely to feel loyal to their organization
- Four times as likely to strongly agree they would recommend their organization as a great place to work
- Four times as likely to feel that they belong at their organization
- Five times as likely to see a path to grow at their organization

These findings highlight the powerful impact that recognition can have on your employees, as those who receive the appropriate level of recognition according to their needs and expectations experience significant positive benefits. Ask yourself and your team—what matters most?

Why do people choose to stay with you? How do you care for your employees—wellness programs, customized benefits programs, flexible work arrangements? How do you recognize and celebrate individual and team wins? How do you help your employees grow and advance? Training? Professional development? Mentorship programs to foster professional growth and knowledge transfers?

Make a list of the ways you could get higher levels of engagement in your company culture. This will serve as your road map for building a dedicated and motivated workforce. You might add things like these:

- Organize volunteer opportunities in your local community and compensate employees for donating their time to causes that align with your company's beliefs and values.
- Plan company events outside the office.
- Prioritize physical and mental health.
- Form an employee resource group, which is a voluntary, employee-led group that aims to create a diverse and inclusive workplace.
- Encourage employee passion projects.

The length of your response is not a cause for concern—every business is unique and will have different needs. If you're a larger organization, your HR department can provide you with a summary of your employee benefits and programs. If you're just starting out, you may not have put much thought into what you can offer. In this section, concentrate on what you can offer and accomplish with your current resources. Keep in mind that the priorities and capabilities of a team of five people will differ from those of a company with 100 employees. The important thing to remember is that you are putting in the effort now. Keep in mind, the connection loop is never ending. It's natural to feel overwhelmed when compared to larger corporations and their offerings. However, as your business expands, you can always return to your loop and incorporate new ways to keep employees engaged and fulfilled. Focus on how you can create a more meaningful culture for the people who believe in you and for your cause by creating the baseline for where you are now.

As a sidenote, it's important to gather feedback from employees on a regular basis to understand their preferences and constantly improve these programs to maintain their effectiveness in fostering engagement. We will discuss methods for conducting an employee engagement survey in the planning section of this book.

WHAT DO OUR EMPLOYEES CARE ABOUT?

In my 25 years of experience, I have seen the significant influence of cultural involvement, or the lack thereof, in both large and small businesses. I have spearheaded communication plans for employee engagement, conducted employee surveys, monitored companies' internal Net Promoter Scores, organized company-wide meetings and workshops, and implemented internal campaigns to boost employee engagement.

Although employee engagement is essential, it has two significant shortcomings. First, it needs to reveal the genuine concerns of your employees, and engagement surveys and company-wide meetings won't give you all the answers. And second, engagement tools don't demonstrate that you genuinely care about your company culture.

The issue with using engagement tools and surveys is that they only gather information from one side—the questions you want to ask. While I recommend making use of these tools, it's important to have two-sided conversations about what truly matters to your employees.

This is about demonstrating genuine empathy for your employees' concerns and interests. It's about gaining a deeper understanding of the significance of your company culture and identifying potential areas that may need improvement. You can take actionable steps toward amplifying successful practices by actively listening to your employees and acknowledging their priorities and what they care about. This is an ideal occasion to express to your team that their thoughts and feelings truly matter to your company.

With so much going on in your workday, it can be difficult for employees to feel valued and appreciated. It's easy to get caught up in your daily tasks and appear too busy for simple conversations. However, taking the time to hold yourself accountable, asking your team members why their work matters, and actively listening will show your employees that they are respected and valued.

So, what do your employees care about? Considering this question, reflect on why your employees are invested in their work and its importance. What aspects of your company's purpose and values resonate with them? How does your work culture positively affect your employees? While it may seem like a given, ask your employees what matters to them. In addition, ask your leaders and managers if they have actively engaged in this conversation recently. Is your work culture meeting the needs of your employees? How does their sense of contribution affect their overall satisfaction at work?

Gathering input from your employees and understanding their priorities shows that you care. Your employees are the backbone of your company, and you carefully selected each one for a reason. You can create a more positive and fulfilling organizational culture by actively showing interest in their personal and professional lives. This also means recognizing what matters most to your employees, which will hold you and your leadership team accountable for maintaining this feedback loop and fostering a thriving work environment.

WHAT IS OUR SUPERPOWER?

When I was a CEO in the past, I was faced with countless ideas, options, and strategies promising even greater success for our company. My email inbox was constantly flooded with individuals trying to grab my attention and pitch solutions that would revolutionize how we provided value to our customers and beat our competition. During the management of daily inbox chaos, it was up to me to provide our teams with clear direction and guidance as we worked toward achieving our goals and making progress.

It was bound to happen—one of my team members would inevitably come up to me and say, "Did you happen to catch what our competitor is up to?" or "Our rival just added a 24/7 chat feature to their website," or "One of our potential customers asked how we stack up against feature X."

Seldom do these conversations focus on our competitors' distinct "organizational advantage." The problem is, when we survey the competitive landscape, we tend to become hyperfocused on solution comparisons. This happens when our sales team alerts us to a rival's latest launch of a new product, service, or feature, and suddenly we are urged to start development on something similar. We fall into the trap of constantly comparing ourselves to others instead of staying true to our own vision and catering to what our customers truly need and want.

To truly differentiate ourselves from our competitors, we must first focus on where we invest our time and energy. To avoid the comparison trap, we should strive to create our own unique value in the market. By constantly benchmarking against what our competitors are doing, we limit our potential and set the bar too low for what our team can achieve. We need to change our perspective and focus on our strengths, doing more of what we excel at.

To achieve this, we must identify and make use of our distinctive strengths and organizational capabilities. In other words, when you bring together your team, processes, and technology, what sets you apart? While your competitors may try to replicate what you're doing, they will always be playing catch-up. You can easily add the same features as them, but what sets you apart is your unique superpower. This is something that cannot be easily duplicated.

Your company has one or two distinct strengths that drive your success. Once identified, these core strengths guide your employees and strengthen your differentiated workplace culture. These strengths are your superpower.

Think of your favorite superheroes, and what sets them apart from the rest of us. When I was growing up, my favorite heroes were Superman and Wonder Woman.

Superman, the popular comic book and movie character, is a symbol of hope, justice, and pure goodness. Along with his impressive abilities, including "flight, superhuman strength, X-ray vision, heat vision, cold breath, super-speed, and enhanced hearing,"[76] his true superpower lies in the unshakable principles of truth and justice that guide him.

With superhuman strength and invincibility granted by her magic bracelets and shield, Wonder Woman can withstand even the hottest of fires. Her expertise in hand-to-hand combat, ability to communicate with all creatures (so cool), and extraordinary agility, stamina, endurance, and reflexes make her a paragon of justice and empathy.

While Superman and Wonder Woman may possess incredible powers, it's what they do with those abilities that truly matters—fighting for truth, justice, and equality. Just like the imaginary superheroes whose strengths contribute to the goodness of humanity, you have distinctive organizational strengths that define who you are and what you stand for. These superpowers set you apart and draw in loyal customers.

In thinking about your superpowers, here are two examples to help guide you:

Adaptability: Your strengths leverage the ability to effortlessly adjust and evolve with the ever-changing market conditions, customer demands, and industry developments. You excel in overcoming obstacles, capitalizing on new opportunities, and maintaining perseverance in a rapidly evolving business environment.

Empathy: Your organizational capabilities enable you to comprehend and empathize with the feelings and requirements of customers and staff, promoting sincere connections and cultivating a caring work environment.

Each of these superpowers can contribute to the success and resilience of your business in a dynamic and competitive market. But before you write anything down, it's crucial that your core strengths represent who you really are. For illustration purposes, let's look at how three small-business owners used their superpowers.

A Train Engine Parts Supplier

Superpower: Negotiation

The owner of a train engine parts supply business wielded negotiation as a superpower, consistently securing favorable deals with suppliers and clients alike. Through adept negotiation skills, they forged strategic partnerships, ensuring a steady supply of high-quality components at competitive prices. This not only boosted their profit margins but also allowed them to offer cost-effective solutions to their clients, solidifying the business's reputation for reliability and efficiency in the competitive market.

A Health Services Organization

Superpower: Grit

At the helm of a health services organization, the owner exhibited grit as a superpower, tackling challenges in the ever-evolving healthcare landscape. Despite facing regulatory hurdles and resource constraints, the owner demonstrated unwavering determination to improve patient outcomes and provide quality care. Their grit-driven approach inspired the team to persevere through adversity, fostering a resilient and patient-focused organizational culture. Ultimately, this commitment to excellence led to improved service delivery, enhanced patient satisfaction, and sustained success in a demanding industry.

A Marketing Agency

Superpower: Evangelizing

The owner of a marketing agency harnessed evangelizing as their superpower, passionately advocating for their clients' brands. Through fervent belief in the power of effective marketing, they transformed clients into enthusiastic advocates for their own brands. This superpower not only led to increased client satisfaction, but it also generated word-of-mouth referrals and long-term partnerships. By evangelizing the unique value propositions of their clients, the marketing agency owner successfully built a portfolio of thriving brands, establishing the agency as a go-to partner for influential and results-driven marketing strategies.

Write down one to two superpowers your business has, how these capabilities provide meaning at work for your employees and customers, and how they will contribute to your success over the next three years.

Coming back to our bakery case study, purpose and values helped to inform the answers for this business owner. To answer the question "Why do people stay with us?" the key is to tie recognition and rewards directly to the core values and purpose of the company, reinforcing the importance of these values in creating meaning for employees.

Bakery

Purpose: To enrich and celebrate life's moments by crafting exceptional, allergen-free baked goods sourced locally, fostering joy, and creating lasting memories for our community.

Core Values

- **Delight with artistry:** We passionately pursue the art of baking, infusing creativity and skill into every confection. Through our commitment to artistic excellence, we aim to delight our customers with visually stunning and flavorful baked goods that surpass expectations.
- **Actively care for allergies and celiac wellness:** With a deep commitment to inclusivity, we actively prioritize the well-being of individuals with allergies and celiac disease. Our dedication to crafting allergen-free baked goods ensures that everyone can enjoy our offerings, promoting a sense of inclusion and care for our diverse community.
- **Foster a joyful community:** We actively engage with our customers, creating a warm and welcoming space where connections are formed. Through events, collaborations, and personalized service, we strive to build a community that shares in the simple pleasure of life's sweet moments, with consideration for diverse dietary needs.

Why Do People Join Us?

People join us because they are passionate about baking, appreciate creativity in their work, and want to contribute to creating special moments for customers. Our employees find joy in the artistry of baking and making a positive impact on people's celebrations.

Why Do People Stay with Us?

People stay with us because of the supportive and creative work environment. Our employees value the opportunity to craft unique, allergen-free baked goods, contribute to memorable celebrations, and be part of a team that shares their commitment to quality and innovation.

1. Recognition and Rewards Program
    - **Creativity awards:** Recognize and reward employees who contribute innovative and creative ideas for new allergen-free

designs, aligning with the company's commitment to artisan-ship and personalization.

- **Customer testimonials:** Implement a program that high-lights and rewards employees based on positive customer tes-timonials, reinforcing the impact of their work on customers' special moments.

2. Skill Development and Training

- **Allergen-free mastery:** Provide specialized training in aller-gen-free baking techniques and recognize employees who excel in mastering these skills, showcasing the company's commitment to quality in allergen-free offerings.
- **Continual improvement:** Reward employees who actively participate in workshops or seek additional training to stay updated on the latest baking trends and techniques.
- **Celebration of milestones:** Recognize employees who actively participate in the creation of baked goods for signifi-cant customer milestones or events, reinforcing the emotional impact their work has on customers' lives.

What Do Our Employees Care About?

Our employees care about producing exceptional baked goods that bring joy to customers with dietary restrictions. They are passionate about con-tinual learning in baking techniques and staying up to date with allergen-free practices. The sense of contributing to meaningful celebrations is a driving force.

What Is Our Superpower?

Our superpower lies in the fusion of creativity and allergen-free exper-tise, and in our commitment to crafting visually appealing personalized baked goods. We empower our employees to express their creativity, mak-ing a positive impact on customers' lives through delicious and memorable experiences.

Chapter 8

PURPOSE-DRIVEN PROSPERITY: HOW YOUR BUSINESS CAN UPLIFT SOCIETY

When thinking about the impact you want to have on your local community or the world at large, take into consideration the following:

- How do we meaningfully serve people?
- How do we benefit our community? Society?

When considering the influence you want to have on the world around you, let your purpose and values be your compass. When envisioning your future, consider the ways in which you can make a positive impact in the world. You may already be contributing to your community through involvement in local organizations and networking events that offer opportunities for meaningful contributions.

When your company takes a stand and supports a cause that aligns with your passions, you will attract like-minded customers and employees who share these values and aspirations. When you dedicate time and resources to making a positive impact, your business will gain recognition from individuals who want to partner with an inspiring and purpose-driven organization.

Now that you've created a simple plan to create meaning inside your business, let's explore the benefits of using your business as a platform for social change.

In a world full of distractions, time constraints, interruptions, work responsibilities, and personal obligations, it's easy for your competitors to focus solely on short-term gains through selling their products and services. They are not considering how they can give back to society and make a positive impact in the world. Their main focus is on meeting quarterly targets rather than on building lasting relationships with their customers through prioritizing social impact. However, as you continued through the loop of connection, you learned that you are not just standing for anything—you have a purpose. This is your advantage and opportunity. You have gained a deeper understanding of the value you bring to individuals both inside and outside your organization. Your journey driven by purpose has brought you to this point, and it's exciting to imagine the ways your business is making a difference and how you can share your story with others.

WHY IS SOCIAL IMPACT IMPORTANT FOR BUSINESSES?

Consumers are becoming increasingly aware and conscious of the social and environmental impact of the products and services they purchase. They want to support businesses that align with their values and are making a positive difference in the world. Based on research by Sprout Social, most consumers (70%) believe it is crucial for brands to publicly support social and political causes. Additionally, 66% of these consumers believe that brands have the power to make a meaningful impact in these areas.[77]

By incorporating social impact into your business strategies, you not only attract potential customers who are looking to make a difference, but you also create opportunities to engage with existing customers on a deeper level. This can lead to increased customer loyalty and even brand advocacy. With 75% of Americans saying it is no longer acceptable for companies just to make money—they must positively influence society too[78]—your business can do good in the world by focusing outward and saying, "This is who we are and what we believe in," and "This is our story, and you can be a part of it too."

Implementing social impact initiatives can also attract top talent when it comes to recruiting new employees. People want to work for companies that prioritize making a positive impact in society, as this gives them a sense of purpose and fulfillment in their work. According to research, 90% of employees who work for companies with a clear and meaningful purpose report feeling more inspired, motivated, and loyal.[79] When your employees believe their efforts are making a meaningful difference in something they value, they become more committed and devoted to your business and cause.

It is widely known that consumers are more inclined to trust and support companies that share their values. As a result, it is logical that businesses focused on social responsibility have experienced the highest profits in recent years.[80] Your brand's reputation speaks volumes about your products and services and is often the first thing that comes to mind for customers. And there are examples everywhere of CEOs making an impact by standing up for what they believe in. Daymond John, the CEO of FUBU, who also appears on *Shark Tank* as an investor, speaks out against racial injustice on Twitter,[81] and Sarah Blakely, the former CEO of Spanx, uses LinkedIn to promote female empowerment.[82] David Green, the CEO and founder of Hobby Lobby, invoked his religious beliefs in his opposition to the Obamacare mandate requiring health insurance plans for employees to cover all forms of birth control, including the morning-after pill.[83] Whether you agree with their views or not, these CEOs' stances fit into the worldviews of people who identify with their causes.

These causes are also encouraging CEOs to band together to fight for what they believe in. In 2021, a group of over 70 CEOs from major corporations pleaded with governments to take stronger action in addressing climate change. These business leaders, including Nestlé's Mark Schneider and PepsiCo's Ramon Laguarta, signed an open letter calling for all governments to implement policies that align with the Paris Agreement's most ambitious target—limiting global temperature rise to 1½ degrees Celsius.[84]

For any fence sitters, don't be mistaken—corporate responsibility goes beyond just empty promises. Corporate social responsibility has a significant influence on how the public views your company, and it can even affect your customers' buying behaviors. Your customers are four to six times more likely to buy from you when you have a strong purpose.[85] As the younger generations, such as millennials and Gen Z, prioritize environmental protection and activism,[86] it's safe to assume that they consider these values when making purchases. They certainly don't want to support a business that stands for self-interest—or worse, is actively harming the environment.

But purpose and values alone aren't enough to create the impact you're hoping for. You've got to talk the talk and walk the walk. Establishing strong partnerships with other businesses is crucial for your long-term success. Building personal relationships with local organizations and members of the community promotes a culture of giving back. By giving back, you will improve your public image, increase engagement from both customers and employees, and fulfill your ethical responsibilities. While it's important to avoid appearing too self-serving, you should not shy away from showcasing your acts of kindness. The most important thing you can do is authentically serve, being true to who you are and pushing forward with the difference you want to make in your community, society, or both.

To make giving back a regular aspect of your business, consider implementing one or more of these three ideas to positively influence your community:

1. **Volunteer time off policy:** Implement a policy that allows employees to take paid time off to volunteer for local charities or community projects. This encourages a culture of giving back and strengthens your connection to the community.

2. **Local product sourcing:** Whenever possible, source products or materials locally. This not only supports local businesses, but it also reduces the carbon footprint associated with transportation. Highlighting local partnerships in your marketing can enhance your local brand.

3. **Seasonal community clean-up events:** Organize or participate in community clean-up events during different seasons. This not

only contributes to a cleaner environment, but it also fosters a sense of community pride. Consider collaborating with other local businesses for a larger impact.

There are countless ways to contribute to your community and make a positive impact. While I was building my business, I had the opportunity to support dedicated volunteers by offering our office for committee meetings and community events, as well as making use of our team's skills in marketing, public relations, and visitor experience to help with the Hill 70 Memorial Park project.[87] This cause was particularly close to our hearts, as several of us had family members who had served or were currently serving our country. My own grandfather was a veterinary surgeon on the front lines during World War I, and his bravery and dedication inspired me. Another colleague of ours had served in Afghanistan, and his service was a source of inspiration for our entire team.

When considering who you meaningfully serve in your community or how you benefit society, think about the causes that align with your company's values and goals. This will help guide your efforts toward making a meaningful difference instead of spreading resources too thin across various causes. As you complete this section of the connection loop, define your specific goals when it comes to creating social impact through your business. This will help you track progress and measure the success of your efforts.

If you're going through this process of giving back for the first time, the first step in creating a social impact strategy is to identify your key stakeholders. These are individuals or groups who have an interest in or are affected by your business, including employees, customers, local communities, and suppliers. Understanding their perspectives and needs will help inform your strategy and ensure that it resonates with them.

For those who are already actively contributing to society and the environment, it is important to assess your current impact. Conduct a thorough review of your operations to pinpoint areas where improvements can be made. This may also involve gathering input from stakeholders to gain insight into their perspectives on your business's impact. With a comprehensive understanding of your existing efforts, develop an action plan that outlines actionable steps toward achieving your desired goals. The plan should include a timeline, designated individuals responsible for each task, and quantifiable targets for each initiative.

Finally, be transparent about your efforts. Educate your staff on the ways in which you are giving back to the community, and ask for their input and suggestions. This will not only build trust and credibility with customers, but it will also inspire pride in your employees as they see the positive impact of their work.

Let's look at how the business owner of the bakery completed this section of the connection loop by answering these questions:

- How do we meaningfully serve people?
- How do we benefit our community? Society?

Bakery

- **Food banks and shelters:** Establish partnerships with local food banks or shelters, donating surplus baked goods to those in need, addressing food insecurity while emphasizing the bakery's commitment to social responsibility.
- **Educational initiatives:** Conduct workshops on allergen-free baking for the community, sharing knowledge and empowering individuals to create safe and delicious treats at home.

Chapter 9

KEEPING SCORE

HOW WE MEASURE SUCCESS

When determining success, there are two main things to think about: (1) the influence you have within your company, and (2) the effect you have on your community or society as a whole.

Evaluating success from within means that you are personally responsible for ensuring that you and your team stick to the plans that have been set. This allows you to pinpoint any potential problems and can also help uncover sources of stress, exhaustion, or discontent among team members. By addressing these issues, it is possible to improve mental health, achieve a better work-life balance, and promote overall well-being.

By measuring the impact on your external community and society, you can show your employees and customers the positive change that your organization is making through its direct actions. For instance, if your company is supporting local shelters, you could track and quantify the quantity of meals provided or the number of community members assisted with shelter and aid.

Your business's contribution to the community can be measured by how well it fulfills its purpose and values through actions, such as donating, collecting, and distributing food. The number of meals served is a tangible way to track progress and determine the positive social impact on health and housing outcomes. It is important to define your purpose and values in order to effectively gauge your social impact and share the results with data.

Let's explore ways you can track and measure success over time.

Internal Evidence

You can measure employee engagement in various ways, including surveys, your internal Net Promoter Score (called eNPS), face-to-face meetings, employee retention rates, and absenteeism metrics.

Survey-Based Approaches

Leadership Alignment Surveys

To measure leadership's unity on purpose, values, and strategic direction, leadership and managers often conduct alignment surveys. These semiannual surveys serve as a self-evaluation tool for leaders to assess their clarity and agreement in the key areas of your business and strategic plan. The surveys also evaluate the level of trust within the team, making it particularly useful for oversight leadership teams, such as C-suite, sales, marketing, HR, IT, or management teams. For leaders, it is important to be open to self-assessment and to hold each other accountable. The leadership alignment survey acts as an impartial third party, providing an unbiased evaluation of your organization's leadership.

Annual Employee Engagement Surveys

Employee engagement surveys are often used to measure employee satisfaction and are distributed annually. These surveys provide valuable data for understanding employee engagement and serve as a benchmark for improvement efforts. However, they can be time consuming, taking up to 20 minutes for employees to complete due to their length.

Note: In the appendix section of this book, I provide a leadership alignment and employee engagement survey that you can use or tailor to fit your specific needs. I also gained insights into team members' and departments' mutual appreciation using Motivosity, (www.motivosity. com) software for creating a culture of community and connection.

Employee Net Promoter Score (eNPS)

The eNPS is a metric based on the Net Promoter Score (NPS) used to gauge customer loyalty. However, in this case, it measures employee loyalty by asking one simple question:

> *How likely are you to recommend this company as a great place to work?*

Responses are given anonymously on a scale of 1–10, with 1 indicating a high likelihood of *not* recommending and 10 indicating a high probability of recommending.

Based on these responses, employees are classified into three categories: detractors (scores of 0–6), passives (scores of 7–8), and promoters (scores of 9–10). Detractors would not recommend working for the company, while promoters are the most enthusiastic supporters. While the eNPS does not explain why employees may not recommend the organization, the eNPS offers a quick overview of their dedication. This assessment can be quickly conducted through annual or pulse surveys.

Nonsurvey Approaches

Here are some ways to measure employee engagement without a survey.

If you're running a small business and engagement surveys are not an option yet, consider using these alternative methods. I encourage you, as well as your leaders and managers, to schedule one-on-ones with your team members regularly.

One-on-Ones

If you're conducting regular one-on-one meetings with your team— excellent! If not, and if this is something you are considering, make sure everyone on your team knows about the new practice of holding regular one-on-one meetings by announcing it at a team meeting.

Make it clear that these meetings are in line with your company's principles, such as valuing the input of employees and your own values as a supportive leader. It's important to stress that these conversations are not meant to criticize the team's work or to micromanage. Instead, they allow you and each member to get to know each other better, discuss challenges, and discuss how your team member is doing. This is also an excellent time to communicate what you expect from your team during these meetings:

- Driving the agenda with key priorities
- Being curious and actively engaged
- Communicating honestly
- Thinking deeply about problems and solutions
- Being open to providing help to others and acting on feedback

You might ask these questions during your regular one-on-one meetings:

- How have you been?
- How did the previous week/month go?
- What's on your mind today?
- Is there something you're particularly proud of?
- Are there any obstacles in your way?
- Do you require any assistance? How can I be of service to you?
- Is there anything else you'd like to discuss today?

Be open, show up, and be consistent. Respect and value individuals—make their time more important than yours.

Measuring Employee Retention Rates

Employee retention rates measure the percentage of employees who remain with your company during a specified time frame. This is usually calculated quarterly or annually and compares the number of employees at the beginning of the period to the number who are still employed by the end. By understanding your company's retention rate, you can determine how many employees you are able to retain, giving insight into overall employee satisfaction and identifying potential areas for growth and improvement.

High turnover can lead to hidden costs such as decreased productivity and lower work quality, with the cost of replacing an employee ranging from half to double their annual salary. By retaining employees for longer periods, your organization can reduce the expenses associated with recruiting and hiring new team members.

The Formula for Retention Rate Calculation
To determine the rate of employee retention, follow this equation:

[Total number of employees at the beginning of a time period] minus *[number of employees who left during that time period]* equals *[original employees remaining at the end of the time period]*

With this information, calculate the final retention rate using the second part of the formula: Divide the number of original employees who remain by the total number of employees, and then multiply by 100. (You can do this by moving the decimal point two places to the right.) The resulting number will be shown as a percentage, which represents the retention rate.

Tracking Absenteeism

To measure the overall health and wellness of your organization, it's important to track the rate of absenteeism. This can be done for the entire organization or for individual employees. When you understand the exact absence rate, interventions can be implemented to improve overall well-being. The absenteeism rate is calculated as a percentage of working days missed during a specific time period, such as a month, quarter, or year. To determine this rate, divide the total number of absences by the total number of available working days for your team. For instance, if you have 10 team members who work 20 days per month, there are 200 total working days available. If they miss a combined total of 10 days due to various reasons, the absenteeism rate would be 10/200, or 5%.

Calculating New Hire Fail Rate

The percentage of new employees who successfully complete their first 90 days at your company, known as the new hire fail rate, is a crucial metric to track. A high fail rate indicates that the organization is investing significant resources in new hires without seeing the desired return on investment. To calculate this metric, divide the total number of failed new hires in the past 90 days by the total number of new hires during the same period. While industry, position, and job market can affect expectations, a fail rate exceeding 30% should raise concerns and prompt a thorough evaluation of the onboarding process and employee retention strategies.

Conducting Exit Interviews

Conducting exit interviews is a crucial part of any effective employee engagement strategy. Exit interviews offer valuable insights into the reasons for an employee's departure and can bring attention to areas in need of improvement in order to retain top talent.

Here are some possible questions to ask during an exit interview:

- Why have you chosen to leave our company?
- What prompted your search for a new job opportunity?
- Can you pinpoint any factors that positively or negatively affected your performance in this role?
- Based on your experience, do you have suggestions for improving the onboarding process for new employees?
- How did you feel about the management of your position?
- Did you feel valued by your team, supervisors, and managers?
- What were the most enjoyable aspects of your job?
- What was the biggest challenge you faced in this role?

It's important to note that not all departing employees may be willing to give open and honest feedback during exit interviews. That is why employee engagement surveys can be helpful in gathering more detailed information about employee satisfaction and engagement while employees are still employed with the organization.

Exit interviews allow for a better understanding of the underlying reasons for each individual's decision to leave and enable proactive measures to prevent similar situations from arising in the future.

External Evidence

Social impacts are causing ripples and bringing about changes in various aspects of our lives. From evaluating ethical business practices to consumer choices, social impact is becoming increasingly significant to all of us. There are numerous ways you can achieve a meaningful and positive community and social impact.

As you move forward, encourage your employees to be involved and to share their ideas on how your company's culture can positively affect your community. Seek feedback from them, as they may have insights on potential programs or areas of need in the community. And, most importantly, act based on this input.

It goes without saying, but having good intentions is not enough to ensure your success. A well-thought-out plan is necessary to accurately measure your accomplishments. Measuring your social impact allows you to gain a deeper understanding, manage effectively, and communicate the societal value that your work creates in a clear and consistent manner.

By evaluating the direct result of your actions, you have begun the process of assessing the effectiveness of your cause. Your purpose and objectives will determine your results metrics, such as hours volunteered, emission reduction percentages, scholarships provided, or community initiatives funded. Your team will be tasked with selecting these goals on a yearly or quarterly basis. This allows you and your team to compare your objectives with actual results, providing valuable insights for future planning. The data gathered from your metrics will help you lead more effective strategies in the future.

The important thing is that you lead with authenticity and support causes that are aligned with your purpose and values, causes that matter to the people you serve.

Here are some ways businesses are giving back:

- During the holiday season, Burlington teams up with Delivering Good, a national nonprofit organization, to provide warmth for members of their communities through the Burlington Coat Drive. Customers, associates, and vendors can donate new or gently worn coats at any Burlington store across the country. These coats are then distributed locally to those in need by Delivering Good. This drive has collected over 2.5 million coats to date, making a significant impact for neighbors who may not have access to warm coats otherwise.[88]

- Success Academy is revolutionizing public education and challenging the notion of what is possible. Their goal is to provide every student with equal opportunities for success, rooted in the belief that all children are capable of achieving at the highest level. They have become the fifth-largest public school system in New York State and are consistently recognized as the top-performing district. Every year, 100% of their high school graduates are accepted into college. Using cutting-edge technology and innovative strategies, Success Academy strives to constantly enhance and empower students, and donations made through their website directly support disadvantaged children in achieving success.[89]

- Dr. Bronner's has been a leader in the organic personal care industry, setting an example for social responsibility initiatives. By implementing fair-trade projects and offering education opportunities, they ensure that farmers and workers around the world are treated fairly. Furthermore, they educate their farming partners on environmentally friendly practices such as carbon-sequestering farming and regenerative organic agriculture. The company prides itself on using natural ingredients without any synthetic preservatives or harmful chemicals, and their products are packaged in 100% recyclable materials. Additionally, they never test on animals, and each product is 100% biodegradable. As part of their mission, 33% of all profits go toward supporting important social and ecological projects.[90]

- Lemonade not only provides insurance but also aims to rebuild its importance as a social benefit. As part of their mission, the company created the Lemonade Giveback program. When purchasing a policy, customers are given the option to choose a nonprofit organization they wish to support. At the end of each year, any unclaimed money from their premiums is tallied up and donated to the selected organization. In 2022 alone, Lemonade donated over $1.87 million to various charities, such as Pencils of Promise, To Write Love On Her Arms, and the Breast Cancer Research Foundation.[91]

- Located in Cardiff, California, Pacific Ink is a small office and facility supply company that is dedicated to giving back to the community. They provide backpacks filled with school supplies to local children, ensuring they have everything they need to succeed in the classroom. In addition, they volunteer with the Elizabeth Hospice of San Diego, supporting their child bereavement programs that aim to help grieving children and teens by promoting social connections and decreasing feelings of isolation. Pacific Ink takes a service-based approach that includes both environmental and social responsibility. They offer over 4,000 eco-friendly products made with postconsumer recycled materials ranging from 30% to 100%. They also actively support the AbilityOne program, which provides employment opportunities for more than 46,000 Americans who are blind or disabled. In fact, Pacific Ink offers over 1,000 items under the AbilityOne name.[92]

- PiperWai is a brand that prioritizes sustainability, offering natural deodorants and hygiene products made with eco-friendly materials and packaging. Their products are gentle on the skin, as they are formulated with plant-based ingredients and are free from harmful chemicals like aluminum, parabens, and synthetic fragrances. To minimize waste, they use recyclable materials for their packaging and offer refillable options. Furthermore, the brand is dedicated to reducing their impact on the environment by using renewable energy sources and implementing sustainable practices throughout their manufacturing and shipping processes.[93]

Each of these scenarios required a decision to be made, whether that involved two business partners discussing their vision for making a positive impact on the world, or an employee who saw the chance to make a difference in people's lives. Currently, there are individuals in companies throughout America seeking out local causes to lend their support to, companies like the ones you just read about, making an impact and sharing their results with their employees, customers, suppliers, and partners.

You also have the power to choose. You can be the difference. You can begin with small steps, using your purpose and values as guidance. Jane Goodall, the renowned environmentalist, often said, "What you do makes a difference, and you have to decide what kind of difference you want to make."[94] The real question is, what sets apart the change you want to create in the world and how will you strive toward it? Every small act of service toward another is like a single raindrop, coming together with others to form a powerful river. Small acts of kindness combine to raise every ship in the harbor. While I'm not asking you to be Jane Goodall, what I am saying is, never underestimate the power you have to make a positive change in the world.

We can keep following the same paths, stepping on the same stones, but our location or routine won't change the fact that there is always an opportunity to positively impact someone's life.

Take responsibility for yourself and your team. Show the positive difference you are making and share it with those who believe in you and want to be a part of your journey. Your actions can create change in those around you, so make sure to measure and communicate that impact.

WHAT ABOUT B CORPS?

B Corp certification is a badge indicating that a company upholds the highest levels of verified performance, accountability, and transparency across various areas such as employee benefits, charitable contributions, supply chain practices, and material sourcing. These companies are the gold standard of social impact. B Corps have chosen to join a worldwide movement toward viewing business as a means for positive change, reshaping the definition of "success" to use profits and expansion for a greater purpose. Their dedication lies in creating an economy that is inclusive and sustainable for all.

To achieve B Corp status, a company needs to prove their dedication to social and environmental responsibility and pass a B Impact Assessment (BIA). B Lab (a "nonprofit network transforming the global economy to benefit all people, communities, and the planet"[95]) takes a holistic approach to business practices, not just addressing one specific social or environmental issue. Depending on the size and type of company, this involves providing documentation on their business model and details about their operations, structure, and various work processes. To be certified, a business makes a legal commitment by adjusting their corporate governance structure to prioritize all stakeholders, not just shareholders. Transparency is crucial—B Corps must allow public access to information about their performance according to B Lab's standards.

For those embarking on a new business venture, there is the option to apply for Pending B Corp status. To meet the legal accountability requirement, your startup must incorporate stakeholder governance into its legal structure. Essentially, this means that your company is held responsible not just to shareholders but also to a wider range of stakeholders such as employees, customers, clients, and the communities in which you do business, as well as to the environment.

More and more businesses are prioritizing the B Corp certification process because it is in line with their values, and they strive to be socially responsible companies.

While going through the BIA, companies inevitably discover areas for improvement. This could involve formalizing their mission statement, creating a charitable-giving program, implementing a community service initiative, evaluating suppliers for diversity, and more. In addition, they typically improve their overall operations. Outdated employee handbooks are updated, long-discussed professional development plans are finally put into action, and complex carbon footprint calculations are completed.

The comprehensiveness of the BIA makes it a valuable tool for business owners to assess all aspects of their operations, set deliberate goals for their impact, and continually improve policies and processes. This leads to a more efficient and streamlined organization in the end.

B Corps show the strongest proof of social impact, proving my case that your community, social impact, and evidence matter. There are many companies moving to this certification—with many more already there. Here are three companies running B Corps and doing good in the world:

1. **The Body Shop:** You may know the Body Shop from frequent trips to the mall, but the retailer has attracted a dedicated customer base for its social responsibility and wide array of ethically sourced body care products. In 2019, the company became a certified B Corp.[96]

2. **Allbirds:** Many people call Allbirds the "most comfortable shoes in the world," a statement I wholeheartedly support. With each new collection, they continue to improve their use of natural materials. The classic sneakers and loungers are crafted from ZQ-certified merino wool that naturally wicks away moisture, regulates temperature, and resists odors. This material is also sustainably farmed with strict animal welfare standards and uses 60% less energy than synthetic fabrics.[97]

3. **Tentree:** Tentree is a company that views itself as a forestry program but also happens to sell clothing. With every purchase made, the company plants 10 trees through carefully curated initiatives that aim to restore the earth's forests and support communities in building sustainable local economies.[98]

Becoming a certified B Corp means joining a global community that uses business as a tool for positive change. You will connect and collaborate with like-minded individuals and organizations who share your values and goals, both within your own community and around the world. This provides an opportunity to exchange ideas and learn from one another in practical ways, whether through the online networking platform known as the B Hive or through in-person meetings with other B Corps in your region, known as B Locals.[99]

B Corps are at the forefront of advocating for economic system reform, and members reap incredible rewards. They establish a foundation of reliability with customers, communities, and suppliers; attract and retain talented employees; and draw in investors that align with their missions. To learn more about the B Corp movement, I encourage you to visit www.bcorporation.net.

THE POWER OF CHOICE

Just like the companies who embrace B Corp certification, you also have the power to choose a transformation, making your business a force for good. You can be the difference by making sustainability a priority and identifying which areas of your business are negatively affecting the planet, your employees, or your customers. Prioritizing sustainable business practices not only helps streamline operations and improve financial stability, but it also ensures that your business is making a positive impact on the community by operating in an ethical and responsible manner.

It's not necessary to completely overhaul your business practices immediately. However, you can't simply hope to make a positive impact in the world without taking action. You have the opportunity to use your business for something meaningful beyond just accumulating wealth. It doesn't matter if you're not a famous CEO or if you don't have a massive following on social media. When you believe you can make a difference for the better, your conviction and determination will lead you to how things could be. In the inspirational words from Ruth Bader Ginsburg, cofounder of the Women's Rights Project at the ACLU and former associate justice of the Supreme Court of the United States, "Fight for the things that you care about, but do it in a way that will lead others to join you."[100]

It's natural to want to see what other companies are doing to find success and make a difference. However, staying true to your purpose and values and making your unique impact is essential as a leader. Be bold, go against the grain, and take a different path. Blaze your trail and leave a mark for others to follow.

While you think about the path ahead, be mindful of how you passionately, persistently, and wholeheartedly support those around you. Never underestimate the power of a small act of kindness. It has the potential to create a ripple effect, spreading positivity and inspiring transformative change in someone's life. Imagine the impact you could make by incorporating these small gestures into your daily work.

Remember, many of the most successful companies were founded by individuals who chose to zig while everyone else was zagging, and creating something new offers an opportunity to become someone new.

The path to your success is a winding road—not a straight line. Be curious. Take chances. Try new things. Get outside your comfort zone and lean into the wrong turns you take. The accomplishments you desire are often found along the imperfect journey behind you, made up of your blunders, trips, and slips. Learn, iterate, and keep moving forward. I can tell you from my experiences that success is not permanent, and failure is not the end; what truly matters is having the courage to keep going. Your purpose will guide you.

Chapter 10

THE BUSINESS OF FEELING DIFFERENTLY

In the words of Carl W. Buehner, "They may forget what you said—but they will never forget how you made them feel."[101]

Leading brands understand the importance of creating a positive experience for customers, whether it's through their products, services, or employees. This is evident in the success of the Apple Store, which became the most profitable retailer in America after reimagining the retail experience in 2001. Before even considering profits, Steve Jobs and his team asked themselves how they wanted customers to feel when entering their stores. By prioritizing emotions, the Apple Store achieved unparalleled success in profitability.[102]

We all want to feel seen, heard, understood, and respected. But we often forget that we're not in the business of selling things—we're in the business of making people feel differently because of our things. Remember, people don't buy what you do or how you do it. They buy why you do it. The best marketers understand that customers don't buy features and benefits, they buy promises and what could be. To truly make a difference, focus on providing meaning and emotional value to others. By helping people become their best selves, you can create a lasting impact that goes beyond just surface-level interactions.

As you journeyed through the infinite loop of connection, you may have identified and acknowledged the emotions that were evoked by the bakery. Each step in the cycle revealed more about your purpose and values, helping you understand the emotional needs of your customers and shaping the internal and external significance you wish to create. With this, you have a concrete plan for creating a positive company culture and a compelling cause that your employees can rally behind—a plan to make a meaningful impact in your community and improve people's lives. You have achieved a deep understanding and gained a clear direction that sets your business apart from others.

You have become meaningful.

Now it's time to make every interaction, every exchange in your business intimate. Before you unlock your office doors in the morning, respond to your first text, or send that first email to a prospective customer, think about the feelings you want to create to guide them toward their destination. Understand that the problem you are trying to solve belongs to a specific person. Your goal isn't to personalize. It's to be personal. The software you want to sell me—it's personal, offering me a brighter outlook for my business, making me feel more confident and less stressed. The earrings at Macy's for my wife, they're personal too. They boost her confidence and enhance her appearance, making her feel more graceful and alluring. The fresh dog food I buy at the pet store, that's personal as well. I want my loyal companion to enjoy a joyous, healthy, and extended life because he brings me solace and peace of mind.

While we commonly believe that we make purchasing decisions after carefully evaluating all available options, the truth is that our emotions play a significant role and often dictate our choices. Our emotional responses are incredibly quick, 3,000 times faster than rational thought. And the parts of our brain responsible for processing emotions work five times faster than those involved in rational thinking. We're emotional creatures with rational thoughts, and our emotions' persuasive power over reason is a ratio of 24 to 1.[103] These findings highlight the strong influence that our emotions have on our purchasing behavior, with our internal narratives looking for places where we think we'll fit in. This is your opportunity.

Your customers are interested in what your company does, why it does

THE BUSINESS OF FEELING DIFFERENTLY ≋ 111

it, and how your values align with theirs. They believe you can help them become the person they seek to be. When your purpose, values, and sense of connection (feelings) intersect, your business becomes meaningful for those of us who envision our narrative unfolding in a manner that enriches us because of you.

What feelings do you want to evoke in your business? Let's look at the bakery. As you go through this case study, reflect on ways you could build stronger connections with people you serve—person to person. These are the experiences behind your brand, the interactions that really matter.

BAKERY

Joy

Feeling: We want our customers to experience joy and delight when celebrating special moments with visually appealing, allergen-free baked goods, contributing to positive emotions associated with their events.

Inclusivity

Feeling: Through our commitment to allergen-free options, we want to create a sense of inclusivity, allowing individuals with dietary restrictions to enjoy celebrations without worry, fostering a feeling of being valued and accommodated.

Appreciation

Feeling: We want to show our customers we appreciate them in every interaction. Through our artisanship, creativity, and personalization in our bakery's creations, we want our customers to feel the sense of caring and effort we put into making their special moments memorable.

To achieve the bakery's objective of creating an emotional connection with its customers and creating an opportunity for new value, the key is to evoke positive emotions tied to your purpose, core values, and offerings. The bakery focuses on creating joy, inclusivity, and appreciation through its allergen-free and visually appealing baked goods. This business recognizes they will not please everyone—they are focused on the people who might share their worldview. In thinking about the feelings you want to create, remember that your authenticity matters to some people. And the "some people" you matter to, that's where you focus all your time and energy. By serving the people who self-identify with your cause and values, who believe in what you believe, you help these people achieve their dreams and live better lives.

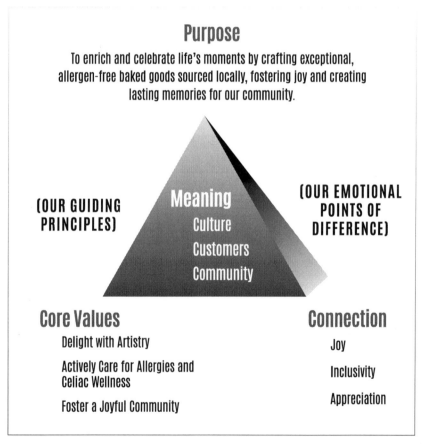

Figure 4

As you complete the loop, write down two or three feelings you want to create in your business. These feelings will become your emotional points of difference. When you go above and beyond, people will take notice. This has a significant impact on their perception of what you do. Your unique emotional qualities matter because they demonstrate your level of care. They will set apart your brand, and as you truly stand for something, you will shape your culture around them, creating devoted customers and brand advocates that no amount of advertisement can match. Ultimately, purchasing decisions are driven by emotions. We want to feel confident in our choices, even if we believe they are based on logic. By appealing to your customers' desire for connection with their purchases, you can unlock greater value, foster strong brand loyalty, and drive repeat business.

Here are some positive emotions you might consider:

- Acceptance
- Belonging
- Bliss
- Calmness
- Caring
- Comfort
- Confidence
- Curiosity
- Delight
- Elation
- Enchantment
- Enjoyment
- Enlightenment
- Enthusiasm
- Excitement
- Fascination
- Friendliness
- Glee
- Gratitude
- Hopefulness
- Intrigue
- Joy
- Kindness
- Nostalgia
- Pride
- Relaxation
- Relief
- Satisfaction
- Sentimentality
- Serenity
- Strength
- Surprise
- Tenderness
- Thrill
- Triumph
- Trust
- Worthiness

Looking inward, you can drive your team toward greater levels of achievement using the power of emotion. By fostering deep connections with your employees, you will also have a direct influence on creating similar connections with your customers. This is because the happiness of your employees directly correlates with the satisfaction of your customers. Multiple studies have demonstrated the positive impact of happiness on business and educational outcomes. Companies who nurture happy cultures see a 37% increase in sales, a 31% boost in productivity, and a 19% improvement in task accuracy. Additionally, happiness has been linked to various health benefits and overall quality of life enhancements. Despite this evidence, many companies fail to consider the role of happiness in effective leadership.[104]

In doing research for the book *The Inspiring Leader: Unlocking the Secrets of How Extraordinary Leaders Motivate*, the authors analyzed data from 25,000 leaders as they went through 360° surveys. What they discovered is those who were most inspiring (the top 10% of the group) shared a common trait: their ability to form a strong emotional bond with their employees.[105] Despite what you may think, I'm here to tell you that happiness at work is serious business. It is your responsibility as a leader to prioritize the well-being of your employees. If this is not currently a part of your job description, it should be. If you have employees who are struggling or if you have a toxic work culture that is causing people to look for other jobs, it's time for some deep self-reflection about who you are and what you stand for. I believe that all of us should be held accountable for ensuring the well-being of our employees. This can be integrated into your performance reviews, 360° leadership assessments, and daily routines at work.

A happy workforce leads to positive customer experiences. With access to a vast database of job insights, salary information, and company reviews, Glassdoor has a wealth of knowledge about employee experience. According to an article published by the *Harvard Business Review*, Shawn Achor, *New York Times* best-selling author of *The Happiness Advantage*, has been able to quantify the effects of employee satisfaction on various aspects such as retention rates, talent recruitment, and even stock performance.[106] The findings indicate a significant correlation between the well-being of employees on Glassdoor and customer satisfaction for some of the top companies in today's market.[107] It is evident that a content workforce directly affects your company's ability to provide customer satisfaction and deep emotional bonds.

Your emotional points of difference say, "We care about you." It's a common refrain in the business world: "We prioritize our customers," "Your satisfaction is our top priority," or "Service is number one." But empty promises can fall flat without tangible evidence. Genuine concern and empathy are crucial for building trust and fostering customer loyalty. In fact, 79% of consumers believe that brands must demonstrate understanding and genuine care before they will even consider making a purchase. Always prioritize the individual behind the customer, rather than just their problem. By focusing on creating meaningful experiences for your customers, you can outshine competitors, cultivate loyal customers through word-of-mouth, and carve out your own successful niche in the market.

Your competitors likely do not prioritize their businesses based on purpose or values. And if there happen to be competitors who do, it's unlikely that they are truly living out their purpose and making a positive impact in society. By placing importance on both internal and external meaning, you are generating value that goes beyond just profit and loss statements. Your efforts may seem small in the grand scheme of things, but you are making a significant difference in people's lives. Your contributions have a lasting effect that can change someone's life forever. Never underestimate the impact you have on others—a simple act of kindness has the power to change someone's day. Your purpose can bring much-needed goodness into a world that craves it.

The connection loop is a powerful tool that helps you discover your purpose and values, establish emotional connections with customers, build a high-performing workforce by prioritizing people, create products and services that meet the needs of consumers, and ultimately make an impact in the minds of your customers. After reading through the case studies and understanding how this infinite loop of connection can be applied, it's time to share it with your team. Use it to delve deeper into your business, identify areas for growth, and devise strategies for success. By applying the insights gathered from this process, you can enhance your offerings and establish meaningful connections both within and outside your company. Let's see how this works for another case study.

Hardware Store

A family-owned chain of hardware stores was looking for a unique advantage in the communities they served in northeast Pennsylvania. The $10 million hardware chain shifted to a purpose-driven business to capitalize on its strengths.

The initial hardware store was established to provide the community with trustworthy assistance in selecting appropriate tools and materials, and their success led to the opening of additional stores.

As they delved into their reason for existence, the revelation of their beginnings transformed into their purpose: to empower people and communities by providing trustworthy advice and top-notch products. At the heart of their business were their core principles, deeply ingrained in the expertise of their staff, commitment to the community, and responsibility to the environment. They understood that customers wanted more than just a run-of-the-mill transaction, so they focused on providing reliable and exceptional customer service for all hardware needs.

Their shared mindset catered to DIY enthusiasts and professionals who valued expert guidance and community. Their customers were those who appreciated high-quality tools and personalized attention.

As they moved through the infinite loop of connection, they recognized the need to improve the customer experience, so they implemented a three-pronged solution. The first was an in-store advisory service that offered personalized guidance and support for DIY enthusiasts. The second focused on building community through DIY workshops and events. Last, their emphasis on exceptional customer service, grounded in strong family values, aimed to instill confidence and trust in every interaction.

They created a simple culture plan that included rewarding dedication with competitive wages, benefits, and opportunities for advancement. A recognition and rewards program was closely tied to the company's core values. Training opportunities focused on learning continually, acknowledging skills, and fostering team cohesion.

Now each hardware store is creating a stronger connection with their communities by hosting workshops, offering advice clinics, participating in improvement projects, promoting green initiatives, organizing youth programs, and providing apprenticeships.

Their goal is for customers to feel confident, have a sense of belonging, and have overall satisfaction knowing they have access to top-quality tools, exceptional service, and successful project outcomes. In addition, their community benefits greatly as each store contributes discounted or free supplies to local renovation and improvement projects for Habitat for Humanity. They donated over $250,000 of tools and supplies to this cause in their first year alone.

This journey embodies the heart of the infinite loop of connection, creating meaning for the people they serve.

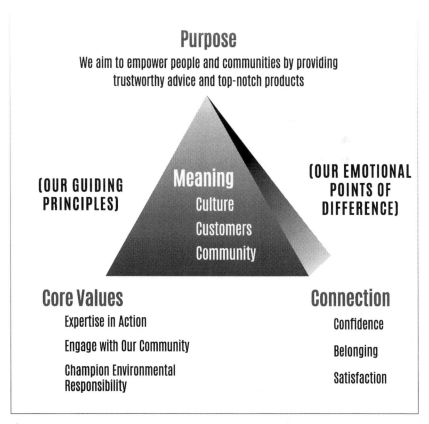

Figure 5

Earlier in the book, I asked you to answer two questions:

1. What is your company's core reason for being?
2. What is the unique, positive impact you aspire to bring about in your community, in society?

Now that you've been through the loop, your purpose, values, and emotional points of difference unite, creating the heart of your company's identity. This seamless intertwining results in a distinctive and captivating story that propels your company toward success and recognition. Guided by purpose, you go beyond profit-seeking and embrace a higher calling that resonates with your customers and employees. This shared cause gives meaning to your interactions, transforming transactions into meaningful exchanges.

THE ENDLESS CYCLE OF MEANING

As products and services continue to improve, customers' expectations are constantly evolving. While initially grateful for better services, they quickly become accustomed to them and start to demand even more. Additionally, every interaction a customer has with *any* organization—not just with your company or others in the same industry—influences their perception of your organization. As organizations across all industries strive for excellence, they set new standards for customer expectations that affect all businesses.

To meet the constantly evolving expectations of customers, businesses must be willing to change the way they do business. This requires a fundamental shift in mindsets and approaches, rather than simply implementing new strategies or processes.

One analogy that can help illustrate this concept is trying to improve grades in school. If a student wants to get better grades, they cannot simply make a few minor changes, like buying new school supplies or studying harder for one test. They need to fundamentally change their study habits and approach to see significant improvement.

Similarly, businesses must be willing to adapt and change to keep up with evolving customer expectations. This can involve making changes in areas such as products, services, processes, policies, and company culture.

Let's consider a fast-food chain that prides itself on providing quick service and low prices. As customer expectations evolve and customers start demanding healthier options from restaurants, this company may need to reevaluate their menu offerings and incorporate healthier choices. Changing their menu may involve overhauling their supply chain and training staff on how to prepare these new items. It may also require changing the company culture from focusing solely on speed and price to also prioritizing health and quality.

As customers continue to evolve, companies must also adapt their processes and services. This may even involve adopting new initiatives or technologies. For example, businesses now need to have an online presence that allows for 24/7 access to products or services. Instead of just focusing on developing user-friendly websites or mobile apps or building compatibility with Amazon's one-click buying experience, the trend is moving toward automated ordering through Internet of Things (IoT) technology or voice-activated systems like Amazon's Alexa or Apple's Siri. Today, a Samsung refrigerator can communicate with your smartphone to create a shopping list, pushing it directly to your favorite online platform.[108] With one click in your Instacart app, your groceries will be delivered right to your doorstep at your convenience.

DoNotPay, a technology startup, has created the world's first robot lawyer that uses AI to fight for consumer rights. This groundbreaking program allows defendants to receive real-time guidance on how to respond to the judge through an earpiece with Bluetooth capabilities, a concept never before seen.[109] It's clear that automation is the way of the future—from home to legal services to Tesla's work with self-driving vehicles, with AI potentially eliminating entire industries of labor.

Your loop of connection will constantly adapt to the changing needs, wants, and desires of your customers. Whether you are just starting out or leading a well-established company, your loop will continue to evolve as you strive to enhance the experiences within your company culture, for your customers, and in your community. This is never ending because we all know that standing still or believing that no other business can surpass you is a recipe for failure. Just look at companies like Blockbuster, RadioShack, and most recently, Bed Bath & Beyond, that were unable to keep up with the shift toward e-commerce.[110]

Regardless of your business or industry, the key to success lies in understanding the needs and wants of your customers. To avoid the same fate as companies that failed to adapt and evolve quickly enough, implementing an infinite loop can create a stronger connection and add depth to the story your brand is telling. When you stand up for something that aligns with your beliefs and resonates with your employees, you embark on a transformative journey that truly matters. You're inviting people in and asking them to participate in your story, a story that helps us all become better versions of ourselves.

With meaning being an endless pursuit for your company, it stands to reason that there would be a mechanism to make sure it's upheld—a system and process through which you can ensure that meaning is baked into everything you do as a company.

Strategic planning allows you to maintain focus on the things that matter, devote resources accordingly, and ensure that the path forward is guided by meaning—that meaning isn't something you do once but every day, every quarter, and every year.

The second half of this book shows how you can carry meaning and purpose forward with strategic planning.

You may have previously participated in strategic planning with your company—and you may not think much of it—but here's a chance to reconsider strategic planning through a different lens.

PART 2:

ACTIONABLE INSIGHTS: ALIGNING STRATEGIC FRAMEWORKS WITH PURPOSE

Chapter 11

A SIMPLE AND LASTING PLAN

Now that you've differentiated your business, it's time to be strategic. Your strategy determines where you will concentrate your energies to reach your objectives and how you will attain the success you're striving for. Strategy is where you play the game and how you win.

Search "strategic planning" on Google, and you'll find articles, step-by-step guides, and templates to guide you through the strategic-planning process. But this thinking and these processes are flawed because they address strategy and planning together rather than untethering them and focusing on strategy first.

In many cases, company executives will engage in strategic planning without a cohesive overall strategy, resulting in disjointed efforts. When viewed only through the lens of strategy, this rote, paint-by-numbers method is ineffective and becomes a yearly planning event with little impact or benefit.

Strategic-planning retreats are typically unsuccessful because they are misguided by facilitators and consultants who, while well-intentioned, may need to gain the necessary expertise in this area. Leaders often over-look strategy and instead focus on the result. For example, a company's strategy may be to enter the European market by establishing an office in Amsterdam with a warehouse for distribution. Although this may seem like a solid strategy, it isn't a strategy at all—it is just an anticipated outcome. Similarly, adding more machinery to the shop floor to increase production capacity is an expected outcome, not a true strategy.

Some of your leaders may think that their business acumen and experience are enough to carry out strategic planning. However, this belief is usually false and can hinder the critical thinking needed to generate good strategies.

I used to be one of those leaders—I believed I was adequately educated and experienced enough to lead strategic planning. Because of my overconfidence, I caught myself in the strategy trap.

After enrolling in and completing a strategy course at the Smith School of Business, I confidently returned to my office, determined to share my knowledge and chart a new course for my business. To gain a competitive edge, I knew I had to complete the strategy workbook given to me by Smith. It seemed like a clear path to success, and I eagerly accepted the challenge. For weeks, I worked diligently, answering each question in the workbook. When I finally finished, I felt a sense of accomplishment and was confident about what lay ahead in my career.

Despite weeks of effort and meticulous planning, my work seemed to go nowhere. I had managed to write 10,000 words, but they remained stagnant on the page. One of the biggest issues was that I had chosen to plan alone. The leadership team at the company was preoccupied with sales and project execution. Not wanting to hinder their revenue generation, I worked independently. However, I quickly realized that my plan lacked credibility without their input and buy-in. This was a crucial lesson learned: when your team isn't actively participating in the process, it's hard for them to have faith in your plans.

The problem was that I had alienated the people responsible for the execution. I developed our strategies without consulting leadership or involving our employees, resulting in a lack of critical thinking and buy-in from those who were needed to understand and support the strategy. I was solely presenting the strategies on paper, but there needed to be more drive and motivation to implement them effectively. I should not have excluded input and involvement from my team, leading to a lack of commitment toward change and achieving the desired outcomes.

The other problem was that my 20 pages of answers to strategic questions caused me to create unnecessary complexity. I proposed key strategies, several strategic tactics, and more outlined actions. As I analyzed the situation, I realized that my actions had caused chaos within my team. Although I had found important information, my plan had unnecessarily complicated matters, causing more harm than good.

Perhaps you have seen a business struggling due to its own self-imposed complexities. I have. I have observed how companies can fall into the same traps that I did. Their strategic plans are overloaded with objectives and an excessive number of tactics, presented in lengthy documents and slide-shows featuring numerous initiatives written in tiny 14-point Arial font. Every aspect of their strategic plan is bogged down with unnecessary intricacies. This level of planning complexity leads to heightened confusion and frustration. Each objective holds equal importance, creating a tangled web that is impossible to unravel. Where do you even begin?

Alternately, not having any plan is just as detrimental as not knowing where to begin. Making decisions without a well-defined strategy or plan can lead to a lack of clear direction. When no strategic goals and objectives are in place, employees may struggle with prioritizing tasks, leading to confusion and inconsistent performance.

So, ask yourself, **"What is our strategy?"** Is our team fully aware of our path, and are they actively using our strengths to gain an advantage in our markets? It's doubtful. In their book *The Balanced Scorecard: Translating Strategy into Action*, authors David Norton and Robert Kaplan note that 90% of organizations fail to execute their strategies successfully.[111] And thought leader and author Steve Andriole, in an article for *Forbes*, writes, "Companies are too busy to strategize, don't know how to strategize, and are too internally focused to even think about strategy....[C]ompanies don't strategize."[112] This invites the question: why?

I have heard business owners say, "We're doing well and expanding, so we don't need a strategy or a plan." However, this belief is far from accurate. Without a well-defined strategy, your company lacks clear business objectives. This lack of focus can hinder your business. When no set goals are in place, it's difficult for your company to have a clear vision for the future. After all, how can you know when you've reached your goals if you haven't defined them?

Another challenge companies face is making plans without taking coordinated action. Whenever CEOs open up about their abandoned plans, I am immediately intrigued and inquire about their reasons. The most common response I receive is that, despite engaging in the strategic-planning process, they were forced to set it aside due to time constraints. With quarterly targets to meet and busy sales, marketing, and operations teams, these CEOs could not take on anything else. Imagine designing the blueprint for a stunning skyscraper, only to never see it come to life. These best-laid plans without focused execution are like birthday wishes—and hope isn't a strategy.

Countless companies create strategies and plans that ultimately never come to fruition. We've all been there, nodding in agreement about the next great initiative or plan that seemingly never materializes. Attempting to achieve success on our own or without the necessary resources, having inadequate communication, or lacking accountability can all lead to failure. As leaders, we need to prioritize the organization's objectives with clear and transparent communication, remain flexible in the face of unforeseen challenges, and empower and hold ourselves accountable when taking action. Ineffective communication and a lack of accountability can lead our teams to pursue the wrong objectives, ultimately wasting valuable time and effort on tasks that do not align with our purpose. I guarantee that, at this very moment, people in your company are occupied with tasks that are ultimately unproductive. And let's face it, unproductive work will never lead to your desired success.

I am here to show you that there is another way. I will guide you through creating a simple and lasting strategic plan for your business, but this is just one aspect of a larger narrative. It's all about effectively using your resources and making wise decisions to reach your goals. Like predicting future moves in a chess game, having a strategic plan is key to winning. Adapting and changing course quickly is crucial, just like how a skilled chess player must be willing to abandon old strategies to gain an advantage over their opponents.

Another perspective to consider is this: strategy entails developing a plan based on informed guesses, using your strengths to overcome challenges or capitalize on opportunities, and through a unified series of steps, progressing toward that goal. According to Richard Rumelt in his book *Good Strategy Bad Strategy: The Difference and Why It Matters*, the key to creating a successful strategy is identifying a significant aha moment that will give a sustainable competitive advantage. This means coming up with a truly meaningful insight on how to achieve victory.[113]

By taking the time to map out a simple plan, you'll gain another advantage over your competitors, enabling you to seize opportunities and anticipate potential risks. Ultimately, the goal is to create strategies that are worthwhile, and, if your hunch is right, achievable.

Before we dive into the framework, let's look at an instance of a bad strategy and then two successful ones.

BEYOND THE BOTTOM LINE: THE HIDDEN COSTS OF GREED

Electronic Arts, or EA, is based in Redwood City, Northern California. They specialize in creating and providing games, content, and online services for various internet-connected devices such as consoles, smartphones, and computers. With a strong following of nearly 600 million active players and fans worldwide, you may know them for games like *Battlefield*, the *Sims*, *Madden NFL*, and *Titanfall*.

What you may not know about EA is that in 2012 and 2013, they achieved the less-than-prestigious honor of being named the worst company in America two times in a row (according to consumer votes in a poll conducted by Consumerist).[114]

EA was viewed by its customer base to be prioritizing profit over producing high-quality products. This perception was reinforced when several employees spoke to the media anonymously about EA's corporate strategy in 2013.[115] Shareholders pressured the company to increase financial gains, but the more EA focused on maximizing profits, the more their sales declined.

Consumerist summarized the results by asking, "When we live in an era marked by massive oil spills, faulty foreclosures by bad banks, and rampant consolidation in the airline and telecom industry, what does it say about EA's business practices that so many people have—for the second year in a row—come out to hand it the title of Worst Company in America?"[116]

Instead of setting customer-centric objectives such as crafting captivating video games that offer exceptional customer experiences, creating groundbreaking titles with a focus on positive social influence, or designing games that promote community inclusivity, EA's approach was to produce subpar games and consistently demand small payments from players to allow them to advance within the games, all to maximize profits. In a similar move, EA required players to have an active internet connection in order to play solo. The company denied that this was a form of anti-piracy digital rights management and instead marketed it as a way for players to experience a constantly evolving social world. However, this also meant that players were constantly online and encouraged to make purchases from the in-game store. In a LinkedIn post, one gamer wrote, "It's become more apparent now than ever that EA is in it for the money…it's one thing to want profit and another to clearly rip-off fans to their face."[117] According to a 2013 *Forbes* article, EA sparked anger from fans for their use of microtransactions. Initially, EA stated their intention to include microtransactions in all their games, even those that already cost $60.[118] However, they later retracted this statement and clarified that they intended for all *mobile* games to have microtransactions.[119]

Despite EA's focus on pleasing shareholders, their financial goals could have been achieved if they had prioritized their employees and customers. Instead, they became one of the most hated companies in America. So, what happened?

You may recall the gaming industry's massive growth in the mobile-gaming sector. With the rise of smartphones and tablets, more and more people were turning to mobile games for entertainment. EA shifted their focus toward this booming market, seeing this as a lucrative opportunity. However, instead of approaching mobile as an opportunity to create innovative and engaging games, EA's strategy was narrowly focused on maximizing profits. This led to the infamous microtransactions and loot boxes in their mobile games, where players were required to pay continually to progress or unlock certain features. While EA wasn't the first game maker to include pay-to-play mechanics, EA came under fire because these actions infuriated their loyal fan base and tarnished their reputation as a customer-centric company. This fixation on profits led to the release of rushed and suboptimal games and adversely affected EA's internal culture. Prioritizing profits above all else created a toxic environment where employees were pressured to take shortcuts and sacrifice quality.

This is a cautionary tale for companies prioritizing profit over fulfilling their core purpose. Thankfully for their players, EA learned from these hard lessons and was able to turn the company around. EA has implemented a more efficient process for gamers to receive refunds on games that fall short of their expectations. They have removed strict anti-piracy measures and started giving players access to upcoming games earlier. This change reflects a shift in the company's focus, prioritizing players' satisfaction as their top priority.

In stark contrast to the Electronic Arts of 2013, EA made *Forbes*'s 2023 Best Midsize Employers list.[120] They are also expanding their programs for social good. EA is committed to supporting the LGBTQ+ community through collaboration with organizations focusing on inclusive legislation and youth support. Their digital learning program, Play to Learn, offers online gaming and simulations for middle and high school students to engage them in STEAM subjects and increase interest in new career fields. Developed with EVERFI, Digital Schoolhouse, and Ukie, "the program reached 15,500 students in North America and the UK last year and helped increase their assessment scores by 77%," according to their website.[121]

MEANINGFUL MOMENTUM: THE KEY TO COMPANY TURNAROUND

Best Buy, the multinational electronics retailer, is an excellent example of how a shift in business strategy can lead to rapid growth. In 2012, Best Buy faced fierce market competition with online platforms like Amazon and big-box stores like Walmart and Home Depot that were able to provide the same appliances Best Buy did but for lower prices. With a decrease in revenue and shrinking margins, the executive team needed clarification on the state of their business and worked to understand the underlying issues. After suffering a staggering $1.7 billion loss, the company brought on Hubert Joly, who had previously led Carlson, a hospitality company, as their new CEO.[122]

To make a significant change, Joly took two months to gather information and analyze what was causing Best Buy's decline in profits. His research discovered that their potential customers were engaging in showrooming—trying out their desired products at physical stores before making a purchase decision. However, instead of buying from the store, these customers would leave and purchase the products online for a lower price, often from retailers like Amazon. With these new insights, the company reevaluated their approach and implemented a strategy to embrace their employees, customers, and community.

Rather than viewing Best Buy employees as mere expenses to be reduced—as his predecessor had done by removing employee discounts—Joly prioritized giving them purpose and meaning.

Joly's first significant impact at Best Buy was creating employee meaning and promoting a culture where managers actively listened to employees' aspirations and connected them with the company's purpose. This was controversial at the time, but by defining purpose and meaning for employees, customers, and the communities they served, Best Buy shifted their focus to become a caring culture.

Best Buy's turnaround strategy included the following:

- Match online retailers' prices—including, of course, Amazon's.
- Turn foot traffic into more sales through expert advice and personalized service.
- Enhance employees' knowledge and skills to create higher levels of engagement.
- Elevate customer experiences by allowing key suppliers to set up store-within-a-store concepts.
- Make a positive impact on the world and change it for the better.

During this turnaround, rather than downsizing or creating new merchandise, the executives at Best Buy chose to make use of a valuable asset that was being underutilized: their physical stores. By transforming their storefronts into "mini-warehouses," Best Buy offered quicker shipping, more convenient customer pickup options, and better product availability, ultimately improving the overall shopping experience for customers.

As Joly said in a December 2018 interview for *Twin Cities Business*, "I don't believe that the purpose of a company is to make money. It's an imperative. It's a necessity. But it's not the purpose....I believe the purpose of a company is particularly to contribute to the common good: its customers, its employees, and to the community in which it operates....If you can connect the search for meaning of the individual with the purpose of the company, then magical things happen."[123]

In just three years, the narrative of Best Buy has drastically changed. Joly streamlined the company, making it more adaptable as a retailer. A glance at their 2015 earnings report showed that comparable-store sales increased by 3.8%, profits skyrocketed, and online sales surged by 17% compared to the previous year.[124]

The result of Joly's tenure as CEO was six straight years of growth and a tripling of earnings.[125] Best Buy was able to turn things around by fostering a sense of purpose and connection for their employees, promoting genuine human relationships between managers and team members, granting autonomy within the workplace, providing personalized feedback through one-on-one coaching, and embracing a mindset of growth and development. What we can take away from this is that prioritizing the quality of your employees ultimately results in your customers' success, which in turn leads to financial success.

Joly emphasized the importance of putting people first as a CEO. He firmly believed that when employees have a strong sense of purpose in their work, they perform at a higher level. In an interview by Marcel Schwantes for his podcast *Leadership from the Core*, Joly explains, "It's all about creating the right environment, being someone caring, vulnerable, and very human."[126]

In the past 10 years, Best Buy has raised a total of $160 million to support St. Jude Children's Research Hospital in their goal to treat the most challenging pediatric cancers and diseases. Additionally, the company is in the process of constructing 100 Team Tech Centers, which provide a safe place for children to learn new skills and stay focused on their education after school. Best Buy also offers other programs that benefit their communities.[127]

STRATEGY REVERSAL: THE UNEXPECTED PATH TO CUSTOMER DELIGHT

Southwest Airlines Co., often known as Southwest, is a major airline in the United States and the largest low-cost carrier airline globally. It was founded on March 15, 1967, by Herb Kelleher under the name Air Southwest Co. In 1971, it changed its name to Southwest Airlines Co. and started offering flights within Texas, traveling between Dallas, Houston, and San Antonio.

During the 1960s, most airlines adopted the widely used hub-and-spoke model. As the name suggests, this model has a central hub where all flights originate from, and different destinations are connected like spokes on a wheel. While this model offers benefits such as fewer routes to manage, its main disadvantage is its inflexibility. Even a tiny change in routing due to weather or other circumstances can have ripple effects on the airline's entire operation.

Southwest instead focused primarily on the point-to-point model and significantly improved its processes. Under the point-to-point model, each flight is a direct journey from one destination to another. This offers passengers more options and flexibility compared to the hub-and-spoke model. However, those traveling beyond their initial destination must retrieve their baggage and recheck it for the next leg of their journey. Despite this extra step, the point-to-point model has dramatically reduced travel time and eliminates the need for connecting flights.

Ranked as the third largest airline in the U.S.[128] and one of the top low-cost carriers worldwide,[129] Southwest Airlines has achieved impressive operational efficiency through a different flight-operations model. Yet this is not the sole factor behind their success. It's worth examining what sets Southwest apart from other airlines in terms of their strategy.

Imagine a company that defies common expectations and still manages to thrive. It may seem absurd, but this is the exact strategy that propelled Southwest Airlines to success in an ever-changing airline industry. While other airlines assigned seats, Southwest allowed customers to choose their own through a first-come, first-serve system. Instead of complimentary meals, customers could purchase alcoholic beverages with complimentary snacks served on flights over 175 miles.[130] And unlike other airlines, Southwest did not participate in transferring luggage between flights. Their unorthodox approach was the key to their success.[131]

As other airlines focus on satisfying the needs of travelers seeking comfort, such as providing first-class or business-class options and assisting passengers with connecting flights while managing schedules, baggage, and in-flight dining, none can match Southwest's unparalleled efficiency.

Southwest, in contrast to their competitors, tailors all its activities to deliver low-cost, convenient service on its routes. Through fast turnarounds of only 15 minutes at the gate, Southwest can keep planes flying longer hours than rivals and provide frequent departures with fewer aircraft. Automated ticketing at the gate encourages customers to bypass travel agents, allowing Southwest to avoid their commissions, and a standardized fleet of 737 aircraft boosts the efficiency of maintenance.[132]

Southwest further differentiates itself from competitors by providing exceptional customer experiences. The airline is implementing important strategies to create a sense of meaning at work. First, they recognize that happy employees result in satisfied customers. And second, their frontline staff goes above and beyond to make sure every passenger feels acknowledged, appreciated, and well cared for.[133] And it's paying off. In J.D. Power's 2023 North American Airline Satisfaction Study, Southwest Airlines ranked highest in customer satisfaction in the economy/basic economy segment for the second consecutive year.[134] It is also worth noting that Southwest was named to the first-ever *Forbes* Customer Experience All-Stars list in 2023.[135] From their welcoming and friendly employees to their simplified booking system, Southwest is making flying easy and pleasant for individuals from all walks of life.

It wouldn't be fitting to end the story of Southwest Airlines without mentioning the lovable and outgoing personality of renowned founder and former chair/CEO Herb Kelleher, who passed away in 2019. In the book *Nuts!: Southwest Airlines' Crazy Recipe for Business and Personal Success*, Kevin and Jackie Freiberg recount a situation where Southwest had to part ways with an unsatisfied customer:

> One woman who frequently flew on Southwest was constantly disappointed with every aspect of the company's operation. In fact, she became known as the "Pen Pal" because after every flight she wrote in with a complaint.

> She didn't like the fact that the company didn't assign seats; she didn't like the absence of a first-class section; she didn't like not having a meal in flight; she didn't like Southwest's boarding procedure; she didn't like the flight attendants' sporty uniforms and the casual atmosphere.

> Her last letter, reciting a litany of complaints, momentarily stumped Southwest's customer relations people. They bumped it up to Herb's desk, with a note: "This one's yours."

> In sixty seconds, Kelleher wrote back and said, "Dear Mrs. Crabapple, We will miss you. Love, Herb."[136]

What can we learn from this?

Southwest has always had a clear understanding of their identity. When a company or brand knows their core values and principles, and all decision-making stems from that foundation, it's a powerful approach. This is the essence of strategy!

Serving their communities, Southwest Airlines partners with over 400 local and national organizations to create positive change, promoting and supporting workforce development, fostering diversity, equity, and inclusion, and supporting environmental sustainability.[137] Since 2007, Southwest Airlines has donated over $42 million in complimentary transportation to 117 hospitals and medical organizations across 28 states. The company is also committed to supporting various other causes, such as raising awareness about human trafficking through educating their employees and partnering with nonprofits dedicated to rescuing, rehabilitating, and restoring survivors of this heinous crime.[138]

These examples of bad strategy versus good strategy show that aiming to increase revenues and profit margins at the expense of people is bad for everyone. When companies fail to address the challenges and underlying reasons for declining sales or underwhelming company performance, they risk losing even more. With open and honest discussions about what impedes progress, meaningful change will be achieved. In the case of EA, they took their customer feedback seriously, turning the company around by putting players before profits. And just like Best Buy's remarkable turnaround, or Southwest's, which began with **a clearly defined purpose** and a well-thought-out strategy for accomplishing it, to lead your organization toward success, it is crucial to thoroughly examine the key obstacles and potential opportunities that lie ahead.

To get you from here to there, your purpose, values, and unique emotional points of difference will guide you in developing your strategy. And your strategy will guide the planning process. We are untethering strategy from planning to avoid the pitfalls of others—when people get so caught up in strategic planning that it replaces actual strategy. Strategy and planning are closely connected, but by placing a focus on strategy before diving into the details of planning, you will engage in strategic thinking that will ultimately make your planning process smoother. When these two components merge, they will create an effective and simple strategic plan.

You might be under the impression that differentiating strategy and planning is a daunting task, but I assure you that you are capable of handling strategy:

1. Focus on your purpose and where you want to go.
2. Conduct a thorough analysis.
3. Uncover key insights.
4. Put forward strategies.
5. Make any necessary adjustments to bring your strategies to the plan.

These steps will put you in a solid position to move forward confidently into the next step—planning. Remember, a strategy is essentially a hypothesis. For it to be effective, you must accurately identify the problem at hand or the opportunity ahead, establish a framework for addressing it, and suggest a series of logical actions to achieve the desired outcome. Then act by moving forward toward your goals—one step at a time. I gained this valuable insight when I had the chance to discover the secrets behind the Canadian women's Olympic hockey team's success.

For those of us who have a competitive nature, winning is exhilarating and losing is crushing. Unfortunately, I was never skilled in team sports, always at the bottom of the talent pool in hockey, soccer, basketball, and any other sport. However, despite my lack of individual talent, I relished the camaraderie of being part of a winning team.

When you're in the game to win, your confidence fuels your motivation and determination to push forward. You take calculated risks, maximize strengths, focus on positive outcomes, and don't dwell on current setbacks. Nothing can stand in your way. But when something unexpected happens, it can throw you off balance, and suddenly, you lose focus.

When I studied leadership at Queen's University, Dr. Peter Jensen stepped into the classroom. He was the team psychologist for the Canadian women's Olympic hockey team and had guided them to back-to-back gold medal wins. Our class sat mesmerized as he spoke.

I had to know—what was the secret?

With a twinkle in his eye, Dr. Jensen leaned forward in his chair and explained that the team wasn't focused on winning the ultimate goal of a gold medal. Instead, they homed their efforts on succeeding in each moment—analyzing what needed to be done in the next 10 minutes of ice time and taking it one step at a time.

Achieving gold medals is not out of your reach. If you incorporate purpose, values, and your unique emotional points of difference into everything you do, then you are already on the path toward victory. And by giving back to others and creating a positive impact in their lives, you are already winning.

As you navigate the process of creating a road map for success, you'll define your strategies and move to planning. The key difference is that you will lead this process with purpose. For a long time, companies have been encouraged to incorporate purpose into their operations. However, purpose has often been viewed as an afterthought—something that can improve employee morale and commitment, create shared value, contribute to the community, and benefit the environment. But a *Harvard Business Review* study revealed that high-growth companies elevate purpose from being a peripheral aspect of their strategy to its core.[139]

By putting purpose at the center of your strategy, you will eliminate unnecessary complexities and provide a straightforward plan that everyone can understand and support. I am thrilled to share the methods and tactics that will take your business from average to exceptional. Your strategic plan will evolve over time, as no one can predict the future accurately. However, when you use this framework, your business will be better prepared to handle any challenges it may face. As you go through this process, your vision for the future will become clearer and more defined.

The outcome of your simple strategic plan is a 10-slide presentation, which includes a title slide for your branding and an end slide to show your appreciation for employees' time. Between these two slides, you'll communicate your purpose, values, emotional points of difference, objectives, goals, and strategy(s) and share what your business might look like three years from now.

Let me repeat this: **Your strategic plan is 10 slides—easy to understand and easy to communicate.**

By simplifying your plan, you will increase employee engagement and nurture a culture that reflects your purpose, fostering loyalty to your fundamental beliefs and sparking enthusiasm for meaningful work. We will examine the structure that affects your main objectives, goals, and strategy(s).

In this guide, you will learn how to engage your leaders and teams in the business by setting annual objectives and goals, supported by quarterly goals that are MEAN (meaningful, exact, actionable, and necessary). The MEAN goal framework emphasizes the importance of creating meaning for your employees, customers, and community while maintaining clarity, actionability, and relevance in pursuit of your objectives.

You're probably accustomed to the SMART (specific, measurable, achievable, relevant, timebound) goal framework, but I want you to discard it and focus on MEAN goals instead. The problem with SMART goals is that they hold you back from reaching higher. If you're using SMART goals, your perception of what is quantifiable (measurable) and within your abilities (achievable) fails to consider your team's potential.

Before you lies a world of unexpected possibilities that can emerge when you expand your perspective. Empower your employees by eliminating the notion of achievable. SMART goals overlook the impact of cooperative, analytical thinking or the valuable achievements that your leaders and their teams can attain by pushing themselves outside their comfort zones.

According to a study by Leadership IQ involving 16,000 people, a mere 15% of employees feel strongly that their goals are capable of propelling them toward great things. Additionally, only 13% of employees have confidence that their goals for the year will allow them to reach their full potential.[140]

But it's not enough to simply set MEAN goals—you must also clearly define what needs to be done, who should do it, and when it should be completed. By fostering a connection between your team and your company's purpose, values, and emotional points of difference, you can ensure that every action aligns with these core elements.

Get ready to transform your business approach by infusing meaning into your strategic plan. In the following chapter, I'm going to show you what this strategic plan looks like and how you can use it to lead with clarity and focus. Your strategic-plan template is designed to be simple—because simplicity is key to improved employee engagement.

Chapter 12
CRAFTING A LEAN STRATEGIC FRAMEWORK

The meeting room was filled with executives and managers from various departments of the company, all gathered for a session on strategic planning. The air was thick with anticipation and nervous energy, as everyone knew that this meeting would set the tone for the entire company's future.

Sitting at the head of the table was a new CEO, a tall, imposing figure with a commanding presence. She had a reputation for being a visionary leader, always pushing boundaries and challenging the status quo. And today, she was about to share her vision with the rest of the team.

"Today, we are going to transform our approach to business," she began, her voice steady and confident. "We are going to infuse meaning into our workforce and prioritize making a bigger difference in people's lives."

All eyes were fixed on her, anticipating her next words. The CEO went on to say, "Our company's focus is shifting from solely chasing profits to putting people first. I believe in making a positive impact and serving our community, and that's what truly matters to me."

She took a brief pause, allowing the excitement to grow, before adding, "The key to boosting employee engagement is simplicity. That's why our strategy and plan will be straightforward yet powerful. Are you prepared to join me on this journey?"

A resounding yes echoed through the room, and the CEO smiled. This was the start of something great, and she could feel it in her bones.

Similar to how the recently appointed CEO opened up by sharing her personal journey, a straightforward planning worksheet also begins with your own story. It starts with your desire to craft a strategic plan that is both straightforward and purposeful. This specially designed worksheet will walk you through the essential steps of creating a concise 10-slide plan that will steer your business toward success with clarity and direction.

The 10-slide strategic plan looks like this:

How We Measure Success	Slide 1: Title Slide: Your Strategic Plan
Slide 8: Scorecard	Slide 2: Purpose statement
	Slide 3: Core values
	Slide 4: Emotional points of difference
	Slide 5: Annual objectives
	Slide 6: Key goals
	Slide 7: Key strategy(s)
	Slide 9: Three years ahead
	Slide 10: End slide: Thank you

The process kicks off with semiannual strategy and planning meetings. The left side of your simple plan worksheet serves as a scorecard, tracking the financial metrics related to your annual objectives. On the right side, you will define your purpose, values, emotional differentiators, and key strategy(s) before diving into the rest of the plan. During the planning meeting, you will establish your annual objectives, set key goals, and share your predictions for the future.

YOUR SCORECARD, LEFT

Slide 8, your Scorecard: How you'll track and measure your financial success and community impact.

It is vital to monitor the relevant metrics to assess both your progress toward achieving your goals and objectives and your community and social impact. A scorecard can be an effective tool for this purpose. You can better understand your performance by tracking various key performance indicators (KPIs). This information will enable you to make informed decisions for your business and position yourself for success.

Regarding financial metrics, several measurements can indicate your current standing and whether you are moving in the right direction. Below is a partial list of 20 financial metrics to keep an eye on:

1. **Sales revenue:** The total income generated from selling products or services.

2. **Revenue growth rate:** The percentage increase in revenue compared to a previous period (for example, same quarter last year), indicating business growth.

3. **Gross profit margin:** The percentage of revenue retained after subtracting the cost of goods or services sold. This measure is typically shown as a percentage of overall revenue, also referred to as the gross margin ratio.

4. **Net profit margin:** The percentage of revenue remaining as profit after all expenses, indicating overall profitability. The net profit margin is a measure of how much profit a company generates for every dollar of revenue it brings in.

5. **Return on investment:** The ratio of gains or losses from an investment relative to its cost, measuring investment performance.

6. **Customer acquisition cost:** The cost incurred to acquire a new customer, highlighting marketing efficiency.

7. **Customer lifetime value:** The total revenue expected from a customer over their entire relationship with a company.

8. **Percentage of repeat customers:** The proportion of customers who make multiple purchases, indicating loyalty.

9. **Churn rate:** The rate at which customers stop using a service or product, reflecting customer retention.

10. **Cash flow:** The movement of money into and out of a business,

indicating liquidity.

11. **Current ratio:** The ratio of current assets to current liabilities, indicating short-term financial health. This financial metric evaluates a company's capability to pay its short-term obligations, which are typically due within a year.

12. **Debt-to-equity ratio:** The ratio of a company's debt to its shareholders' equity, measuring financial leverage.

13. **Inventory turnover:** The number of times inventory is sold and replaced in a specific period, indicating efficiency.

14. **Accounts receivable turnover:** The number of times receivables are collected and replaced in a period, measuring collection efficiency.

15. **Average order value:** The average amount spent by customers in a single transaction.

16. **Conversion rate:** The percentage of website visitors who complete a desired action, such as making a purchase.

17. **Employee productivity:** The efficiency of employees in generating output or results.

18. **Customer satisfaction:** A metric measuring customer contentment with a product or service.

19. **Employee satisfaction:** The level of contentment and engagement among employees within an organization.

20. **Net promoter score:** A metric gauging customer loyalty and likelihood to recommend a product or service to others.

Community and Social Impact

Using the infinite loop of connection, you were tasked with showing the evidence of your community and social impact. Here are 10 metrics you may consider when striving to fulfill your purpose:

1. **Donation amount:** Measure the total monetary contributions made to community initiatives, charities, or social impact projects over a specific period.

2. **Volunteer hours:** Track the amount of time employees dedicate to volunteer work, showcasing the commitment to social causes.

3. **Community reach:** Evaluate the extent of the organization's impact by measuring the number of individuals or groups positively affected by community giving efforts.

4. **Influential projects:** Identify and measure the success of specific projects or initiatives undertaken, focusing on the tangible outcomes and benefits for the community.

5. **Partnerships established:** Gauge the number and quality of partnerships formed with local organizations, nonprofits, or community groups to amplify the social impact.

6. **Employee engagement:** Assess the level of employee involvement in community giving or social impact activities, reflecting a culture of corporate social responsibility.

7. **Media impressions:** Monitor the reach and exposure of community giving efforts through media coverage, showcasing the organization's commitment to social responsibility.

8. **Environmental impact:** Evaluate the ecological footprint of community giving initiatives, measuring contributions to sustainability, conservation, and environmental stewardship.

9. **Skill-development metrics:** Measure the acquisition and enhancement of skills among community members through educational programs or skill-building initiatives sponsored by the organization.

10. **Socioeconomic progress:** Gauge the socioeconomic progress within your community, considering factors such as reduced poverty rates, increased employment opportunities, and enhanced economic stability.

Every metric offers insight into the state of your business, steering your choices and aiding in refining your plans. Your KPIs are tailored to your specific business—you will not monitor all the listed examples. The number of KPIs that your company monitors and shares with its employees depends on the size of the organization. Typically, senior management will track numerous financial metrics, while I recommend that you limit the number of KPIs shared with employees to a range of five to 10.

TIP: As I launched my first business, the phrase "Cash is king" echoed in my ears from everyone around me. It became my top priority to generate cash and keep it flowing. For those just starting, this concept of a scorecard may seem daunting. The best approach is to seek help from experts in areas where you need more knowledge, such as hiring a bookkeeper or accountant. Be bold, ask questions, and continue learning along the way.

As my business continued to expand, I heavily relied on the knowledge and expertise of others. I always asked questions and ensured I fully understood the answers before making any decisions. Learning is a never-ending process, so don't be discouraged by unfamiliar concepts or data—instead, use the questions you may have about financial metrics as an opportunity to broaden your understanding further.

Before we move on to the next step of your plan, let's share a clear understanding of your objectives and goals. Even highly experienced executives can struggle to differentiate between the two, so I want to ensure we agree before proceeding further.

Objectives are the broad, overarching aims that you strive to achieve. In contrast, goals are specific and tangible targets that help you reach those objectives. They serve as markers and checkpoints along the way toward the final goal. When you break down the larger strategy into smaller, measurable steps, goals provide a clear road map for your team. These targets often have set timelines and can be tracked and monitored to measure progress. They also provide a sense of accomplishment once they are achieved.

Now that we share a common understanding of objectives and goals, let's move to the right side of your worksheet.

YOUR STRATEGIC PLAN, RIGHT

Slide 1, Title Slide: The strategic plan

Slide 2, Purpose (Why You Exist): Now that you've defined your why, write your purpose statement on the top right of your worksheet.

Slide 3, Core Values: Beneath your purpose statement, write the three to four core values that everyone in your organization lives.

Slide 4, Connection: Write two or three emotional points of difference, the feelings you want to create through your customer interactions.

Slide 5, Your Annual Objectives: Define your annual objectives. Here are 10 examples of objectives your company could strive to achieve:

1. Revenue growth
2. Market expansion
3. Customer satisfaction
4. Operational efficiency
5. Innovation
6. Employee development
7. Brand awareness
8. Sustainability
9. Market leadership
10. Community engagement

Taking your organization's size into consideration, your company should narrow its focus to a few objectives. When you narrow down the objectives to two to five key areas, employees will have a clear understanding of their priorities and how they align with the overall plan. We all know the risks of taking on too many objectives—it becomes difficult to make meaningful progress toward any of them. In the fast-paced corporate world, there's constant pressure to do more in less time. But by prioritizing your goals and focusing on the most important ones, you can make significant progress toward your aspirations. This approach to planning communicates clear expectations for what needs to be accomplished, sets the tone for a productive work environment, directs the allocation of resources, and promotes efficient prioritization. To quote Kathleen Eisenhardt of Stanford University, "There must be a balance in the number and kind of aims and objectives: too many goals are paralyzing; too few, perplexing."[141]

Slide 6, Your Key Goals: Let's take the next step in defining key goals using our 10 examples of broad objectives.

1. **Revenue growth:** Increase annual revenue by 20% through new customer acquisition and upselling to existing customers.
2. **Market expansion:** Enter two international markets, France and Germany, by the end of the fiscal year, expanding our global reach.
3. **Customer satisfaction:** Achieve a Net Promoter Score (NPS) of 55 by enhancing customer support and service.
4. **Operational efficiency:** Reduce production costs by 15% through process optimization and supply chain improvements.
5. **Innovation:** Launch a new product line leveraging emerging technologies and addressing customer pain points.
6. **Employee development:** Increase employee engagement by implementing a professional development program and achieving a 75% employee satisfaction rate.
7. **Brand awareness:** Increase brand visibility by 30% through targeted digital marketing campaigns and social media engagement.
8. **Sustainability:** Implement eco-friendly practices to reduce the company's carbon footprint by 10% and achieve green certification in 18 months.
9. **Market leadership:** Secure a 25% market share within the industry by positioning the company as an authoritative thought leader.
10. **Community engagement:** Contribute to social responsibility initiatives by volunteering 1,000 hours of community service and supporting local charities.

As you'll recall, MEAN stands for meaningful, exact, actionable, and necessary. Let's break down what this means in the context of your key goals:

- **M**eaningful: Ensure your goals contribute to employee, customer, or societal significance, aligning with your values and contributing to your greater purpose. Don't prevent your leaders from reaching high. Make your goals heartfelt and challenging.
- **E**xact: Define your goals with precision, leaving no room for ambiguity, and specify exactly what you intend to achieve. Empower your team by enabling them to picture the outcome and how great it will feel when the goals are achieved.
- **A**ctionable: Make your goals actionable so your leaders and managers can break them down into specific, manageable steps that lead to progress. Be bold and open to learning—and possibly failing. You can adjust along the way.
- **N**ecessary: Ensure that your goals are essential and relevant to your overall objectives, eliminating distractions and focusing on what truly matters. Empower your leaders to do the critical thinking. Will this goal get you closer to fulfilling your purpose?

By ensuring your key goals adhere to the MEAN criteria, you create a framework that promotes clarity, meaning, and accountability for what truly matters, as well as a focused pursuit of winning to fulfill your purpose. The MEAN framework becomes a signpost for your organization, helping everyone understand what needs to be achieved, how, and when—and why their work matters.

Slide 7, Your Key Strategies: Your well-constructed strategies form the foundation of your plan, and it's important to define those strategies before diving into the planning process. Strategy acts as a road map for your organization, guiding you toward your goals and helping you navigate through challenges, competition, and unknowns. This involves making strategic choices and decisions that position your business for long-term success. An effective strategy clarifies your purpose, shapes your actions, and ensures that every move you make is in line with your purpose.

If you're looking to expand your business, there are countless strategies at your disposal. A simple online search will yield over a hundred examples of different approaches. There are numerous paths to growth, including providing exceptional customer service, making your products and services unique, or using the latest technology. The key is to select the strategies that align with your goals and set you up for success. Here are 20 options to consider exploring.

1. **Acquisitions:** Grow by acquiring other businesses.
2. **Cross-sell more products:** Sell additional products or services to existing customers.
3. **Diversify products and services:** Expand your offerings to new areas.
4. **Distribution:** Optimize how you get your products to customers.
5. **Exceptional customer service:** Stand out by providing outstanding support.
6. **Improve operational efficiency:** Streamline processes for better productivity.
7. **Increase customer retention:** Focus on keeping existing customers satisfied.
8. **Intellectual property:** Leverage intellectual property for competitive advantage.
9. **Joint ventures:** Collaborate with other businesses for mutual benefit.
10. **Low-cost:** Compete on price by minimizing costs.
11. **Market expansion:** Enter new markets to reach more customers.
12. **Outsource to focus on core competencies:** Delegate noncore projects and tasks to external experts.
13. **Pricing:** Set prices strategically to attract customers.
14. **Product differentiation:** Make your product unique in the market.
15. **Quality:** Emphasize high-quality products or services.
16. **Sourcing:** Optimize where and how you get your resources.

17. **Technological advantage:** Leverage technology to gain an edge.
18. **Talent:** Attract, develop, and retain skilled employees.
19. **Transform your business model:** Rethink your fundamental approach.
20. **Vertical diversification:** Expand into different parts of the supply chain.

The Art of Selectivity: Opting for Quality, Not Quantity

As I mentioned earlier, focusing on a limited number of annual objectives, goals, and strategy(s), typically two to five, is a strategic approach that optimizes your chances of success. Here's why this approach is highly recommended:

Clarity and focus: When it comes to your team's objectives, goals, and strategy(s), keeping them limited allows for a clear focus on the primary purpose, avoiding any confusion over the intended direction and promoting teamwork toward achieving desired results. However, having too many objectives and goals can create distractions and lead members offtrack.

Resource allocation: Successfully accomplishing your objectives, goals, and strategy(s) relies on wisely allocating resources such as time, money, and personnel. By prioritizing what's most important to your business, you can effectively and efficiently distribute resources. This focused approach prevents dilution of resources among numerous tasks and improves the chances of achieving meaningful outcomes.

Quality over quantity: Having too many objectives, goals, and strategy(s) can result in rushed and mediocre outcomes—or complete misses. Instead, by prioritizing a select few and dedicating time and attention to them, you can ensure high-quality results that will have a significant impact on driving your business forward.

Manageable execution: Having a limited number of objectives, goals, and strategy(s) makes them more manageable to execute. This allows for better attention and planning for each individual objective, goal, and strategy, reducing the risk of tasks being forgotten or overlooked. Additionally, tracking progress and holding individuals accountable for their contributions becomes easier with a concise, straightforward plan.

Flexibility and adaptability: In a volatile market, things can change rapidly. By having a limited number of objectives, goals, and strategy(s), your organization becomes more flexible and better equipped to handle unexpected situations and take advantage of new opportunities. A manageable plan allows for easier pivoting without being weighed down by an extensive list of objectives, goals, and strategy(s).

Motivation and engagement: When you accomplish your objectives and goals, it brings a sense of achievement and drive. By staying focused and dedicated as a team, you can increase the frequency of success, which in turn raises morale, productivity, and enthusiasm. This positive spiral motivates everyone to keep striving for future strategic objectives and goals.

When you home in on two to five strategic objectives, your business can harness the power of synergy between clarity, resource optimization, quality, execution, adaptability, and motivation. This focused approach allows for strategic and powerful energy to be channeled toward achieving success and fulfilling your overarching purpose.

Slide 9, Three Years Ahead: How do you envision your company in three years? What advancements will you have made in terms of solutions, and what additional services will you offer? Where do you hope to be? While predictions may not be definite, what are your goals for growth and success? Having a clear sense of the path ahead is the only way to turn your vision into a reality.

Create a concise list of objectives outlining the vision for your business in three years. This can be a powerful tool to motivate and inspire your employees. Remember to keep the list on one slide for easy comprehension.

When it comes to planning, there are various approaches for anticipating the future. Some advocate for creating a vision that extends 25 years into the future. However, when it comes to building a business, I find that setting a three-year target is more realistic and achievable. Of course, if you want to aim higher or envision an even further future, go for it! Set ambitious goals and don't limit yourself.

In essence, what your worksheet includes is the full set of elements necessary to create an effective yearly plan.

How We Measure Success	Slide 1: Title Slide: Your Strategic Plan
Slide 8: Scorecard (Financial and community impact metrics)	Slide 2: Purpose statement (Why we exist)
	Slide 3: Core values (How we act, think, communicate, and make decisions)
	Slide 4: Connection (How we make customers feel)
	Slide 5: Annual objectives (What we want to accomplish)
	Slide 6: Key goals (The results we want to achieve, when)
	Slide 7: Key strategies (How we're going to achieve our goals)
	Slide 9: Three years ahead (Where we want to be in three years)
	Slide 10: End slide: Thank you

While planning to win works for larger businesses with time, money, and resources, how does this all come together for a small-business owner? Let's look at Wayne, a solo business owner. His story begins with his childhood fear of dogs. To overcome his fears, he wanted to help people overcome their anxieties and provide them with the skills necessary to confidently handle their pets, as evident by the positive reviews from his customers.

Wayne is a driven, passionate advocate for building confidence in dog owners, and he wanted to expand his dog-training service. Still, he needed to make sure there was enough money coming in to keep his venture alive. Wayne was constantly balancing his schedule, handling multiple appointments, overseeing his camps, and keeping a close eye on expenses and cash flow. On top of that, he was always on the lookout for local partners who could lend a helping hand. He jumped from one task to another in an attempt to keep his business afloat and bring in revenue. However, more often than not, he would get sidetracked by daily tasks like updating his website, responding to emails, filling out contracts, and offering free lessons to attract new customers. As a result, he lacked focus and struggled to determine the best path forward.

Wayne had a goal in mind—make his business profitable within one year—and he needed a solid plan to achieve it. He dove into this framework and focused on defining his purpose, values, and what made his brand unique from others—his emotional differentiators. He methodically developed a straightforward plan that outlined his aims, goals, and strategy, as well as his vision for the business three years down the line. Wayne was determined to see his business thrive, and he dedicated himself to putting in the necessary work to make it a reality.

Wayne had a concrete grasp on the specific numbers he needed to reach for bookings; boarding and training sessions lasting one, two, or four weeks; weekly private training sessions; and his weekend training camps. These metrics provided inspiration, giving him a clear path to profitability for the next 12 months. Next, he predicted his growth targets over three years. These simple metrics eventually morphed into what his business could be and where he saw new opportunities to train others on how to train dogs (and their owners).

Within just a few months, his startup blossomed into a thriving small business with big dreams, all thanks to his clear path forward and effective execution of his plan. He added two new staff members to his business and steadily progressed toward achieving his objectives. Rather than relying on just cash, he kept track of six metrics: sales revenue, gross profit margin, cash flow, employee productivity, the conversion rate from free private lessons that converted into new customers, and his volunteer hours at the animal shelter. By continually monitoring these indicators, he was able to ensure that his business continued to move forward and stayed on track.

You could be in a similar situation—trying to manage multiple roles, investing your time and energy in keeping the company running, leading a group of five, and having sleepless nights as you worry about upcoming payroll. I've been through it all, struggling with the overwhelming daily tasks of operations. A simple plan and a scorecard can be a perfect remedy by providing precise goals to aim for, and this applies to your team too. Scorecards are useful for monitoring your development over time, offering clarity and motivation, which are vital for success.

It doesn't matter if your team is small, medium, or large—every business requires a plan to track progress toward its objectives. A scorecard enables you to evaluate your achievements and make necessary adjustments to stay on course.

After thoroughly reviewing the strategic plan, it is time to act. Let's move forward with planning and strategy meetings by preparing beforehand, conducting the meetings, and communicating afterward. This involves selecting your team, scheduling meetings, and executing the necessary tasks for successful strategy and planning.

Chapter 13

BLUEPRINTS FOR HARMONY: ALIGNING ORGANIZATIONAL GOALS AND ACTIONS

The order of strategy and planning is a highly debated topic. Some argue that strategy must come before planning, while others suggest the opposite. However, your purpose and values serve as the foundation for your strategy—the "how" behind your "why." For this reason, your purpose and values inform strategy, which then in turn informs planning.

By identifying your potential advantages over competitors by conducting a SWOT analyses (strengths, weaknesses, opportunities, and threats), evaluating your internal capabilities, considering external factors that could affect your strategy, and uncovering potential opportunities to leverage your strengths, you'll be in a much better position to plan accordingly.

Strategy.

Then planning.

This process is straightforward to grasp and easy to implement.

Now that you're ready to begin the strategic-planning process, it's time to assemble your team for your upcoming strategy and planning meetings. There are certain tasks that must be completed to ensure full readiness for these meetings, but I will provide guidance on what needs to be accomplished.

The key to achieving success through this process is having a thorough grasp on your status, or where your business stands at present. This will enable your strategic-planning team to come fully prepared for brainstorming sessions, offering well-informed recommendations and valuable insights during your strategy and planning meetings. The preparation work requires your leaders to meet with their teams, collecting and analyzing data from surveys and having a clear picture of where their teams are with development projects, revealing any areas that may need improvement or change. Since your strategy and planning meetings complement each other, here's a simple way to communicate the difference: strategy involves making a cohesive and coordinated set of decisions that puts your organization in a winning position, while planning focuses on outlining specific projects with timelines, goals, budgets, and assigned responsibilities.[142]

To kick off the strategic-planning process, I suggest scheduling your strategy and planning meetings about 10 weeks before the beginning of a new fiscal year. For example, if the fiscal year starts on January 1, aim to have these meetings in late October. This allows enough time to finalize your strategic plan for the first quarter. Adjust the timeline as needed. Smaller businesses with five to 10 team members can speed up the process, but larger organizations with over 50 employees should make sure there is sufficient time to prepare and distribute all necessary materials to the entire company.

For those who are new to this process and wish to give clear direction to their teams to drive their business forward after the start of the fiscal year, I suggest implementing your new plan prior to the beginning of the following quarter, making the necessary adjustments to objectives and goals for a partial year.

As I mentioned, there is work to be done beforehand, and to help you get there, I have divided the strategy and planning meetings into four steps:

1. Before the Meeting
2. Strategy Meeting
3. Planning Meeting
4. Communication Afterward

Before booking meetings, it's time to gather your team. Selecting the right team members involves considering role, skill, expertise, and diversity to create a well-rounded and capable group. When choosing your team, consider these elements:

- **Aligning roles and team composition:** Select employees whose roles align with your organization's goals. These individuals should have a deep understanding of their specific areas of expertise, allowing them to offer valuable insights to the team.

- **Prioritizing representation and inclusivity:** A successful team is made up of members who can effectively express their department's viewpoints, concerns, and objectives during discussions. It is also important to have a diverse group that incorporates different perspectives, backgrounds, and ideas to enrich the strategy and planning process.

- **Balancing professional experience:** Experience is critical in building a strong team. When you bring together individuals with diverse backgrounds, the well-rounded mix of fresh perspectives and expertise creates an environment for dynamic exchanges. Choose team members with varying levels of experience who can prioritize overarching goals and collaborate efficiently.

- **Selecting for professional development:** During the early years of my career, I held a sales position at a computer manufacturing company. It was during this time that I had the opportunity to learn from Brad, who served as the director of marketing. We often worked together on various projects, including developing customer personas and improving value propositions specifically for our retail sales partners and distributors. Brad's guidance and encouragement were crucial to my professional growth—he recognized my abilities and even advocated for me to join the strategy team.

  Through these strategic meetings, I gained valuable skills in translating high-level plans into tangible actions. I also had the chance to contribute my perspectives on enhancing customer and partner experiences and was encouraged to explore potential avenues for expansion beyond our usual retail markets. These discussions ignited my passion for strategy, leading to a significant change in my professional aspirations.

I am incredibly appreciative of coworkers like Brad, who recognize that being a strong leader means supporting others to achieve their goals and succeed.

The experience taught me the valuable lesson of acknowledging and nurturing talents within my teams. Allowing individuals to take on higher roles can be incredibly motivating, drive their growth, and have a positive impact on both their careers and your company's success. Often, these individuals are in the thick of things and can provide valuable perspectives that your team may have yet to consider. Who are the individuals in your company who you can guide and help grow?

OUTSIDE HELP

Identify board members, top executives, and key individuals from your staff who can assist with strategic planning. Keep the team size manageable—a group of 10 to 15 individuals is ideal for larger businesses during these meetings. For smaller businesses, consider seeking guidance from advisers and essential contributors to your business growth. Some potential contacts to consider for support and assistance could include business partners, suppliers, local advisers, and angel investors who may be interested in investing in your company in exchange for a stake in your business.

When searching for individuals with strong strategic-planning capabilities, desirable skills to consider include research, analysis, critical thinking, problem-solving, market development, communication, leadership, technology proficiency, and deductive and inductive reasoning abilities.

Once you feel you've got the right team in place, we're ready to move to step 1, Before the Meeting. As the saying goes, "Give me six hours to chop down a tree and I will spend the first four sharpening the ax." This highlights the importance of preparation in achieving success—so it's important to choose someone to champion this process so you can focus on leading your business.

STEP 1: BEFORE THE MEETING

In preparation for your strategy meeting, there are three tasks to complete:

1. Hold a road map discussion if you are responsible for creating and providing products, platforms, solutions, or services to customers.
2. Get feedback from both leaders and employees covering topics such as views on leadership, the focus and direction of your business, workplace culture, employee engagement, and job satisfaction.
3. Leaders gather with their teams to have targeted discussions about the current strategic plan (or potentially a new one if this is the first time going through the process).

Keep in mind that every company is unique, so this process can be adjusted to suit your specific needs. If you're a small business with a team under 10, you may want to skip ahead to the strategy meeting. You are welcome to modify this method to optimize its success.

The Road Map Discussion

The leader of your solutions team, whether that is the head of products or chief technology officer, oversees this meeting. Its purpose is to ensure that your road map aligns with your objectives, goals, and strategy(s). If you run a service-based business, the leadership role may be filled by the chief customer officer, while for smaller businesses, it could be the CEO. For a business with 50 employees, I typically book a 90-minute meeting.

Include these key topics to address at this meeting:

- Updates on solution, platform, and service developments
- Progress toward the key initiatives outlined in the road map

- Changes in the competitive landscape
- Shifts in strengths, weaknesses, opportunities, and threats
- Overview of the future for our solutions and services
- Highlights from ongoing projects and customer requests
- Long-term strategies for our solutions and services
- Further questions and discussion

The purpose of the road map meeting is to give the strategy team a comprehensive understanding of where you stand on products, services, and the competitive landscape, as well as valuable insights for the upcoming strategy session. By the end of the meeting, all attendees should be prepared to actively participate in constructive conversations about strategy and the road ahead.

Organizational Feedback

To gain a full picture of your organization's status, potential areas for growth, and alignment concerns, the strategy meeting includes feedback from leadership, managers, and employees. In these meetings, your leaders and managers encourage open communication with their employees. They dedicate an hour to discussing possible obstacles and possibilities within their teams' responsibilities, actively asking meaningful questions to pinpoint areas of achievement and areas that need development. In team meetings, your leaders will gather information to create short presentations lasting five to 10 minutes. These presentations will summarize important points from their discussions at the strategy meeting.

Department-Specific Discussions (Team Setting)

Each leader is responsible for having a discussion with their respective team about your current strategic plan (or possibly a new one). If this is your first time leading this process, you'll be referring to a different set of questions. Obtaining input from employees on your strategic plan can provide valuable insights for both strategy and planning purposes. This will help you determine the level of support and alignment with your plan and will reveal the effectiveness of your plan's communication and understanding, as well as its perceived importance for achieving your goals. Instruct your leaders to record the thoughts and ideas of their team members during the discussion so that they can later compile them into individual presentations for the meeting.

Here are a few questions your leaders and managers can use to start the conversations:

- What aspects, if any, require further clarification regarding our objectives, goals, and strategy(s)?
- How do you see the connection between our strategy(s) and our purpose?
- What aspects of our strategy(s), objectives, or goals resonate with you or pique your interest?
- What are some potential challenges or barriers that may impede our progress towards reaching our goals?
- What areas of growth do you think we might be overlooking with our current strategy(s)?
- In what way do you believe your actions have contributed to our progress in achieving our goals?
- In your opinion, how successful have we been in communicating our purpose and core values?
- How would you describe our working culture?
- What can we do to make you feel like your daily tasks are making a difference?
- If you could change one thing, what would you change and why?

If you haven't created a strategic plan, ask these questions:

- Do you think the organization has your best interests in mind when making business decisions?
- How satisfied are you with how we manage the business? How can we improve?
- In your opinion, how well do you think our communication

successfully conveys the crucial information and goals of our business?

- How would you describe your experiences with collaboration, both within our team and with individuals outside of our department?
- Which elements of leadership drive you to give your best effort and inspire you the most?
- How do you determine the amount of information necessary to make informed decisions about your work?
- Do you have a plan in place for unexpected situations, and do you know where to seek help?
- How do you view our informal procedures and processes? What can we improve?
- If you could change one thing, what would you change and why?

The value of honest and open communication cannot be overstated. Research shows that leaders who foster an environment of vulnerability also create a psychologically safe workplace where individuals can freely express themselves. This type of authenticity leads to meaningful contributions that can only thrive in a culture built on trust and inclusivity and to a willingness to share diverse perspectives without fear of repercussions.[143] The goal of every leader in your organization is to earn trust. And the most effective way to encourage others to take ownership of their actions and share open and honest feedback is to sincerely model the behaviors you want them to adopt.

As a leader, it is important to gather feedback from employees on your plan. This feedback should be compiled into notes and key points for the strategic-planning team to consider. It can be helpful to involve the HR department or a senior leader in conducting surveys on the employee experience and alignment on your company's direction. These surveys measure the effectiveness of your plan, the level of alignment among leaders, and employee engagement within your workplace. This will provide a clear understanding of how well your plan is working and will identify your strengths and any areas that may need improvement.

There are two types of surveys: the annual employee engagement survey and the leadership alignment survey. After an overview of each of the surveys, I have generated a list of questions to accompany them, which I have included in the appendix of this book, so they are easy to find and reference, if you choose to use them. To conduct surveys, there are several online resources available, with no-cost and subscription-based options. Some commonly used solutions include SurveyMonkey, Zoho Survey, and TINYpulse. For businesses working on a small budget, Google Forms is an alternative zero-cost option.

ANNUAL EMPLOYEE ENGAGEMENT SURVEY (ANONYMOUS, INDIVIDUAL)

The purpose of the annual employee engagement survey is to evaluate and gauge the level of motivation and dedication each employee has toward their work. The survey contains both qualitative and quantitative data, providing your employees with the opportunity to anonymously share their opinions on your objectives, goals, and strategy(s). Collecting feedback from employees offers a range of viewpoints and ensures that everyone is working toward the same goals. It also provides valuable insights for enhancing planning processes and gives individuals a platform to discuss the company's objectives, core values, and plans for achieving success. The survey should address the following six key aspects of your workplace culture.

1. **Perspectives on leadership:** This section of the employee engagement survey seeks to understand your staff's opinions on their leaders, their communication skills, and how well they uphold your company's values. It assesses the level of trust that employees have in leadership, the clarity of internal communication, and whether everyone is aligned with shared goals.

2. **Focus and alignment:** The focus and alignment category evaluates employees' understanding of your company's plans and how their daily tasks contribute to your larger organizational purpose. It also gauges their understanding of their own personal objectives

and how well your company works toward achieving its goals.

3. **Workplace culture:** This category delves into the overall environment of your workplace, including diversity and inclusivity, teamwork, transparency, and work-life balance. It examines how valued employees feel, how much collaboration is encouraged, and the level of support for maintaining a healthy work-life balance.

4. **Learning and growth:** The learning and growth section of this survey measures your company's dedication to employee development and career advancement. It assesses opportunities for skill enhancement, career progression, and continual learning as well as whether your business prioritizes professional development.

5. **Recognition:** This section focuses on employee recognition and feedback mechanisms. It looks at the frequency and effectiveness of your recognition efforts, whether employees feel appreciated for their contributions, and if recognition aligns with your company's core values and objectives.

6. **Job satisfaction:** Job satisfaction measures employees' contentment with their current roles and responsibilities. It evaluates factors such as motivation, clarity of job expectations, autonomy, and relationships at work. This section aims to gauge overall job satisfaction and fulfillment within employees' roles.

How can you use the survey results to enhance employee engagement in your company? Let's look at how Sarah, the CEO of a five-million-dollar consulting firm located in St. Louis, Missouri, used the engagement survey to identify areas for improvement. Sarah prides herself on running a well-managed organization where employees enjoy coming to work. However, she wanted anonymous feedback to confirm her beliefs about the company's environment. Sarah shared the engagement survey with her team of 35 employees and encouraged them to participate in providing their perceptions of the workplace culture. The response was overwhelming, with an abundance of insightful feedback coming from various voices and perspectives.

After the survey results were compiled, Sarah was pleased to see that her company had received high scores in five out of the six categories for employee engagement. However, she and her leadership team were disappointed to find that they fell short in learning and growth. Many employees expressed feeling like there were limited opportunities for professional growth within the company.

Sarah assembled her leadership team and made sure everyone was on board with her plans for helping employees succeed. She began by having her leaders run meetings, focus groups, and team huddles to learn more about why her employees felt they weren't growing professionally. Through this feedback, the leadership team learned that several employees wanted to continue their education through workshops, courses, and college programs. So, Sarah teamed up with HR to create internal training programs and a tuition reimbursement program, giving employees access to outside resources such as courses, workshops, conferences, and mentors, so anyone could take advantage of opportunities for growth.

However, she didn't stop with tuition reimbursement to address her employees' concerns. Sara wanted to show employees that they were valued and understood, which led her to introduce a new program called Purposeful Pathways. This initiative aimed to assist employees in identifying their individual aspirations and creating a plan to reach them while still fulfilling their duties at the consulting firm. Each employee who opted into the program was matched with a mentor who specialized in their desired field of development. Together, they collaborated on honing skills, forging connections, and pursuing new opportunities.

Sarah's commitment to developing her employees did more than just boost their morale and increase productivity—it also had a positive impact on the overall profits of the business. When employees feel appreciated and motivated, they tend to work harder to achieve success. Seeing the successful outcomes of her investment in her team, Sarah made it a priority to set aside two hours each month for mentoring sessions with aspiring managers. During these sessions, they could discuss any topics of their choosing.

Sarah understood the significance of acknowledging accomplishments along the journey. She ensured that her team's achievements, regardless of size, were acknowledged and rewarded, fostering an atmosphere of gratitude and recognition. This approach resulted in continual success for Sarah's consulting firm. Her employees felt appreciated and motivated, their commitment to the company's goals only increasing.

When compiling the results of your survey, take a page from Sarah's book and look for areas where improvement can be made. To get a complete picture, it's helpful to include two or three open-ended questions in your survey. These questions should focus on identifying what your business is excelling at as well as any potential areas for improvement. When I conduct engagement surveys, I make sure to share the results openly with the entire company during a designated meeting. Before this meeting, I prepare to discuss the bright spots as well as the identified areas for improvement, sharing the leadership team's action plan for addressing those areas. This includes allowing for an open question-and-answer session so that everyone understands the next steps, why these decisions were made, and when any proposed changes are expected to be completed.

One of the biggest mistakes a company can make is conducting an engagement survey and keeping the results hidden from their employees. Transparency builds trust, so if you have no concrete plans to address any issues found in the survey, it's better not to conduct one at all. However, if you are like me, you are constantly searching for ways to enhance workplace culture. And it's not just about employees—leadership must also be taken into consideration.

In the next step, you will assess the effectiveness of your leaders and gather input from top-level managers. The leadership alignment survey focuses on how well your organization is aligned among leaders and managers. Alignment refers to a state of harmony and unity among individuals or groups who share a common purpose or perspective. When your organization achieves this, all members, from frontline employees to every leader, are aligned and actively working toward your shared goals. This alignment assessment spans across six key areas that work together to propel your business toward its purpose.

LEADERSHIP ALIGNMENT SURVEY
(ANONYMOUS, INDIVIDUAL)

Ensuring organizational alignment in your company is key for achieving speed and driving accelerated growth. Studies show that highly aligned organizations experience a 58% increase in revenue and are 72% more profitable than their unaligned counterparts.[144] These organizations also excel in customer satisfaction, effective leadership, and employee engagement. Alignment creates a shared understanding of your organization's purpose, strategies, goals, and tactics for success, fueling motivation and empowering individuals to work toward a common goal. In addition, alignment promotes autonomy in decision-making, while fostering trust among team members.[145]

Twice a year, the leadership alignment survey provides your team with valuable insights into their alignment with your purpose, values, objectives, goals, and strategy(s). This survey follows a quantitative approach, guaranteeing anonymity through individual responses. By gathering feedback from each leader, it offers your senior team a comprehensive understanding of the leadership perceptions within your company.

As the surveys are completed, the results are used to enhance alignment among leaders. You may believe that your leadership team is already in complete harmony with your strategic plan, but this may not be the case when you learn how your employees truly feel. According to a Leadership IQ survey of more than 21,000 employees, the majority feel that their leader's vision for the future does not align with the organization's goals. Specifically, 29% said their leader's vision always seems to be aligned, while 16% said it is rarely or never aligned.[146]

By using various sources of feedback, you'll demonstrate your commitment to conducting a thorough and informed strategy and planning process. Here are the key areas of leadership alignment:

- **Leadership unity:** An essential aspect of achieving organizational alignment is ensuring that all members of the leadership team are working toward the same goals. This requires establishing a shared understanding and commitment to your company's purpose, core values, and strategic objectives. Your leaders and managers must be dedicated to championing your purpose and setting an example by embodying the desired values and behaviors to inspire others.

- **Strategic harmony:** For a purpose-driven approach to thrive, it is essential that the strategy is closely aligned with the organization's purpose. Every decision made should contribute directly to fulfilling your higher purpose, from customer-centric product development to overseas market expansion. This level of alignment ensures that all actions taken by leadership serve the difference you seek to make.

- **Cultural congruence:** The culture within your company is a critical factor in reinforcing its purpose-driven ethos. The core values and behaviors that uphold your purpose should be deeply rooted in your company's culture. Employees should feel a strong sense of alignment between their personal values and those upheld by your business, fostering a sense of belonging and unity.

- **Operational alignment:** Day-to-day operations must be in alignment with your purpose to effectively turn abstract ideals into actionable steps. All operational choices, methods, policies, and protocols should reflect your company's core values and cause. This coherence guarantees that the entire organization remains devoted to its overarching vision.

- **Employee support:** When employees are engaged in their work with a sense of purpose, it means that they recognize the impact their roles have on the overall goals of the organization. This connection between individual tasks and the company's purpose provides motivation and a sense of empowerment, resulting in more meaningful and powerful outcomes.

- **Stakeholder alignment:** Achieving success with a purpose goes beyond the boundaries of your organization. Creating alignment with customers, partners, suppliers, and other stakeholders is fundamental. When these stakeholders identify with your company's purpose, they are more inclined to support your initiatives and participate in mutually beneficial partnerships. If you maintain a strong code of conduct, it is important to ensure that every supplier within your network is upholding the same high standards of safe working conditions, fair and respectful treatment of employees, and ethical practices.

By combining these six elements within your business, you create a complete and comprehensive sense of purpose and focus. Each aspect of the company works toward achieving its ultimate objective, fueling passion, drive, and dedication at every step. Thus, your organization is motivated to achieve notable successes and the desired results that were determined in the never-ending cycle of connection.

When conducting leadership alignment surveys, my first step is to establish a benchmark for leadership views to compare future results. Using Microsoft Excel, I input and tabulate the results for each of the six key areas of leadership alignment as a radar chart. This type of chart compares three or more variables relative to a central point and scores them on a scale of one through five for each category. I arrive at these numbers by dividing each category's overall score by six. This helps to visually represent performance based on survey data and allows for comparison over time in a spider web–like format.

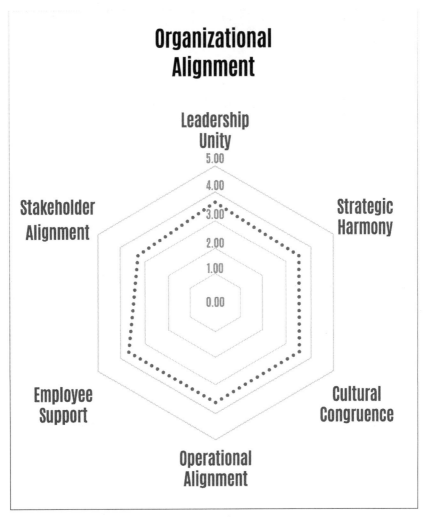

Figure 6

You can download the radar map, surveys, and other resources on my website by visiting www.simplestrategicplans.com/resources, using the password WinningAtPurpose#1.

After establishing a benchmark for leadership alignment, you will quickly realize that there are areas in need of improvement. If your weakest score is in operational alignment, have open discussions with your team about how to work together and improve the score before the next survey. I recommend prioritizing one leadership category for improvement at a time, as taking on too much can hinder your progress. By monitoring your results over time, you can target all aspects of alignment and concentrate on the key areas where you are making strides while addressing any weak points in your leadership.

As you review the surveys and gather feedback from your employees, it's important to start preparing for your upcoming strategy and planning meetings. To ensure that you are fully prepared, we will establish guidelines and create agendas for these meetings.

As you schedule your strategy and planning meetings, your team is getting ready to set the course for your business, assess the resources needed to reach your objectives, and channel their efforts toward achieving success. This is an ongoing process and requires regular evaluation. Your strategic-planning team will convene biannually to ensure a solid foundation for the future of your business. During these sessions, creative and critical thinking will guide decisions about the direction of your company. Strategies will be crafted in the strategy meeting and translated into objectives and key goals during the planning meeting.

Six months later, you will regroup for a meeting to review your strategic plan. This meeting will be more focused and should only take a part of the day. The purpose of the review meeting is to evaluate your progress halfway through the year and make any necessary adjustments to your tactical plans. In this chapter, we will explore the specifics of the strategy and planning meetings themselves, providing valuable insights on where your time and focus should be directed. Additionally, I will guide you through the critical tasks to tackle as you kick-start this process. Remember, this is not a one-time event—it's an ongoing cycle that drives your business toward its goals.

WHO LEADS THIS PROCESS?

Select an individual or team to oversee the strategy and planning process, making sure all necessary arrangements are taken care of. Determine whether you want to hold your strategy meeting on-site or off-site. If financially feasible, opting for an off-site location offers numerous advantages for strategizing, including these:

- **Change of scenery:** Holding a strategy meeting in a different location can stimulate new ideas and viewpoints. Being outside the typical work setting can inspire creativity and bring new perspectives to the table.
- **Focused attention:** Moving the team out of the traditional office environment and into a secluded location can aid in maintaining their focus on the task at hand. This uninterrupted period of dedicated discussion can foster more meaningful conversations, resulting in more productive outcomes.
- **Team bonding:** Switching up the location can facilitate breaking the ice and encourage people to talk. The environment becomes more laid back, fostering a stronger sense of unity and teamwork within the group. It also helps cultivate stronger bonds between team members.
- **Reduced interruptions:** Being out of the office removes potential interruptions, such as phone calls, emails, and tasks, that can disrupt discussions and decision-making. This allows participants to fully concentrate on the matters at hand without any external distractions pulling them away.
- **Strategic immersion:** Moving away from daily work obligations allows those involved in strategizing to fully immerse themselves in the process. This distance from day-to-day tasks allows for deeper examination and reflection and fosters a mindset for strategic thought.

When deciding on the length of your strategy meeting, consider your team's knowledge and experience with strategic thinking. Allowing for two days will give those new to strategy ample time for detailed discussions and strategizing. However, if you have seasoned strategists on your team, a full day followed by a debrief the next morning may be more appropriate. It is important to ensure that the allotted time allows for the thorough exploration of strategies while also considering attention spans and energy levels.

DO YOU NEED A MODERATOR?

Having a moderator for your strategy meeting is beneficial in keeping everyone on track and focused. The choice of who to appoint as the moderator will depend on your budget and specific needs. A professional and experienced moderator can ensure that discussions stay on topic, provide an unbiased perspective, and effectively manage the meeting schedule. A moderator is responsible for ensuring equal participation from all members, facilitating smooth conversations, and promoting a collaborative environment. While an internal staff member can fulfill this role, bringing in an external expert offers a more impartial viewpoint and increases the potential for successful outcomes in your meetings.

If you are still contemplating your options for who should lead and manage the discussions, here are some other possibilities to consider beyond your current connections. These alternatives can bring new viewpoints and skills to assist in guaranteeing that your conversations go smoothly:

- **Professional associations:** Research and reach out to professional organizations that are relevant to your industry or business sector. These associations often have members who specialize in strategy and facilitation, which can provide valuable insights and a wider perspective on current industry developments.
- **Consulting firms:** There are consulting firms that focus on offering strategy and facilitation services. Take the time to research and connect with firms that align with your overall goals and principles. These firms employ seasoned consultants who can offer an external perspective and use structured models to help achieve a successful outcome for your strategy.
- **Academic institutions:** You may want to consider reaching out to universities or business schools that offer programs focused on strategy and leadership. Professors or instructors who specialize in these fields could potentially serve as moderators for your meeting, bringing both academic knowledge and real-world experience to the discussion.

If you need assistance, don't hesitate to contact me by visiting my website (www.simplestrategicplans.com/contact). Considering these alternatives will give you a range of viewpoints and the opportunity to achieve success at your strategic planning on- or off-site, aiding in the achievement of your business objectives. Whichever direction you decide to go, ensure that your moderator is briefed on your strategy session's goals and objectives ahead of time. This will help them align with your approach and facilitate a successful meeting.

YOUR RULES OF ENGAGEMENT

The first step in your strategy and planning meetings is to present the team with a set of guidelines known as the rules of engagement. These rules serve as a framework for productive discussions and help to maintain a respectful and transparent atmosphere. Typically, these rules are discussed at the start of the day's meeting, so here is an overview of what they cover:

- **Equal valuing:** All team members' perspectives are equally valued, regardless of their position or role. Each person's input is integral to the conversation.
- **Confidentiality:** Discussions during the retreat are held in confidence. Open dialogue is encouraged, and team members can express diverse opinions without fear of retaliation.
- **Majority consideration:** Decisions are made with the majority's best interests in mind. The goal is to find solutions that resonate with the larger group.
- **Focus on controllable factors:** Attention is directed toward areas that are within your control or sphere of influence. This ensures that discussions stay relevant and actionable.
- **Respectful differences:** Differing viewpoints are welcomed, and disagreements are handled respectfully. The emphasis is on understanding before being understood.

- **Positive dialogue:** Avoid phrases that halt constructive conversations, such as "It won't work" or "We've tried that before." Instead, focus on contributing positively.
- **Individual ideas, collaborative contributions:** Team members are encouraged to share individual ideas while actively participating in collaborative contributions that drive the discussion forward.
- **Parking Lot:** The designated "Parking Lot" area is reserved for topics that are not immediately relevant to your strategy. Here, your team can store potential opportunities and challenges that may be addressed later.

MODERATING AND MANAGING THE PARKING LOT

In your strategy and planning sessions, the term "Parking Lot" refers to a designated spot for off-topic conversations. This area acts as a temporary storage for ideas that may not pertain to the main purpose of the meeting but are still valuable to discuss. During your team's discussion of current plans, new ideas may come up. However, it may not be efficient to address them right away. Instead, these ideas can be noted by your moderator and added to the Parking Lot for future consideration during subsequent meetings.

Select a team member to oversee the Parking Lot during these meetings. Once your planning session is complete, the list of items in the Parking Lot will be distributed to your leaders for evaluation and prioritization. They will determine if these topics should be pursued, postponed, or canceled. The focus of the meetings should be on your strategy(s), objectives, and goals, while the Parking Lot is used as a place to store potential ideas for future development.

The Parking Lot serves as a valuable tool to ensure that all ideas brought up during the process are not lost and can be revisited later once your plans have been finalized.

When you adhere to the principles outlined in these rules of engagement, your team meetings can cultivate an environment conducive to open communication, collaborative decision-making, and innovative thinking, leading to a more successful and revealing outcome.

As you prepare for your first meeting's strategy, it is natural to think about what you can do for your employees, customers, and community. However, you must also consider the value of their stories and how you can align with them. Your team may prefer to take the easier path, where your ideas are well received by those in the room. But as a leader, it is your responsibility to understand your customer's narrative and to be there when they need you. Gain their trust by delivering on your promises and helping them become the people they aspire to be.

As you move forward with this internal process, define your strategy, set out your objectives, and establish your goals, keeping in mind that your internal plan will lead to an external impact. Like a chain reaction, your plan will inspire action toward the movement you want to create, driven by your good intentions and desire to make a meaningful difference for those you seek to serve.

The next chapter will cover steps 2 through 4. It will provide suggested agendas for the strategy and planning meetings, offer examples of strategic plans, and give tips on how to communicate after the meetings are over.

Chapter 14

CRAFTING PRECISE QUARTERLY TARGETS

W. Chan Kim and Renée Mauborgne, known for their book *Blue Ocean Strategy: How to Create Uncontested Market Space and Make the Competition Irrelevant*, state that, during a typical strategic-planning process, "managers spend the majority of strategic thinking time filling in boxes and running numbers instead of thinking outside the box and developing a clear picture of how to break from the competition."[147] While moving on to the second step, the strategy meeting, remember that big-picture thinking isn't just for those in top leadership positions. It's a valuable skill for all employees to cultivate within your organization. Big-picture thinking means expanding your perspective beyond your immediate role and understanding how your choices and actions affect your employees, customers, and community. By acknowledging the interconnectedness of your work with the greater world, you can recognize opportunities to contribute positively, anticipate potential obstacles, and make well-informed decisions that align with your beliefs and values.

STEP 2: STRATEGY MEETING

Put purpose at the very heart of your strategy discussions. Reflect on your origins and the qualities that set you apart. You have an advantage. By prioritizing purpose in your strategy, you will guide a more cohesive team, inspire stakeholders, and make a greater positive impact on society. As you plan and shape your business, it's important to keep in mind that you can't predict with absolute certainty what lies ahead.

Instead of fearing the unknown, embrace it as a natural part of the process, even if doing so may be uncomfortable at times. Fear and discomfort are components of effective strategy. If you feel completely at ease with your plan, it's likely not very strong. True strategy involves taking calculated risks and making difficult decisions. The goal is not to eliminate risk entirely but to increase your chances of success.

Concentrate on making powerful decisions that will positively influence your employees, customers, and community. Why should customers choose you over others? How can you relate to their perspectives and values? What beliefs do you hold about your customers, and what is necessary for them to believe in your company? How is your industry changing, and what actions are your competitors taking? How can you use your strengths or develop new ones to address a significant obstacle or potential advantage?

During this meeting, focus on answering these central questions:

- **What are the aspirations of our company and how do our overall goals fulfill our purpose?** Putting your purpose at the core of strategy means caring for your employees, customers, and community.
- **Where do we want to focus our efforts, and where will we say no to investing our resources?** Think of Southwest and how they were laser focused on serving only the customers who valued low-cost fairs and exceptional service.
- **In our selected market [where you choose to play], how will we win against our competitors?** Think of Best Buy when they matched prices with giant online retailers, implemented

store-within-a-store concepts, and provided customers with personalized expert advice and guidance.

- **Which abilities must we develop and maintain to achieve victory in our chosen approach?** Think about EA's shift from profit driven to player driven. Being branded as the worst company in America was a pivotal turning point for EA, forcing executives to recognize the need for change in how they treated their customers. Thus, EA took on the challenge of transforming its culture.
- **What operational frameworks must be in place to effectively manage and sustain these key abilities?** To illustrate this point, your company may create a sustainability framework with specific objectives and methods for promoting fair and equitable trade in developing countries. Another company might implement an operational framework to eliminate silos between departments to improve communication and collaboration.

When it comes to creating a strategy, having the right attitude can make all the difference. Instead of viewing strategy as a daunting and overwhelming task, see it as a valuable tool that can bring fulfillment. A strong strategy should be embraced with enthusiasm, as it offers a clear path toward reaching your business objectives.

As I mentioned before, being prepared to handle strategy is necessary for overcoming obstacles and leading your company to victory. Embrace the journey, share the strategy meeting agenda with your team, and keep living your purpose.

CRAFTING CLARITY: BUILDING YOUR STRATEGY MEETING BLUEPRINT

As you prepare for your strategy creation meeting, I would like to provide a two-day meeting agenda that you can use and personalize as necessary. I hope this will help you save time and effort. This is only a suggested timeframe and can be adjusted to fit your specific requirements.

Day 1: Full-Day Strategy Creation Meeting

Morning Session (9:00 a.m. to 12:30 p.m.)

Welcome and Introduction (1 Hour)

- Briefly introduce the purpose and goals of the meeting.
- Set the tone for open and productive discussions.
- Discuss the importance of alignment and collaboration.
- Review the rules of engagement.

Review of Current State (2.5 Hours)

- Review the organization's performance in the past year.
- Review your scorecard (financial metrics, social impact, KPIs). Are you on track? If not, why?
- Leaders present employee feedback. Review and discuss the key insights.
- Review and discuss your survey results (employee engagement and leadership alignment).

During this review, here are the three most important questions you can ask:

1. What should we stop doing?
2. What should we continue doing?
3. What should we start doing?

Any concepts that do not align with the focus of the strategy discussion should be moved to your Parking Lot for later consideration. As you proceed with the afternoon schedule, remember to reference the five central questions that need to be addressed.

Afternoon Session (1:30 p.m. to 5:30 p.m.)

Economic Environment and SWOT (1.5 Hours)

- Discuss your industry's current economic environment and trends.
- Discuss the key points from the competitor's SWOT analyses that were presented during the road map meeting.
- Participate in creating a SWOT analysis for your organization.

Conducting the SWOT Session

- **Strengths and weaknesses:** Begin by identifying internal strengths and weaknesses. Encourage open discussions and gather input on what your organization excels at and where it faces challenges.
- **Opportunities and threats:** Transition to external factors by discussing potential opportunities your organization can leverage and threats that may hinder progress.
- **Group discussions:** Encourage participants to share their insights and perspectives for each SWOT category. Use brainstorming techniques to stimulate creative thinking.
- **Capture key points:** Record all significant points raised by participants on a whiteboard, flip chart, or digital tool for everyone to see.
- **Consolidate and prioritize:** Review the recorded points and facilitate a discussion to combine and rank the most powerful strengths, weaknesses, opportunities, and threats.

SWOT matrix: Organize the collected insights into a SWOT matrix, categorizing them into the respective quadrants.

Crafting Your Key Strategies (2.5 Hours)

- **Discuss implications:** Engage the group in analyzing the implications of the SWOT findings. What do the strengths and weaknesses mean for the opportunities and threats identified?

- **Formulate key strategies:** Ask the five central questions. As a group, propose strategies that will leverage your strengths, overcome weaknesses, strike at opportunities, or minimize potential threats. Write down your proposed strategies. You'll refine them on day 2.
  o Limit the number of key strategies to the number of offerings or markets you serve. This means if you manage one entity, in one market, in one geography—you'll have one strategy.
  o Having multiple unique offerings in various markets requires a strategy for each one. For instance, if you have accounting software that is sold in both the United States and Japan, you'll need a separate approach for each geographical region. Likewise, if you offer solutions in both the aerospace and rapid transportation industries, you'll need to have a distinct strategy for each market.
- **Review your results:** Ask participants for their final feedback and gain alignment from everyone on your team.

Day 2: Half-Day Strategy Refinement and Alignment Meeting

Morning Session (9:00 a.m. to 12:30 p.m.)

Review and Refine Key Strategies (2 Hours)

- Revisit the key strategies identified on day 1.
- Analyze and refine each strategy based on additional insights or feedback.
- Ensure alignment with your organization's overarching purpose and values.
- Discuss potential challenges or risks associated with each strategy.

Consensus Building and Alignment (1.5 Hours)

- Facilitate open discussions to address any remaining concerns or differing perspectives on your key strategies.
- Encourage team members to express their views and collaborate on finding common ground.
- Put each strategy through a simple process called possibilities, appraisal, capability, execution, and significance (PACES).
- Seek consensus on the finalized key strategies.
- Confirm alignment among the leadership team regarding the chosen strategies.
- Move your key strategies into your strategic plan.

The effectiveness of your plan rests on the thoroughness of your assessment and the reasoning behind your decisions. Your team will make this choice based on the PACES criteria. Ultimately, the success of this process will determine if the proposed strategies are accepted by the team and put into action.

- **P (possibilities assessment):** Key insights and analysis on overcoming challenges or going after new opportunities.
- **A (appraisal):** Is it worth pursuing?
- **C (capability evaluation):** Do we have the capability—or can we develop the capability—to execute?
- **E (execution planning):** Can we move this to action and create the policies and processes to support it?
- **S (significance determination):** Is this how we win? Why? Discuss the logic behind your proposed strategy.

The success of a strategy relies heavily on the decision to continue, adapt, or stop its implementation. This pivotal choice is made by your team, based on the PACES criteria. Ultimately, the outcome of this process will determine if the key strategy put forward gains consensus from the group and moves forward.

The oldest and most essential aspect of strategy is the ability to focus. In military terms, this means directing all forces toward an enemy's weakness. More broadly, it involves coordinating resources and effort toward a significant but achievable goal. Strategic focus requires harnessing sources of power and aiming them at a specific target. Without enough power, nothing can be accomplished. If power is dispersed across multiple targets, no meaningful progress can be made. And if power is directed at the wrong target, there will be no positive results. However, when power is focused on the right target, breakthroughs become possible.[148]

Use this knowledge to your advantage, apply strategy, and keep learning. Strategy is constantly evolving, and it's never set in stone. It's not like placing three bets on a spinning roulette wheel, hoping it lands on black 17 every time. Your adaptability is key. Take advantage of every experience as a chance to learn and prepare for what may come. For instance, if employees are resistant to new software, use this learning as an opportunity to educate them on its importance and create advocates within your company, along with implementing training plans. It's difficult to anticipate unpredictable events, but having a mindset of continual learning can help you in adjusting strategies as needed.

As your strategy meeting draws to a close, take a moment to reflect: Do our strategies align with our overall purpose and values? For instance, if one of our core values is sustainability, then a key strategy may be prioritizing suppliers who are Rainforest Alliance certified. This shows that you are committed to collective action for both people and nature, rather than solely focusing on cutting costs by using noncertified suppliers to increase profits. By staying true to your purpose and values, you can better prioritize and adapt when faced with change.

And finally, don't be afraid to be wrong. Make mistakes, learn from them, correct them, and then keep moving forward. Make at least 10 mistakes if you're trying to solve a big problem. Don't be afraid to take risks, pursue opportunities, and continue pushing yourself. Because if you're not making mistakes, you're not truly learning. If your strategies remain unchanged, then it is safe to say that you are not learning enough.

Here are five mistakes people make when working on strategy:

1. Regurgitating last year's plan
2. Not sticking to simplicity
3. Not using data to guide and inform strategy
4. Not knowing the numbers
5. Not implementing review and learning cycles to adjust the strategy's direction

How can you tell if your strategy needs adjusting after making a decision? If your intuition is telling you something doesn't feel quite right, trust your gut. Or, if trusted colleagues within your company have expressed concern about the decision, it's worth considering adapting your strategy. And finally, if you've been trying to convince yourself that the decision was the right one ever since you made it, it may be a sign that things are not going according to plan.

Always keep in mind that it's impossible to make everyone happy. Having said that, my advice is to never underestimate the significance of your team when implementing strategic change. As the leader of strategy, you are the driving force behind change, but it's ultimately the individuals in your organization who will bring your vision to life and make it a reality.

If you want to learn more about strategy, here are some must-read books (in no particular order):

- *Built to Last: Successful Habits of Visionary Companies* by Jim Collins and Jerry I. Porras
- *Blue Ocean Strategy: How to Create Uncontested Market Space and Make the Competition Irrelevant* by W. Chan Kim and Renée Mauborgne
- *Leadership Strategy and Tactics: Field Manual* by Jocko Willink
- *Good Strategy Bad Strategy: The Difference and Why It Matters* by Richard Rumelt
- *Playing to Win: How Strategy Really Works* by A. G. Lafley and Roger L. Martin

Now that your key strategies have been established, it's time to focus on planning. During the planning meeting, your team will need to shift their mindset and adopt a strategic-planning perspective. This is where your strategy informs planning.

It's important to emphasize that strategy and planning require continual effort, not just a single meeting. The process of setting objectives and goals will prompt you to reflect on your journey and consider the various road maps that can guide your business and reveal its potential.

STEP 3: PLANNING MEETING

According to James Clear, the author of *Atomic Habits*, most goal-setting exercises involve a well-paid expert writing on a whiteboard and asking questions, like "What does success mean to you? Specifically, what do you want to achieve?" But if we want to accomplish our goals, we should approach goal setting differently. Instead of focusing on what kind of success we want, we should ask ourselves, "What level of discomfort am I willing to tolerate?"[149]

Although James Clear's method may seem unconventional, I believe he brings up a valid and compelling argument. This is why SMART goals often fall short—we are not pushing ourselves far enough, striving for high-enough goals, or deeply considering the significance of our objectives and how they align with our purpose and values.

Frequently, the objectives and goals that are meant to drive companies forward become empty and uninspiring words to their employees. Employees need a reason to believe in the direction of the company, but often, these objectives are only mentioned once a year at the annual meeting. They lack substance and are not accompanied by any concrete plans for how they will be achieved.

Many business owners and CEOs express their desire to increase profits and share the company's wealth with their employees, yet these goals typically remain unfulfilled. Worse, these goals often get stuck at the heralded table of senior management, who meet monthly to expound on progress without ever speaking to or empowering the people capable of achieving them. When you clearly and effectively convey your objectives, goals, and strategy(s) to employees, everyone will share a common understanding of the bigger picture. This includes explaining why your plan is important and how it will be achieved. By doing so, you can tap into the creativity and expertise of your leaders and their teams as you work together to fulfill your purpose.

During the planning process, I encourage you to reach higher, to strive for greatness by helping others achieve their full potential. When we shift our focus from ourselves to those we serve, with support and motivation, it's amazing what we can accomplish when we choose to change things for the better.

Now that you have your key strategies in hand, it is time to start your planning meeting. Get your slides prepared because today we will complete them!

Similar to the strategy meeting, I have prepared a meeting agenda that you can use or modify according to your requirements.

Two-Day Planning Meeting Agenda
Morning Session (9:00 a.m. to 11:30 a.m.)
Welcome and Introduction (15 Minutes)

- Briefly introduce the purpose of the planning.
- Set expectations and goals for the day.
- Communicate your purpose and key strategy(s) that will inform planning.

Brainstorming Annual Objectives (1 Hour)

Your vision can only become a reality with a clear set of objectives to guide you. Determine two to four strategic objectives that align with your purpose. To recap, here are three examples of potential objectives to help get you started:

- **Operational Excellence**
  - o Objective: Streamline internal processes to improve efficiency, reduce costs, and enhance overall operational performance.
- **Customer Experience Enhancement**
  - o Objective: Deliver an exceptional customer experience to build loyalty and increase customer retention rates.
- **Sustainability and Corporate Social Responsibility**
  - o Objective: Integrate sustainable practices and contribute to social responsibility, aligning with the organization's values.

Facilitate a collaborative brainstorming session to define annual objectives. Pose key questions to guide the discussion:

- What are our strategic priorities for the upcoming year?
- What objectives do we aim to achieve?
- How do these objectives align with our purpose and long-term strategy?
- What resources are required for these objectives?
- Are these objectives ambitious and challenging?

Evaluation and Alignment (1.25 Hours)

- Evaluate and discuss each proposed objective.
- Ensure alignment with your broader strategic direction.
- Discuss the feasibility and resources required for successful execution. Do you need to develop new capabilities?
- Analyze and refine each objective based on additional insights or feedback.
- Discuss potential challenges or risks associated with each objective.
- Finalize your two to four key objectives and ensure that all members of the leadership team agree.
- Move your key objectives into your strategic plan.

Afternoon Session (1:30 p.m. to 5:30 p.m.)

Defining Key Goals (2 Hours)

Determine two to four strategic goals that support your objectives. Here are three examples of potential MEAN goals to help get you started:

1. **Operational excellence:** Achieve a cost reduction of 6% through process optimization by Q4.
2. **Customer experience enhancement:** Increase customer satisfaction scores by 15% within the next year.
3. **Sustainability and corporate social responsibility:** Reduce carbon footprint by 5% through eco-friendly initiatives over the next 18 months.

Define key goals that support each annual objective. Address questions such as these:

- What are our organization's top priorities for the upcoming year?
- How do these goals align with our purpose and long-term vision?
- Are these goals MEAN (meaningful, exact, actionable, necessary)?
- What challenges or opportunities do these goals address?
- Do these goals require cross-functional collaboration and resource allocation?

As with key objectives, propose, review, and finalize two to four key goals. Ensure that all members of your leadership team agree. Then move your key goals into your strategic plan.

Three Years Ahead (1 Hour)

Explore the organization's vision for the next three years. Ask questions like these:

- Where do we want to be in three years?
- What do we want to build? (Technological capabilities? Expanded reach? Social impact? Other strategic factors?)

Move your vision for the future to your strategic plan.

Finalizing the Plan (1 Hour)

- Your strategic plan now includes your purpose, values, emotional points of difference, key strategy(s), key objectives, key goals, and vision for the next three years.
- Review the strategic plan, addressing any gaps or overlaps.
- Consider any potential risks and opportunities.
- Ensure alignment and feasibility of objectives, goals, and strategy(s).

Wrap-Up and Next Steps (Day 2: Morning, 9:00 a.m. to 10:30 a.m.)

Summary and Outcomes (30 Minutes)

- Review the finalized strategic plan.
- Summarize the key outcomes of the retreat.

Timeline and Implementation (45 Minutes)

- Discuss the timeline for implementation.
- Establish the schedule for the upcoming strategic-plan review in six months.

Closing Thoughts (15 Minutes)

- Celebrate the win!
- Encourage commitment to the plan and move forward to the next step—an effective communication plan to be shared across your organization at the start of your next fiscal year (or when you want to introduce your plan).

By centering your strategic-planning meeting on these specific topics and questions, you can ensure that your discussions will be thorough and will result in a well-defined strategic plan.

Striving for perfection should not be your primary focus in strategic planning. The goal is to create a process that can grow and adapt over time, allowing room for adjustments and improvements. As your planning meeting ends, take a moment to revel in your success—you have established clear objectives, goals, and strategy(s)! And even if there are some imperfections, it's important to acknowledge and appreciate what you have achieved.

You may feel as if there is still much to accomplish, but take a moment to look back at how far you have come. You have set the foundation for your team's future and have provided them with a clear direction and vision for the organization's future. And here's something to celebrate: While, shockingly, 95% of employees don't understand their companies' strategy, [150] fortunately, your business is not one of those companies—giving your business a competitive edge. For those who are new to this process, keep in mind that the benefit of having an incremental strategic plan is the ability to adjust as you go. Your leaders will meet monthly to discuss strategy and alignment. And six months from now, you will receive feedback and guidance during the strategic-plan review meeting. Make the most of your journey and allow your experiences to be opportunities for learning, growth, and adaptation. With each new experience, gain knowledge. You will find that you will ultimately succeed as you continue on your path.

Revisiting the strategic plan slide deck, let's review how the plan has evolved since we have reached the end of this initial stage.

YOUR STRATEGIC PLAN

Example 1

Scorecard	Strategic Plan
Revenue	**OUR PURPOSE**
Revenue growth rate	At XYZ Manufacturing, our purpose is to engineer innovative solutions that drive industries forward, contributing to economic growth and sustainability.
Gross profit margin	
Return on investment	
Customer acquisition cost	
Inventory turnover	**OUR CORE VALUES**
Volunteer hours	**Pioneer excellence:** Continually push the boundaries of quality and performance in every product we create.
	Foster collaboration: Foster a collaborative environment that harnesses the collective expertise of our teams, partners, and customers.
	Embrace integrity: Uphold the highest ethical standards in all business dealings, building trust and credibility with stakeholders.
	Empower sustainability: Integrate sustainable practices across our operations, minimizing environmental impact and promoting responsible manufacturing.
	OUR CONNECTION
	Attentive and inspired: Our top priority is to ensure our customers feel deeply supported and appreciated. We aim to inspire customers with innovative solutions that fulfill their current needs while anticipating and fulfilling their aspirations for the future they envision.

ANNUAL OBJECTIVES

Operational efficiency: Streamline our production processes to reduce waste and enhance productivity, resulting in a 12% reduction in production costs.

Market expansion: Penetrate two new international markets, increasing global market share by 10% through strategic partnerships and market analysis.

KEY GOALS

- Implement lean manufacturing principles in the production line, reducing material waste by 20% within 12 months.

- Rapidly develop and launch two new smart city product lines that leverage cutting-edge IoT and automation technologies within the next fiscal year.

- Create a supplier code of conduct to ensure all partners adhere to ethical and sustainable business practices by the end of Q3.

- Reduce energy consumption by 10% within the next year through facility upgrades and process optimizations.

KEY STRATEGIES

- **Technological innovation:** Invest in research and development to incorporate IoT and automation solutions into our products to *open the smart city market* and create new demand.

- **Global expansion strategy:** Collaborate with European distributors to tailor our products to specific regional needs and regulations, entering new markets successfully.

- **Sustainability integration:** Develop a sustainability task force to assess and implement eco-friendly practices throughout the supply chain, from sourcing to manufacturing.

THREE YEARS AHEAD

- Be a global manufacturing leader, recognized for pioneering excellence and innovative solutions, achieving high growth through our investment in solutions for smart cities.

- Be seen as an operational efficiency champion, with streamlined production processes that reduce waste and increase productivity.

- Be working with strong distribution partners in the United Kingdom, Germany, the Netherlands, and Spain.

- Secure commitments from all of our partners to our supplier code of conduct for ethical and sustainable business practices.

- Lead the industry by reducing CO_2 emissions by 15% through facility upgrades, process, and maintenance optimization.

Example 2

Scorecard	Strategic Plan
Revenue growth rate	**OUR PURPOSE** Empowering dogs and owners for lifelong happiness through compassionate training.
Gross profit margin	
Cash flow	**OUR CORE VALUES**
Employee productivity	**Respectful partnership:** Foster respectful relationships between trainers, dogs, and owners, ensuring a collaborative and positive training experience.
Conversion rates	**Excellence in education:** Strive for excellence in canine training methods and education, delivering exceptional results and knowledge to every dog owner.
	Courageous growth: Embrace challenges with courage, pushing boundaries to achieve transformative growth for both dogs and their human companions.
	OUR CONNECTION
	Confidence and pride: We aim to instill confidence and pride in our customers by equipping them with the tools and knowledge they need to foster healthy relationships with their dogs.
	ANNUAL OBJECTIVES
	• **Enhance training programs:** Elevate the quality and variety of training programs to cater to different dog needs and training goals.
	• **Increase client satisfaction:** Boost client satisfaction by providing personalized training solutions and exceptional customer service.
	• **Expand community outreach:** Extend our influence by engaging in educational initiatives and community events to promote responsible dog ownership.

KEY GOALS

- Launch an advanced obedience training program for working dog breeds in the next six months.

- Achieve a minimum 90% satisfaction rate in post-training client surveys.

- Host at least two free dog-training workshops in collaboration with local animal shelters by the end of Q2.

- Develop an online resource hub with training tips, videos, and articles to support dog owners by the end of the year.

- Increase annual revenue by 15% through new client referrals and expanded training services.

KEY STRATEGY

- **Virtual training:** Develop a software as a service platform, an online dog-training academy targeting new dog owners to help them master puppy training.

THREE YEARS AHEAD

- Be a key online resource for new dog owners with 1,000 active subscriptions for mastering puppy training.

- Be a local community hub for weekend camps offering owners' training and agility courses meant to create closer bonds between owners and their dogs.

- Have 10 trainers solely focused on private in-home lessons for dog owners, expanding our geographic reach throughout the state.

- Be the strategic partner of the community police forces in our region as their number one choice for K9 scent and protection training.

- Be the community partner for local shelters and rescue organizations, providing free rehabilitation training for fearful dogs.

Example 3

Scorecard	Strategic Plan
Revenue	OUR PURPOSE
Revenue per mile	Empowering journeys: enhancing lives through safe and reliable transportation experiences.
Cost per mile	
Gross profit margin	**OUR CORE VALUES**
Return on investment	**Safety first:** Ensuring the well-being of passengers and staff through rigorous safety protocols and continuous training.
Contract rejection and acceptance rates	
Environmental impact	**Accountable excellence:** Taking responsibility for delivering top-notch service that exceeds expectations every time.
	Dependable partnerships: Building lasting relationships founded on trust, reliability, and mutual success.
	Caring connection: Nurturing a compassionate environment where every interaction is marked by genuine care and consideration.
	OUR CONNECTION
	Friendliness and caring: In every customer interaction, we strive to convey friendliness and care by greeting each customer with a smile and consistently demonstrating courtesy and respect.
	ANNUAL OBJECTIVES
	Enhanced customer experience: Elevate passenger satisfaction by delivering exceptional service and personalized experiences.
	Operational efficiency: Streamline processes to optimize fleet utilization, reduce costs, and minimize environmental impact.

Safety enhancement: Implement advanced safety measures to ensure the well-being of passengers, staff, and assets.

Market expansion: Explore new markets and partnerships to broaden our reach and contribute to economic growth in our region.

KEY GOALS

- Achieve an 85% customer satisfaction rating through post-trip surveys within the next year.

- Reduce fuel consumption by 5% through driver training and route optimization by the end of the fiscal year.

- Implement advanced safety technology, resulting in a 15% reduction in accident rates within two years.

- Establish service to three new high-demand routes, increasing revenue by 15% over the next 18 months.

KEY STRATEGIES

- **Sustainability:** Deliver premium shuttle services on electric vehicles to capture college campus ridership.

- **Training and development:** Invest in comprehensive training programs for staff to enhance customer service, safety, and operational efficiency.

THREE YEARS AHEAD

- Be the pinnacle of customer satisfaction, aiming for a 95% customer satisfaction rating, reflecting our commitment to delivering exceptional service and personalized experiences, setting the company apart in the transportation industry.

- Be a leader in fuel efficiency, having reduced fuel consumption by 20% with 15 electric shuttles in our fleet.

- Be at the forefront of safety innovation with plans to implement advanced safety technology. This initiative is expected to result in a 15% reduction in accident rates within two years, ensuring the well-being of passengers, staff, and assets.

- Add three new high-demand routes to our services, with a 25% increase in revenue over the next 36 months.

- Invest in comprehensive training programs, enhancing skills in customer service, safety, and operational efficiency.

- Strengthen community ties through charitable initiatives, local events, and partnerships.

The next step in achieving your strategic plan is to keep your attention on the immediate next steps. Success is built upon commitment to your purpose and clear understanding of the necessary actions to reach it. Your leadership team will outline these actions during quarterly planning, as they prepare for the execution of your plan. This requires careful examination of each strategy, anticipating potential obstacles and challenges, and remaining flexible in adapting to overcome unexpected hurdles. In the next chapter, I will explain how to divide your plan into achievable tasks.

It's important to remember that a strategic plan is not a one-time document to be stowed away and neglected. It's an ongoing process that demands persistence, determination, and self-control. You can transform your visions into tangible results by staying true to your purpose, aligning your aspirations with your values, and executing key activities. With a well-defined road map and a drive for success, you are on the path toward making a lasting impact and experiencing meaningful growth.

STEP 4: COMMUNICATION AFTERWARD

Proper dissemination of your strategic plan to everyone in your company is vital in promoting a culture of effective communication and guaranteeing that every team member is aligned with your plan's overall objectives. Your leaders are responsible for demonstrating transparent communication, stressing the importance of clarity, honesty, and genuineness. Transparent leadership builds trust and encourages open dialogue, empowering employees to share their thoughts and concerns.

Your leaders should use various methods to communicate the strategic plan effectively: your 10-slide presentation, video updates, and an accessible internal dashboard for employees to view the plan. These mediums aid in understanding and accessibility, enabling team members to fully comprehend your organization's purpose, values, objectives, and goals. Regular progress updates and a scorecard help reinforce alignment with your strategic objectives. Additionally, a kickoff meeting, monthly and weekly updates, weekly meetings with your team, emails, success stories, discussion forums, infographics, and other materials can be used to emphasize key aspects of the plan and ensure that each team member understands their role in achieving your purpose.

Maintaining focus is crucial for effectively carrying out a strategic plan. Your leaders must prioritize tasks that align with the plan and must ensure that everyone in the organization understands and supports the purpose behind their actions. I recommend creating an internal communication plan for this effort, being clear about goals, target audiences, key messages, communication channels, time frames, responsibilities, and ways to measure progress. Regularly updating and engaging with employees through workshops and feedback processes makes the strategic plan a living guide for your company's progress. It promotes a unified approach to your shared objectives.

Chapter 15

STRATEGIC AGILITY: FINE-TUNING YOUR BUSINESS COURSE

With your plan approved by leadership and distributed across your organization, it's time to focus on the execution phase. So let's dive into executing your plan!

Here's a review of your strategic plan:

How We Measure Success	Slide 1: Title Slide: Your Strategic Plan
Slide 8: Scorecard (Financial and community impact metrics)	Slide 2: Purpose statement (Why we exist)
	Slide 3: Core values (How we act, think, communicate, and make decisions)
	Slide 4: Connection (How we make customers feel)
	Slide 5: Annual objectives (What we want to accomplish)
	Slide 6: Key goals (The results we want to achieve, when)
	Slide 7: Key strategies (How we're going to achieve our goals)

	Slide 9: Three years ahead (Where we want to be in three years)
	Slide 10: End slide: Thank you

Your leaders will complete execution planning with the following process:

How We Succeed	Departmental Quarterly Goals
Communication Empowerment Transparency Accountability	Quarterly goals (Each department is dedicated to achieving quarterly goals by supporting the objectives, goals, and strategy(s) outlined in the plan.)
	Key activities (How each department achieves quarterly goals)
	Action items (What each team needs to get done to achieve key activities)

The execution planning process is a guide for getting everyone in your organization on the same page. It helps to create vertical and horizontal alignment in your company. Vertical alignment means that, from executives to frontline workers, everyone understands and works together to achieve the plan. A good way to think of this is like a pyramid with objectives at the top, goals in the middle, and strategy(s) at the bottom. This ensures that management has clarity on these levels and creates an environment for success.

Horizontally, all departments of the organization need to work together, like a band playing music. All the instruments need to be in sync with each other or else it won't sound right. It's like a puzzle where every department plays a vital role in completing the bigger picture. Horizontal alignment requires collaboration and effective communication in all areas of your business.

Why is this relevant? Imagine your company as a precisely calibrated machine, with all its components working in perfect harmony. This creates strength and durability. When everyone knows their role and collaborates seamlessly, you can achieve greater results in less time. Alignment is maintaining the efficiency and effectiveness of your organization, top to bottom and side to side.

To stay on the right track, your leaders will focus on quarterly execution planning. This involves homing in on your objectives and goals and breaking them into achievable steps for each quarter. Your leaders have an essential role here: they set goals with their teams, divide responsibilities, and make sure everyone agrees.

This isn't a one-person job. Your leaders and managers take charge to guide their teams, collaborating on short-term goals, ensuring they align with the overall strategic plan. It's like assembling different pieces of a puzzle to create a cohesive picture.

It's important to keep in mind that this synchronization is not solely for the purpose of streamlining business operations. It also contributes to fulfilling your company's purpose. When all individuals have tasks that correlate with your company's plan, everything falls into sync.

The opposite of alignment is misalignment. Here are two examples for illustration purposes.

EXAMPLE 1

When Mathew, an HR manager, met with his direct supervisor, he realized that his team was not aligned with the company's strategic plan. His team had been focusing on administrative tasks, reviewing company policies and onboarding guides, which were not a priority. As a result, they were not contributing to the company's overall goals.

After Mathew's supervisor noticed the problem, they decided to create a quarterly execution plan to make sure that his team's efforts were in line with the company's overall strategy. First, Mathew and his team carefully reviewed the plan and had a thorough conversation about the company's objectives, goals, and strategy(s). Then, they broke down the plan into more manageable quarterly goals for the HR department. Finally, they assigned tasks to each team member and established deadlines for completion.

As they worked on the plan, Mathew's team became more engaged and motivated. They understood how their work contributed to the company's overall success, and they felt a sense of purpose. The team's alignment with the company's strategic plan also led to better communication and collaboration across departments.

In the end, the company achieved its goals for the quarter, and Mathew's team felt proud of their contributions. This is the power of alignment—it not only helps your organization achieve success, but it also boosts employee morale and job satisfaction.

EXAMPLE 2

Misalignments, like the one Mathew experienced, are not always clear cut. In some cases, there is a deeper issue at play—such as a toxic work culture. This was the unfortunate reality for Emily, a marketing manager at a startup company.

Emily had been struggling to meet her team's quarterly goals, despite putting in long hours and sacrificing her personal life. She couldn't figure out what was going wrong until she realized that the company's culture was toxic. The CEO and other executives were constantly pressuring employees to perform by pitting the high achievers against the low performers. There was no sense of shared purpose or collaboration in Emily's company.

Emily was aware that her team's lack of harmony with the company's strategic plan was a result of poor management. Her team was losing motivation and felt that their work was insignificant. Emily acknowledged that she needed to make a change if she wanted to improve the situation.

Emily began by engaging in conversations with her team, attentively listening to their worries. They shared the negative atmosphere of their workplace and how it was impacting their well-being and efficiency. Realizing the urgency of the situation, Emily knew she needed to take immediate action before her team members lost all drive.

After arranging a meeting with the CEO and other top-level employees, she addressed the concerning issue of hostile behavior from leadership and its detrimental effects on the company's progress. To her pleasant surprise, the CEO was open to her feedback and recognized the need for a shift in the workplace culture. Together, they devised a course of action to transform the company's culture and align it with the overall strategic plan.

The transformation in Emily's team was evident to all. They sensed that their manager and the company's leaders were actively listening and providing support. Their efforts felt valued, and they saw the impact of their work on the company's achievements. This newfound sense of purpose boosted their efficiency and overall morale, leading them to successfully achieve their quarterly targets.

Emily took great pride in the progress her team had made and the positive influence she had on the company's overall culture. She understood that alignment went beyond just setting goals and plans—it also meant creating an atmosphere of support and collaboration. Emily knew that her team's accomplishments were a direct result of the culture she had helped cultivate, one where employees felt appreciated and motivated to do their best work.

As time passed, Emily's team continued to thrive in this new and improved environment. They worked together seamlessly and achieved even greater success than before. Emily's strong leadership and unwavering commitment had a profound impact on her team's morale and job satisfaction. They were confident in her ability to stand by them, listen to their concerns, and guide them through any obstacles they faced.

Although the story of Emily's workplace is exaggerated (turning around a toxic culture is a long-term process and takes coordinated action by leadership), it serves as a reminder that even small misalignments caused by a hostile work environment can significantly affect employee productivity and engagement. As you may recall, a staggering number of employees left their jobs in early 2021, and many others left as well as the year progressed. Between April and September 2021, an unprecedented 24 million Americans left their positions. This trend, known as the great resignation, had business leaders scrambling to understand the underlying causes and find ways to retain their top-performing employees.[151]

Unfortunately, the main reason for resignations during this time was toxic work environments. Early on in my own career, I worked in an environment that was incredibly damaging to my well-being. Every day after work, I felt drained and empty. Despite the high salary for my age (I was only 21 at the time), I eventually sought out lower-paying jobs just to avoid working under supervisors who treated me poorly.

Viewing alignment within your workplace as the foundation of focus and direction can greatly benefit your progress toward goals. When your leaders align quarterly goals with the overall strategy, it unites everyone's efforts and gives purpose to each step taken. This synchronization helps keep everyone on the same page and allows for more efficient progress toward your goals.

Before diving into quarterly planning and execution, it's important to have a solid game plan in place. Throughout the three weeks leading up to each quarter, (allowing individuals adequate time in their schedules to prepare for, schedule, and attend meetings with their teams), all leaders within the company should be actively communicating with their teams about the upcoming 90 days. In this section, I will demonstrate what this process looks like and how your leaders can effectively lead the way.

YOUR QUARTERLY GAME PLAN

Think of this as your team's quarterly playbook. Leaders, break down your strategic plan into smaller steps for each quarter. It's like plotting out moves for every game in the season. It keeps you on track and inching closer to your strategic plan's goals.

A crucial aspect of supporting your strategic plan and encouraging each department to prioritize the work that will drive your business forward is to prevent anyone from becoming complacent with where the business currently stands. As soon as you find yourself content with the present state, take it as a signal to shift focus toward achieving the next stage of growth. It's important to never let your business coast along. Instead, maintain an attitude of constant development and welcome new goals and challenges. By involving their teams in a compelling vision of the future, your leaders can ignite creativity and passion within their team members. This vision should give purpose to their work and bring meaning to their individual contributions.

Here are some suggestions to assist your leaders in effectively supporting their teams and aligning everyone's efforts for successful quarterly execution.

- **Lead as coaches:** Your leaders and managers act as coaches, guiding their teams toward success. They communicate the goals of the organization and help team members understand how their actions contribute to the plan. Just like a sports coach works with players, leaders support their teams in setting challenging goals that align with your larger vision.
- **Brainstorm as a team:** This is not a solo leadership performance. Each team member has a voice and input. It's like a group huddle where everyone discusses and establishes goals collaboratively. This is how you get everyone involved and motivated to bring their best effort.
- **Fit the puzzle:** Think of goals like a puzzle. In a puzzle, each piece fits snugly to complete the picture. With goals, they must slot into the strategic plan. That's alignment—ensuring everyone's pieces line up and you see the whole picture.
- **Enable purpose:** When all teams are aligned with your strategic plan, it brings your purpose to life. It's like the cogs of a well-oiled machine working seamlessly together. This alignment propels your purpose forward, turning words into tangible actions and victories.

It's also important to remember that to win, everyone needs to be thinking MEAN.

BE MEAN ABOUT YOUR QUARTERLY GOALS

While it may seem that executives in all types of businesses are well-versed in setting quarterly goals, my experience has shown otherwise. I have observed some less-than-effective practices when it comes to setting goals. In some cases, there are no quarterly targets at all, or the targets require further clarification. Here are a few examples of quarterly goals I have come across in areas such as sales, marketing, operations, engineering, product management, technical support, and HR.

- Increase sales by 10%.
- Improve customer service.
- Gain more social media followers.
- Be a thought leader in our space.
- Improve the recruitment process for new hires.
- Ship our products faster.
- Increase operational efficiency.
- Release new features.
- Write the product-requirements documentation.
- Launch a new product.

Did you spot the issue? These goals may appear straightforward, but they lack exactness. Having ambiguous goals can greatly hinder productivity. It can lead to confusion, frustration, and disorganization as team members struggle to understand what they should be striving toward. It's like trying to solve a puzzle without all the pieces—it's difficult to put everything together when you're unsure of the outcome. When employees need more clarification about their priorities, they spend time on tasks that might not contribute to the bigger picture. It's like spinning your wheels in mud—you're working hard but not making progress. And it's costing businesses wasted time and money.

Unclear goals present a final challenge for leaders—you can't effectively measure progress. Imagine measuring how far you've come on a journey without any milestones. It's like walking in the dark without a flashlight—you're moving but can't gauge your progress. During regular team meetings, discussing progress becomes a guessing game.

This is where your MEAN goals come into play. As I mentioned, MEAN goals are meaningful, exact, actionable, and necessary. They provide a structured framework that enables you to monitor, measure, and guide your team's efforts. It's like having a GPS for your goals—you can track your progress and make necessary adjustments to reach your desired destination.

In a nutshell, goals need to be MEAN to ensure a smooth flow of work and the clear measurement of progress. In looking at the earlier examples of unclear goals, how would you turn these into the clarity you need for your team?

- Increase sales by 10% → Increase product X sales by 10% by the end of Q1.
- Improve customer service → Reduce first response time for customers seeking support to two hours by Q2.
- Gain more social media followers → Increase LinkedIn followers by 15% by the end of June to expand our cause.
- Be a thought leader in our space → Publish a biweekly blog post about the technological advancements of AI in our industry.
- Improve the recruitment process for new hires → Optimize the hiring process by implementing a new software platform by Q3.
- Ship our products faster → Ship 90% of customer orders within 24 hours by the end of April.
- Increase operational efficiency → Reduce returns on sales by 10% by the end of the year.
- Release new features → Launch the e-commerce one-click shopping cart on July 1st.
- Write the product-requirements documentation → Write the first draft of the product-requirements document by February 15th.
- Launch a new product → Launch XYZ solution by October 31st.

In each of these instances, we've transformed unclear goals into MEAN goals for the companies seeking to move their plans forward. Collaborating with your team to establish MEAN goals ensures everyone is on the same page and understands what needs to be achieved, and why these goals are meaningful and necessary. With MEAN goals in place, tracking and measuring progress becomes feasible, and adjustments can be made along the way as required.

MEAN goals provide focus and direction, fostering accountability among leaders and managers in attaining their goals.

Just as you do with your strategic plan, you should consider your team's capacity when setting quarterly goals. It's advised to keep the number of quarterly goals manageable, ideally between two to four goals per quarter. Remember that the focus should be on creating meaningful outcomes, aligning with the strategic plan, and ultimately supporting the fulfillment of your purpose.

ROLLING UP QUARTERLY GOALS TO YOUR STRATEGIC PLAN

With your organization now dedicated to achieving its quarterly goals, each department head should collaborate with their team to ensure that each quarter brings specific advancements that align with your purpose. One effective way to do this is breaking down your quarterly goals into your team's key activities.

Empowering Teams with Key Activities

Your leaders and managers should meet with their teams to determine three to five key activities required to achieve each quarterly goal. This method involves collaborating with team members to ensure that everyone is well informed and understands their assigned tasks. Working together in this way ensures that everyone is on the same page regarding the key activities they have identified.

Let's look at the following three examples:

Example 1: Marketing Quarterly Goal

Publish a biweekly blog post about the technological advancements of AI in our industry.

Marketing Key Activities

- **Research and gather information:** Compile relevant data, studies, and industry trends related to AI advancements in our field.
- **Content creation and writing:** Develop well-researched and informative blog posts highlighting the latest AI developments, ensuring the content is engaging and easy to understand.
- **Visual enhancement:** Create engaging visuals, such as infographics or images, to complement the blog posts and visually communicate the key points about AI advancements.
- **SEO and publishing:** Optimize the blog posts for search engines by incorporating relevant keywords and metadata and publishing them on our website, ensuring they are accessible to our target audience.

Example 2: Operations Quarterly Goal

Ship 90% of customer orders within 24 hours by the end of April.

Operations Key Activities

- **Streamline order processing:** Implement an efficient order-processing system that quickly verifies and confirms customer orders, reducing delays caused by manual data entry or errors.
- **Inventory management:** Ensure optimal stock levels for popular products and maintain effective communication with suppliers to prevent shortages and delays in fulfilling customer orders.
- **Expedited shipping integration:** Collaborate with shipping partners to set up an expedited shipping option and integrate it seamlessly into the checkout process, enabling faster order dispatch and delivery.

Example 3: Sales Quarterly Goal

Increase product X sales by 10% by the end of Q1 to make a greater social impact.

Sales Key Activities

- **Launch promotional campaign:** Develop and execute a targeted marketing campaign to highlight the unique features and benefits of product X. Use various marketing channels, such as social media, email marketing, and online ads, to create awareness and generate interest.

- **Enhance sales training:** Provide comprehensive training to the sales team focused on product X. Equip them with in-depth product knowledge and objection-handling techniques so that they can confidently engage with potential customers and close sales.

- **Offer incentives for upselling:** Implement a sales incentive program that rewards sales representatives for achieving higher product X sales targets. Encourage upselling and cross-selling by offering bonuses, commissions, or recognition for exceeding sales goals.

By implementing these key activities, sales can work toward achieving the goal of increasing product X sales by 10% by the end of Q1, enabling the organization to contribute more to the causes they support.

These key activities, devised by the sales department, emphasize the importance of cross-functional collaboration and teamwork to attain the quarterly goal. You may be curious as to why sales is involving other departments in extra tasks. In this situation, sales has assigned the marketing team with additional responsibilities. This collaborative effort is progressing because of a discussion between sales and marketing on how they can work together to advance the plan.

In all these scenarios, leaders within the department oversee and advise their teams during the implementation-planning phase. They play a crucial role in connecting short-term goals to the overall objectives of the organization. Your leaders and managers give direction and encourage active involvement from team members, promoting a unified and cooperative approach. To further streamline the planning process, just as goals are divided into key activities for each team member, these key activities are then broken down into tasks known as action items.

ACTION ITEMS: FOSTERING ACCOUNTABILITY THROUGH EMPOWERMENT

An action item is a task that needs to be completed to achieve a key activity. This is where the real work happens. Your leaders and managers must delegate these tasks to their team members and hold them accountable for their completion. Team leaders track the progress of individuals toward completing their assigned tasks to ensure the success of the team's overall goals. Leaders are also there to offer support and assistance with any challenges that arise during the execution of these tasks.

Assign two to four action items for each key activity. Your action items may cover multiple activities with some requiring teamwork or involvement from different departments. Make sure to collaborate with your colleagues to ensure departments are aligned with the work.

Action items are short-term tasks that can be achieved in a reasonable amount of time.

Meeting the key activities within the next three months will lead you to achieve your quarterly goals. While discussing the necessary action items for each key activity, ensure that everyone is clear on their assigned tasks and time frames. Setting specific deadlines for each item will help keep track of when they need to be completed.

Assign action items to team members who possess the necessary skills for completing tasks efficiently. As each item is completed, it gets crossed off the list, making room for new ones. This strategy increases the team's productivity and ensures that all necessary tasks are taken care of.

THE ROLE OF LEADERSHIP

The role of a leader in managing quarterly goals, key activities, and action items is vital for driving team success and achieving organizational objectives. Your leaders and managers play a pivotal role in guiding their teams, removing obstacles, fostering open communication, and motivating team members. Here's a breakdown of their responsibilities:

- **Facilitating clarity and alignment:** Leaders take the initiative to communicate and collaborate with their teams on quarterly goals, key activities, and action items. By ensuring every team member understands their roles and responsibilities and how their tasks contribute to the larger objectives, leaders create alignment within the group.

- **Removing obstacles:** Leaders identify potential roadblocks or challenges that might hinder the progress of key activities and action items. They work collaboratively with their teams to develop solutions, allocate resources, and make necessary adjustments to ensure smooth execution.

- **Weekly progress meetings:** Leaders facilitate weekly meetings to discuss the progress of key activities and action items. These meetings offer an opportunity to provide updates, share insights, address challenges, and celebrate wins. Like football coaches on the playing field, leaders and managers direct their teams. They guide those under their care to ensure everyone understands how their actions affect the overall outcome. As coaches work with players, leaders help their groups relate to the bigger picture. Finally, your leaders keep score. Tracking progress allows everyone to realize if their efforts are paying off or slipping away.

Being a part of a winning team is a goal for every member, and keeping each other updated on progress serves as a major source of motivation to ensure that everyone's efforts directly contribute to achieving victory. While challenges may arise and cause temporary setbacks, they should be viewed as opportunities for personal growth and learning rather than as failures.

ACTION ITEMS GET THE MOST IMPORTANT THINGS DONE

In our quarterly goal example involving the sales department (example 3), I outlined the three key activities required to attain the goal. Here's a recap:

Sales Quarterly Goal

Increase product X sales by 10% by the end of Q1 to make a greater social impact.

Key Activities
- Launch promotional campaign
- Enhance sales training
- Offer incentives for upselling

Key Activity: Launch Promotional Campaign

- **Action Item:** *Create Marketing Content*

  Develop engaging and informative content highlighting product X's unique features and benefits. The first action item could include writing compelling copy, creating visuals, or crafting catchy headlines.

- **Action Item:** *Select Marketing Channels*

  Identify the most suitable marketing channels to reach the target audience effectively. Evaluate social media platforms, email marketing, online ads, and other relevant channels.

- **Action Item:** *Design Campaign Material*

  Design visually appealing marketing materials such as brochures, webinars, graphics, and images to be used across the chosen marketing channels. Ensure consistency in branding and messaging.

- **Action Item:** *Schedule and Execute Campaign*

  Set up a detailed schedule for the campaign, including release dates, frequency of posts, and specific times for maximum reach. Execute the campaign as planned, monitoring engagement and making adjustments as needed.

By breaking down the key activity into these action items, the team can systematically work toward successfully launching the promotional campaign for product X. Remove and add action items as the key activity moves forward to completion.

Key Activity: Enhance Sales Training

- **Action Item:** *Develop Training Materials*

  Create detailed training materials that cover all aspects of product X, including its features, benefits, use cases, and potential objections. These materials can include presentations, product guides, and objection-response scripts.

- **Action Item:** *Conduct Training Sessions*

  Organize interactive training sessions for the sales team led by subject-matter experts. These sessions should provide a deep understanding of product X and offer practical scenarios for practicing objection-handling techniques.

- **Action Item:** *Implement Assessment*

  Design an assessment or quiz to evaluate the sales team's understanding of the training content. This can help identify areas requiring further clarification or reinforcement and ensure the team is well prepared.

By breaking down the key activity into these action items, the sales team will be equipped with the knowledge and skills to effectively promote and sell product X to potential customers.

Key Activity: Offer Incentives for Upselling

- **Action Item:** *Design Incentive Program*

  Develop a comprehensive sales incentive program that outlines the criteria for earning bonuses, commissions, or recognition based on achieving higher product X sales targets. Clearly define the goals and rewards to motivate the sales team.

- **Action Item:** *Communicate Program Details*

  Create a communication plan to inform the sales team about the new incentive program. Prepare presentations, emails, or announcements highlighting the benefits of upselling and how the incentive program works.

- **Action Item:** *Monitor Sales Performance*

  Implement a tracking mechanism to monitor the sales representatives' performances and track their progress toward the upselling targets. Regularly update the team on their achievements and progress using visual aids or dashboards.

- **Action Item:** *Evaluate Program Effectiveness*

  Periodically assess the effectiveness of the incentive program by analyzing its impact on sales performance. Gather feedback from the sales team to identify any challenges or improvements needed and make necessary adjustments to optimize the program.

When these action items are assigned, the sales team is motivated to focus on upselling and cross-selling product X, leading to increased sales, enhanced performance, and greater social impact.

Action items can take various forms to suit different tasks. The examples given were intended to illustrate this point. Action items can also be simple, direct tasks to support key activities, such as these tasks:

- Update a PowerPoint template for a webinar on product X.
- Kick off the product launch checklist for Alpha deliverables and complete the first five tasks.

Depending on your business type or department, you can break down action items into manageable chunks that team members can efficiently handle. These action items can encompass both internal tasks and cross-functional collaborations. They can involve discussions with salespeople about customer worldviews or collaborations with the operations team on product label branding.

Team unity is strong when team members come together to make commitments. This isn't just about working in tandem—it's about each person taking individual responsibility for the task at hand. Everyone needs to take ownership of the outcome and produce results within tight timelines, not just offering general words of support. And this can't be a one-way system. Your leaders need to switch their roles from supervisors to partners, collaborating with their colleagues and making sure everyone is marching toward the same goal.

This process instills the essence of personal ownership for the team's triumph. Your leaders and teams convene weekly, scrutinizing their progress and facing the pivotal question: Is the team winning or losing? Engaged team members, dedicated to their action items, are intrinsically motivated to win. Their commitment isn't just verbal—it's a solemn vow to their team to fulfill their action items because, at their core, engaged employees yearn for recognition and triumph.

It's important to note that action items aren't mere assignments—every team member's contribution matters. Action items drive progress, ensuring a smooth workflow. They are chosen by team members who mutually hold each other accountable for completing the work. This collective commitment nurtures a culture of responsibility and shared ambition.

As tasks are completed, new action items are assigned to maintain the momentum. External action items involve working with partners, vendors, and suppliers. For instance, marketing might outsource tasks like public relations or website enhancements. Collaborations between team members on a single action item, called interdependencies, are also common. Examples are content and email-automation managers teaming up for a campaign or finance collaborating with a sales director on pricing strategy. Remember, action items aren't limited to your team—leaders and managers guide their teams and ensure deadlines are met across the organization.

Achieving key activities is a reason to celebrate, and these accomplishments contribute to your quarterly goals. Key activities aggregate into quarterly goals, which, in turn, support your strategic plan. This method instills focus, direction, and alignment within the organization vertically and cross-functionally.

Example

Let's look at one last example of a small-business owner, Gloria, who recently defined the purpose of her business, her core values, her emotional points of difference, and her strategic plan. Gloria runs a flower shop with $675,000 in annual revenue in State College, Pennsylvania.

Gloria's small flower shop aims to foster a stronger bond with the local community by actively participating in community events and hosting collaborative workshops. Her staff strives to create meaningful connections through these activities, share their passion for flowers, and spread joy to their neighbors. This flower shop has taken its first steps into living its purpose.

During the execution planning process, she and her employees had a quarterly goal to become more involved in their community.

Purpose

To spread joy and beauty through flowers, creating memorable moments and connections that brighten people's lives.

Quarterly Goal

Become more involved in the community over the next six months.

Key Activities

- Participate in community events: Engage actively in local events, festivals, and markets to showcase our flowers and build a stronger presence in the community.
    - ○ **Action Item:** Event Calendar Planning
      A team member commits to research and compile a list of upcoming community events and festivals (with a deadline).
- Host collaborative workshops: Organize workshops that bring community members together to learn about floral arrangements, fostering connections and a sense of belonging.
    - ○ **Action Item:** Define How Many Workshops and When
      The team discussed the potential for one workshop a month beginning in three months. Katie, a florist, volunteered to work on this action item with Gloria.
    - ○ **Action Item:** Workshop Creation and Promotion
      Katie and Paul (another florist) volunteered to collaborate and design three floral workshop concepts that appeal to different age groups and interests (with a deadline).
    - ○ **Action Item:** Develop a Plan for In-Store, Website, and Social Media Promotion
      Gloria's marketing manager, Ashley, is assigned to write a promotional plan for an in-store banner and point-of-sale flyers, social media, and a new events page on the website to attract participants.

Although navigating this process for the first time may seem daunting, the key lies in its simplicity. Visualize your quarterly goals as four concise three-month routes to achieving the objectives from your strategic plan. Your key strategies serve as your road map for achieving these goals. By breaking down your quarterly goals into smaller key activities, you create opportunities to move forward and to celebrate.

Team members make a personal commitment to each other to accomplish action items, which propel key activities forward, leading to achieving your quarterly goals.

This streamlined process empowers the leaders in your business to monitor progress and make necessary adjustments to stay on track. Through collaborative effort within this simplified system, you unlock the potential to fulfill your purpose and propel your business forward. This bite-sized approach to strategic and execution planning equips teams to tackle challenges effectively.

If you've faced challenges with strategic planning in the past, you're not alone. Many businesses need help because complex plans often go unused. If this resonates with your experience, adopting this straightforward framework can unify your teams, fostering a shared understanding of how to execute tasks while fulfilling your purpose and your plan.

CHAMPIONING A MINDSET OF ACCOUNTABILITY

As you transition to quarterly progress, make sure to hold yourself and your team responsible for meeting the goals set for each quarter. Establishing a culture of accountability in the workplace not only ensures completion of tasks, but it also promotes a sense of ownership, involvement, and overall success for both individuals and teams. Accountability goes beyond simply completing a checklist—it involves taking responsibility for end results, achievements, and the impact of your contributions. When leaders embrace this mentality, employees become more engaged, proactive, and driven to deliver their best work as they understand the importance of their role in your organization's success.

222 ≈ PURPOSEFUL PERFORMANCE

Your leaders and managers must set an example of accountability by embodying it themselves. A captain leads by steering the ship, and in the same way, your leaders must take responsibility for their decisions and actions. By acknowledging their contribution to both successes and setbacks, leaders foster a culture of authenticity and transparency that encourages others to do the same.

Some managers may feel that it is not their responsibility to hold their peers accountable. However, holding peers accountable effectively and respectfully requires tact and expertise. Your leaders should educate their teams on how to properly hold each other accountable and should emphasize that this is a crucial part of the company's culture, rather than an attempt to control others.

Trying to control every little detail never yields success, yet it's a common approach. However, holding someone accountable means trusting them with responsibility and can be a powerful incentive to excel. Accountability and successful outcomes often go hand in hand, and teams that consistently produce high-quality work have a strong culture of accountability.

So, what should you do if a team member is struggling to complete their assigned tasks? Start by addressing the issue directly: "I've noticed that you've been taking longer to finish your work lately." Give specific examples and then ask, "How can we support you in getting back on track?" For a team member who hasn't met their action items, try asking, "How do you think your work helps the team succeed?" and observe their initial response.

Open dialogue—initiate a conversation to inquire about your employee's performance, and actively listen to their response. This gives them a chance to share their perspective on the issue and identify any underlying causes they may be aware of.

Take a moment to consider your role in the situation. To determine whether you may be at fault, ask yourself reflective questions, like these:

- Did I give an excessive amount of work?
- Were the tasks I set for this person unattainable?

- Did I not clearly define their responsibilities?
- Was I available to provide proper guidance when they needed it?

If a team member is not meeting expectations, devise an action plan that addresses their specific needs. Set clear tasks with deadlines to improve their performance. Involve the employee in this process so it is seen as a solution rather than a punishment. Be crystal clear about what you expect. This means being clear about the outcome you're looking for.

From the start, it is important to ensure that your employees have all they need to succeed. Support is crucial—make sure your team has access to resources, knowledge, and assistance in completing their tasks. This will help them develop their skills, boost their confidence, and take ownership of their work.

Demonstrating accountability for your team is a way to convey trust in their abilities and appreciation for their efforts. Give them the tools and support they need to feel empowered and motivated to achieve success:

- **Clear expectations:** Set clear expectations for each team member. Clearly defined roles and responsibilities mean that employees can align their efforts accordingly when they know what's expected of them.
- **Ownership mentality:** Encourage employees to approach their tasks and projects as if the employees were business owners. This mindset instills a sense of pride and commitment. When employees take ownership of quarterly execution, they consistently drive their action items to completion, and you create a winning team mindset.
- **Collaborative goal setting:** Involve employees in setting quarterly goals, key activities, and action items. This empowers them to take ownership of their work and moves your strategic plan and purpose forward.
- **Regular check-ins:** Schedule regular one-on-one meetings to discuss progress, challenges, and where you're tracking against your goals. These check-ins allow employees to share updates and seek

guidance while knowing the score.

- **Opportunities to celebrate wins:** Recognize and celebrate big and small achievements. Acknowledging successes reinforces the value of accountability and encourages continual effort. When employees complete their tasks, reach key milestones, and achieve goals, acknowledge their efforts and celebrate their successes. This recognition can come in different forms, such as verbal praise during team meetings or formal shows of appreciation during awards ceremonies. By celebrating achievements, you reinforce that each person's contribution is valuable. Just like when scoring a touchdown in a football game, getting cheered on by your teammates fuels your desire to score even more. We are motivated to achieve greater success when our coworkers and superiors celebrate our victories with us.

My spouse maintains a designated "Gratitude" folder in her Outlook account where she stores emails from her boss and coworkers expressing their appreciation for her leadership skills. Whenever she feels her motivation slipping, she reads through a few of these messages to reenergize and realign her focus. It's a powerful reminder that her efforts have a positive impact on those she works with.

Encourage your leaders and managers to collaborate with their teams in order to establish a safe and open environment where team members feel comfortable expressing themselves without the fear of being judged or disciplined. Use teamwork when multiple skill sets are required, giving team members the chance to expand their abilities. When everyone feels secure enough to be genuine and openly share their thoughts and evaluations, there are various approaches you can take to elevate your team's performance levels:

- **Open feedback loop:** Create an environment where feedback is welcomed and valued. Employees should feel comfortable providing and receiving feedback, which enhances accountability.
- **Team accountability:** Empower employees to make personal promises to each other to complete action items. Pair team

members together to complete action items that require different skills and expertise. When employees work together to achieve action items, they can support and motivate each other to complete the work.

- **Transparent communication:** Communicate openly about the organization's performance and challenges and where you are against your plan. Transparency fosters trust and encourages individuals to take ownership. If you only share the good news, you'll create skepticism and mistrust when the company meets only some success metrics.

- **Problem-solving mindset:** Encourage employees to approach challenges as opportunities for growth. This mindset shifts the focus from blame to finding solutions.

- **Recognition and rewards:** Recognize and reward employees who consistently demonstrate accountability. This reinforces the behavior and motivates others to follow suit.

When your leaders and managers embrace accountability, it creates a ripple effect throughout the organization. Employees are more likely to take initiative, work collaboratively, and take pride in their contributions. This leads to higher morale, enhanced productivity, and greater feelings of purpose.

Leading through actions, establishing concise guidelines, promoting a mindset of ownership, and offering chances for development foster a workplace where individuals are driven to take ownership of their assignments. When a culture of responsibility is ingrained in your company's core values, it sets the stage for continual achievement and creativity and establishes a flourishing environment where all individuals are empowered to thrive. In an article published by *Forbes*, Mike Scanlin, CEO of Born to Sell,[152] shared his perspective: "Accountability breeds trust. Managers need to have open communication and stand by their decisions and actions, so that all members of the team know the rules, know they will be applied equally to all, and have transparency."

KEEPING SCORE

In organizational accountability, keeping score is a fundamental practice that holds the power to drive performance and foster a culture of transparency. Throughout my professional journey, I've observed instances where leaders grapple with deciding whether to share financial information with their teams. Some choose to withhold crucial metrics, believing that revealing the true situation might lead to unwanted demands for increased resources or benefits. Others opt to restrict the flow of information, fearing that transparency could be overwhelming. Both approaches, however, result in a need for more clarity and trust.

Imagine a sports game where spectators are denied the knowledge of goals or touchdowns—chaos would ensue! The importance of knowing whether your team is winning or losing is universal. Just as in sports, employees crave a clear understanding of their contributions and impact. This is where your strategic plan scorecard comes into play, functioning as a vital tool to keep score for both leadership and every team member.

Your strategic plan scorecard empowers everyone to comprehend where they stand, promoting a shared sense of direction and achievement.

Department heads play an important role in this accountability framework. They establish a pathway for success through their collaborative efforts in creating quarterly goals and driving key activities forward. Weekly meetings serve as a platform for open dialogues on progress, where keeping score is central. Every team member desires to be on a winning team, and the scorecard is a primary motivator to ensure their work directly contributes to success. Challenges may arise, leading to moments of defeat. However, these moments are not setbacks but opportunities for growth and learning.

Accountability extends to leadership, and the responsibility to lead by example falls squarely on the shoulders of executives and business owners. Transparent discussions, informed by financial insights, guide organizations toward effective decisions. Unfortunately, instances arise where the accountability discourse remains stunted, with leaders avoiding tough conversations. For accountability to flourish, leadership must candidly discuss wins and losses.

Maintaining a scorecard and openly addressing success and challenges fosters a culture of growth and improvement. It encourages dialogue around solutions and adaptations when obstacles arise. Accountability is not merely about celebrating victories—it's about acknowledging setbacks, dissecting them, and leveraging the learning opportunities they present. The scorecard provides a clear canvas for analysis, enabling teams to assess their performance, identify trends, and fine-tune their strategies.

Leadership accountability requires more than simply acknowledging subpar outcomes. Excuses may abound, but true leaders accept ownership of their decisions and actions. Blaming external factors or waiting for market dynamics to shift are not signs of effective leadership. Instead, they underscore a lack of accountability. This is where your strategic plan takes center stage—it provides focus and direction and sets up for clear metrics and goal alignment.

To champion accountability, you must embrace transparency, share financial insights, and foster a culture where every team member is invested in the scorecard's success. Every win and loss present an opportunity for collective growth and improvement. Keeping score is not just about numbers—it's about building a resilient and adaptable organization where accountability is the cornerstone of success. So, let us lead by example, uphold accountability, and steer our teams toward victory, learning, and continual improvement.

As you begin quarterly planning and move into team execution, how can you keep your team focused on their goals, monitoring your progress along the way? I will discuss a variety of resources that can help you oversee your goals, key activities, and action items. These tools will ensure everyone is informed and will provide transparency for your team as you work toward achieving your plan and fulfilling your purpose.

TOOLS FOR TEAM TRANSPARENCY

In the fast-paced digital age, technology can be a valuable ally. Using tools such as emails, project management software, and collaboration platforms can keep everyone connected and up to date. These resources are useful in streamlining communication, preventing any information from slipping through the cracks, and facilitating easy information sharing. However, it's important to remember that technology should not replace face-to-face conversations or personal connections—it is simply a tool to aid in these interactions.

If you want your organization to be more transparent and accountable, you may have already implemented or considered efficient project management methods. This is where project management software platforms come in, digital tools specifically designed to simplify, organize, and improve project workflows. Popular platforms include Monday. com, Jira, Basecamp, Smartsheet, and Asana, among others. These allies can greatly benefit your business by increasing productivity and fostering collaboration.

One of the most significant advantages of using project management software is the heightened transparency it brings to the table. Gone are the days of sifting through piles of emails or juggling spreadsheets to comprehend a project's status. With these platforms, teams can access a centralized hub where all project-related information, updates, and tasks are readily available. This transparency translates to enhanced communication and a clear understanding of a project's progress. Every team member is on the same page and aware of project timelines, milestones, and responsibilities—including quarterly goals, key activities, and action items. This newfound clarity fosters a sense of unity and cohesion among team members, ensuring everyone is aligned with your goals.

The use of project management software greatly enhances accountability within a team. These platforms offer tools for task assignments, setting deadlines, and tracking progress, giving each individual a sense of ownership over their responsibilities. As tasks are completed, team members can update their status on the platform, providing a real-time overview of key activities and goals being met. This emphasis on accountability is a game changer—it eliminates blame-shifting, promotes a culture of responsibility, and empowers team members to deliver their best work. By keeping a digital record of tasks, deadlines, and outcomes, the software ensures transparency and recognition for each team member's contributions.

Project management software platforms are instrumental in promoting collaboration. By breaking down traditional barriers like location and time zone, team members can seamlessly work together on tasks, share important files, and exchange valuable insights. These platforms also offer various communication tools such as discussion boards, comment sections, and real-time chat features to facilitate easy and efficient communication. Moreover, these collaborations are not limited to team members. Stakeholders and customers can also be granted controlled access to the platforms, allowing them to stay updated on project progress and contribute their ideas. This collaborative environment fosters creativity, encourages innovation, and promotes collective problem-solving, resulting in successful project outcomes.

The beauty of project management software platforms lies in their versatility and customization. Each platform offers various features, allowing your organization to tailor the software to your specific needs. For instance, if your project thrives on visual representation, platforms like Monday.com offer intuitive, visually appealing boards that display project progress. Alternatively, if you need a tool geared toward software development, Jira provides specialized features such as bug tracking and agile planning. This flexibility empowers organizations to select a platform that aligns with their unique workflows and industry demands, ensuring seamless integration into their processes.

The advantages of implementing project management software are clear. Businesses experience a boost in productivity when routine tasks are automated, information is centralized, and communication is streamlined. This allows team members to focus on more important tasks, leading to faster progress on projects. Additionally, the decreased likelihood of human error and misunderstandings results in fewer delays and interruptions for projects. These efficiency gains not only improve project outcomes but also contribute to overall business success by allowing for quicker completion times and gaining a competitive advantage in the market.

When it comes to choosing a project management software platform, the game has changed for organizations. These platforms have revolutionized the way projects are executed and how goals are managed and measured. No matter if you're coordinating a marketing campaign, developing software, or planning events, project management software platforms offer a comprehensive solution that simplifies processes and empowers your business in today's fast-paced business landscape. With the right platform at your disposal, you can streamline your projects, encourage collaboration, and unleash the full potential of your team, all while driving toward achieving your strategic plan.

I've used Jira, Monday.com, Smartsheet, and Asana. Most recently, I implemented Monday.com (www.monday.com) to create employee dashboards for purpose, core values, objectives, key goals, and key strategies, as well as to track and measure quarterly goals, key activities, and action items, cultivating employee empowerment and accountability across departments. Updated weekly, the company scorecard informed every employee precisely where we were against the plan.

I am not encouraging you to invest in one platform over another. I encourage you to research options to find the right platform that works for your organization based on your business and its unique requirements.

For small-business owners who are unable to invest in a project management platform right now, there are still effective methods for tracking and evaluating the success of key activities and action items. There are alternative options that can keep you organized, track progress, and hold individuals accountable without any added expenses. Here are five strategies to consider:

1. **Spreadsheets and templates:** Use spreadsheet software like Microsoft Excel or Google Sheets to create customized templates. Create columns for task names, responsible team members, deadlines, and progress updates. This approach allows you to track tasks, milestones, and completion dates in a structured manner. Spreadsheets are accessible and can be easily shared and updated by team members.

2. **Task management apps:** Leverage task management applications like Trello, Google Tasks, or Microsoft To Do. These apps

offer basic features for creating tasks, setting due dates, assigning responsibilities, and tracking progress. These tools provide a user-friendly interface and are often free or offer affordable pricing plans.

3. **Online calendars:** Use online calendars like Google Calendar to schedule and track deadlines for goals, key activities, and action items. Create events for each task and set reminders to ensure important milestones are noticed. This approach provides a simple way to manage action items and deadlines while integrating seamlessly with other tools you might already use.

4. **Communication tools:** Leverage communication tools like Slack or Microsoft Teams to foster transparency and collaboration among team members. Create dedicated channels or threads for different projects and encourage team members to provide regular updates on their progress. While these tools are primarily designed for communication, they can also serve as a makeshift platform for tracking and discussing tasks.

5. **Regular check-ins:** Implement regular check-in meetings or video conferences with your team to discuss progress on key activities and action items. During these sessions, team members can share updates, address challenges, and provide feedback. This approach helps ensure that everyone is aligned, accountable, and informed about the status of tasks.

Despite the comprehensive features offered by project management software, there are other options available that can help you effectively monitor and measure the success of your strategic plan, quarterly goals, key activities, and action items. By using spreadsheets, task management apps, online calendars, communication tools, and regular check-ins, you can establish a reliable system for managing assignments, promoting teamwork, and ensuring responsibility without exceeding your budget.

MONTHLY STRATEGY AND ALIGNMENT MEETINGS

Set aside 45 minutes each month for the leadership team to go over their performance against the plan. Each leader should report on what their department has accomplished and how it aligns with the strategic plan.

Ask these questions:

- Is our strategy(s) working? Yes or no.
  - If not, what needs to change? Policies, resources, timeline, workability, risk?
- Are we in alignment? Yes or no.
  - If not, what needs to change?

The objective is to identify any discord within the team as it relates to strategy and leadership alignment. The act of evaluating strategies provides valuable insights into their effectiveness. Through evaluation, you can determine if a policy is achieving its intended outcomes, identify areas for improvement, and make necessary modifications. Additionally, evaluating strategy and leadership alignment monthly means anticipating potential challenges and adjusting, such as shifting resources to overcome challenges before they become major obstacles. At this meeting, everyone agrees on the direction of quarterly goals and the key activities driving goals forward, which in some cases requires cross-functional support. There will be a handful of occasions where something must change. Let me give you an example.

Product management had planned to launch a new product in Q3, but unforeseen problems with compliance had led to a two-month delay. This meant that sales and marketing had to reevaluate their key activities and action items to align with the new timeline.

The leadership team took this opportunity to explore what went wrong with cross-functional communication regarding the delay and how they could improve it in the future. They also discussed how sales and marketing could adjust their strategies to optimize the launch of the new product.

By asking the simple question of "Are we in alignment?" the team was able to identify areas for improvement and work together to address them. This practice of reviewing performance and identifying areas for improvement on a regular basis helps your team maintain a high level of organizational effectiveness.

The leadership team continued to work together, using this monthly review process to regularly reassess their progress toward the strategic plan. Through this practice, they were able to identify and address any discrepancies before they became major problems.

Over time, the team became more cohesive and better aligned toward achieving their collective goals. They also gained a deeper understanding of each other's departments and how they fit into the larger picture. As a result, they were able to make more informed decisions and work more collaboratively toward the success of the organization. By consistently assessing their progress and addressing any discrepancies, your leaders can ensure that their teams are working together toward a common goal.

Thanks to your leadership and the guidance of your managers, you have completed a full cycle. You have established your purpose, core values, and unique emotional strengths. Together, you have navigated through strategic planning and now have a concise 10-slide plan that can be shared with your entire organization. Each member of your team is actively involved in quarterly planning, with their goals, key activities, and action items aligned to support your overarching strategies.

Your leadership team meets monthly to ensure that your strategies are effective, and the team is in sync with the plan. As you approach the six-month mark, you make any necessary adjustments to the plan. Then you gather for a morning meeting to review its impact and discuss your strategic plan going forward.

Chapter 16

THE ADAPTABLE STRATEGIC PLAN REVIEW

As you enter the meeting to review the strategic plan, you've reached a major milestone. The journey has been filled with determination, diligence, and a strong dedication to your purpose and values. This is a moment to rejoice in your accomplishments—transforming a business is no easy task!

Transforming your business requires immense determination and focused work. Whether you're a seasoned pro or embarking on this journey for the first time, acknowledge the difficulty of this task. It takes unwavering commitment to shift the direction of an organization, and it may take longer than anticipated to reach your objectives. Keep your resolve strong and remember that change often requires patience.

In order to truly see the impact of aligning and focusing your organization, larger businesses may need to go through a complete planning cycle. As employees fully internalize your purpose and core values, open communication and accountability must be nurtured. Eventually, you will witness significant changes in motivation—employee involvement will soar, hard work will lead to tangible results, and the daily operations of the business will become more consistent.

Let's take a real-world instance of a company that implemented this model. In just two years, they made significant progress in aligning their

236 ≈ PURPOSEFUL PERFORMANCE

leadership and increasing employee engagement, resulting in an impressive internal Net Promoter Score of 60.[153] Their eNPS score was just as impressive as that of global giants such as Google, Netflix, and Microsoft. With a score of 60, they were recognized as market leaders, surpassing excellence to achieve a world-class rating. Thanks to their unwavering commitment to the strategic plan, quarterly goals, key activities, and action items, they emerged as pioneers and swiftly grew due to their focused drive toward their purpose.

When your company is guided by a clear purpose and consistently provides exceptional value to customers, success becomes an inevitable result. To stay on track, your strategic-planning team should come together for a thorough review session, ideally scheduled halfway through the fiscal year. For those unfamiliar with this process, don't worry about the length of the review and plan update meetings. As you become more familiar with the process, you will develop more efficient ways of conducting them and have a better understanding of how much time they require.

In this meeting, you will have the chance to discuss your recent developments, obstacles, and future prospects in an open dialogue. It's important to keep in mind that your strategic plan remains the backbone of your organization's success and will not be significantly altered. Your planning cycle allows for small enhancements to the strategic plan two times per year.

The strategic-plan review meeting is a chance for the strategic-planning team to acknowledge and applaud their progress. The meeting covers the following areas of discussion:

- **Share and celebrate the wins:** In the strategic-plan review meeting, the team acknowledges and celebrates their successes. This is a chance to recognize the positive outcomes they've achieved and appreciate the hard work that's been put in.

- **Discuss strategic-plan outcomes:** The team discusses the results and progress of your strategic plan's objectives, goals, and strategy(s). Review what has been accomplished and examine how well the team has aligned with their intended outcomes.
- **Evaluate the scorecard:** The team reviews the scorecard, discussing the key metrics and performance indicators. Assess whether you're on target with your goals or if adjustments are needed.
- **Reflect on what you've learned and where you can improve:** Team members share their experiences and outcomes, considering what they've learned. They identify areas where they can improve and make necessary adjustments to goals and strategies.
- **Reexamine and update the strategic plan:** In this activity, the team revisits the strategic plan itself. Review each element of the plan to ensure it still aligns with your objectives, goals, and strategy(s). Then update the plan if needed to reflect any changes in the organization's direction.
- **Assess leadership alignment:** The team must agree that everyone is on the same page regarding the strategic plan. Discuss how well leadership has aligned with the plan's objectives and address any discrepancies.
- **Review the strategic-planning process and recommendations:** The team takes time to review the overall strategic-planning process. Evaluate the effectiveness of the process in achieving your goals and discuss any recommendations for improving the process moving forward.

Depending on the size of your business and the number of people on your strategic-planning team, your one-day agenda may be shorter. I've included a condensed version for smaller teams.

ONE-DAY STRATEGIC-PLAN REVIEW

Session 1: Celebrating Achievements and Reflecting on Success (9:00 a.m. to 10:00 a.m.)

Welcome and Introduction (15 Minutes)

Sharing and Celebrating Wins (45 Minutes)

- Team members highlight successful outcomes and achievements.
- Acknowledge hard work and efforts that contributed to the wins.

Break (10 Minutes)

Session 2: Assessing Progress and Alignment (10:10 a.m. to 11:30 a.m.)

Review of Strategic-Plan Outcomes (30 Minutes)

- Discuss progress made toward the goals and objectives outlined in the strategic plan.
- Evaluate whether the intended outcomes are being achieved.

Scorecard Analysis (30 Minutes)

- Examine key metrics and performance indicators on the scorecard.
- Determine if goals are being met and identify areas for improvement.

Reflection and Improvement Opportunities (20 Minutes.)

- Discuss lessons learned throughout the execution period.
- Identify areas where improvements can be made for greater success.

Lunch Break (11:30 a.m. to 12:30 p.m.)

Session 3: Enhancing and Updating the Strategic Plan (12:30 p.m. to 2:00 p.m.)

Review and Update of the Strategic Plan (1 Hour)

- Evaluate each element of the strategic plan.
- Determine if adjustments or updates are needed to reflect current goals and values.

Leadership Alignment Discussion (30 Minutes)

- Assess how well leadership has aligned with the strategic plan. Share the results from the leadership alignment survey and compare the results to those of previous surveys.
- Address any discrepancies or challenges in alignment, including opportunities for improvement.

Break (10 Minutes)

Session 4: Reflecting on the Strategic-Planning Process (2:10 p.m. to 3:00 p.m.)

Strategic-Planning Process Review (30 Minutes)

- Evaluate the effectiveness of the strategic-planning process.
- Discuss what worked well and areas for improvement.

Recommendations for Process Enhancement (20 Minutes)

- Brainstorm ideas to enhance the strategic-planning process.
- Gather feedback and suggestions from team members.

Closing Remarks and Next Steps (3:00 p.m. to 3:15 p.m.)

- Summarize key takeaways from the meeting.
- Discuss any action items or follow-up tasks.
- Express appreciation for participation and contributions.

This agenda provides a structured framework for a one-day strategic-plan review meeting, ensuring that each topic is covered thoroughly and allowing time for discussions, reflections, and planning for future actions.

Here's a condensed version of the agenda, suitable for smaller teams or businesses:

CONDENSED STRATEGIC-PLAN REVIEW

Session 1: Celebrating Achievements and Progress (9:00 a.m. to 10:00 a.m.)

- Welcome and brief introduction (9:00 a.m. to 9:10 a.m.)
- Sharing wins and milestones (9:10 a.m. to 9:55 a.m.)
- Acknowledging contributions (9:55 a.m. to 10:00 a.m.)

Session 2: Assessing Progress and Aligning Goals (10:00 a.m. to 11:00 a.m.)

- Review of strategic-plan outcomes (10:00 a.m. to 10:20 a.m.)
- Scorecard analysis and discussion (10:20 a.m. to 10:40 a.m.)
- Reflection on progress (10:40 a.m. to 11:00 a.m.)

Lunch Break (11:00 a.m. to Noon)

Session 3: Enhancing the Strategic Plan and Process (Noon to 1:30 p.m.)

- Updating the strategic plan (noon to 12:30 p.m.)
- Leadership alignment and feedback (12:30 p.m. to 1:00 p.m.)
- Reflecting on the process (1:00 p.m. to 1:15 p.m.)

Closing Remarks and Next Steps (1:15 p.m. to 1:30 p.m.)

- Summarize key insights and takeaways
- Assign action items and follow-up
- Express gratitude and adjourn (1:30 p.m.)

This shortened schedule retains the essential elements of the strategic-plan review meeting but offers a more efficient method for smaller teams. It enables targeted conversations about accomplishments, advancements, consistency, and improvements without compromising the overall objective of the meeting.

The strategic review meeting helps your team stay on track and aligns with your adaptability goals. However, it's important to continually improve this process to fit your unique business needs. I believe that there is always room for growth and development in the workplace. That's why I encourage you to take this system and customize it to make it even more effective for your company's success!

If you've been making changes to this process, I would appreciate hearing about them and how your team has improved it. If there are any areas where you feel the process could be made more efficient, please let me know. I will highlight the most successful ideas on my blog, acknowledging you as the source and spreading your concepts with our community.

Speaking of improvement, I want to raise the point that we are all improving every day. In my last position, working as a chief experience officer, one of the hardest and most rewarding internal processes we enacted was 360° leadership assessments. 360° reviews are a form of feedback that provides individuals, teams, and managers with valuable insights on their strengths and areas for improvement. By gathering feedback from various viewpoints, these reviews offer a holistic view of performance and highlight important skills while identifying opportunities for development and progress.

After my 360° assessment was finished and I went through the results, I had a strong reaction to the criticism. My initial thought was "This isn't who I am." But after reading the assessment, I asked my wife to review it, and she concurred with the feedback, stating, "I think that is accurate." The evaluation highlighted both my strengths as a leader and my areas for growth, revealing hidden talents and weaknesses. One suggestion noted that I can be overly talkative, and another stated I may benefit from trying to connect with all employees within the company.

After I prioritized my rational self over my emotional self, I saw these areas of weakness as chances for growth. Self-awareness is indispensable in both life and leadership, so I crafted a plan of action to enhance my leadership abilities and track my progress along the way. As human beings, we must stay true to our values and lead with sincerity—owning up to our flaws while constantly striving to better ourselves.

LEADING YOUR PLAN WITH AUTHENTICITY

We all aspire to be the leader who guides others toward becoming the best versions of themselves. As I experienced with my 360° assessment, the journey of being true to your purpose and values begins with knowing and accepting yourself. This means recognizing your strengths and weaknesses, being honest about your values, and staying true to your beliefs even when faced with obstacles. When you lead with authenticity, you build trust with those who follow you—and trust is the cornerstone of any successful organization.

As you move forward, strive to cultivate genuine relationships with your customers by establishing meaningful connections rooted in your purpose, beliefs, emotional points of difference, and values. In today's world, consumers demand these connections, and brands strive to attain them. Some cultivate them effortlessly, while others must search for them, and there are brands that fabricate them solely for financial gain.

Unlike many companies today, where leadership is often associated with power, titles, and fitting in, I encourage you to lead your business with sincerity and intentionality. By defining your purpose and values, going through the connection loop and creating meaning, then strategizing and executing with a quarterly plan to fulfill your purpose, you have set your business apart from the rest. When you lead from a place of authenticity, it enables you to connect with your audience on a deeper and more personal level, more than you may have imagined possible.

It takes guts to be true to who you are. As Brené Brown says in her book *The Gifts of Imperfection: Let Go of Who You Think You're Supposed to Be and Embrace Who You Are*, "Authenticity is the daily practice of letting go of who we think we're supposed to be and embracing who we are. Choosing authenticity means cultivating the courage to be imperfect, to set boundaries, and to allow ourselves to be vulnerable; exercising the compassion that comes from knowing that we are all made of strength and struggle; and nurturing the connection and sense of belonging that can only happen when we believe that we are enough."[154]

Taking a stand for something you believe in takes guts. I suspect that's why some people choose not to run purpose-driven companies. It's harder to stick to your convictions and much easier to brush aside the causes and movements that matter. Once you have established your stance, your business will inevitably face complex social and political challenges. As the world continues to change, consumer behavior evolves accordingly. These issues will test your principles and morals, but they do not define you. How you choose to address them, however, does.

Ben & Jerry's decided to cease selling ice cream in Israeli settlements, stating that "it is inconsistent with Ben & Jerry's values for our ice-cream to be sold in the Occupied Palestinian Territory."[155]

Bob Chapek, the former CEO of Disney, encountered a significant obstacle during his leadership after the company received backlash for their mishandling of an anti-LGBTQ+ bill in Florida. In an internal memo, Chapek explained that Disney did not take a stance on the bill because it could have been "counterproductive." This caused controversy as the bill, informally known as the don't say gay bill, aimed to restrict discussions about sexual orientation and gender identity in schools. Despite pleas from LGBTQ+ employees for the company to stop donating to lawmakers who supported the bill, Disney remained silent on their stance. As a result, employees felt betrayed by the company's lack of support for the LGBTQ+ community.[156] Bob Chapek later apologized to his staff, acknowledging that he should have been more supportive. However, for some employees who were deeply troubled by the company's lack of action on the bill, the apology was too little too late.[157]

In the year 2019, Gillette displayed their support for the #MeToo movement through a short film campaign titled *We Believe: The Best Men Can Be*.[158] The campaign highlighted instances of violence between boys and sexism in popular media and in the workplace, and it posed the question "Is this truly the best a man can be?" The ad quickly gained traction and went viral with over four million views on YouTube within 48 hours.[159]

These examples all demonstrate a significant change in the way businesses in America present themselves, as they now market not just their products but also their beliefs and values. This wasn't always the case. In the past, during the civil rights movement, when the *New York Times Magazine* questioned if corporations had a responsibility to voice their opinions, the leader of U.S. Steel stated that such actions were "beyond what a corporation should do."[160] Times have clearly shifted since then.

In our fast-paced digital era, where information is shared quickly among individuals glued to their smartphones, there is a trend of "canceling" people or organizations for perceived wrongdoings or negative effects and actions. That's why it's important to have the courage to stand up for what you believe in and weather any adversity that may come your way.

When faced with social and political issues that conflict with your beliefs, you are confronted with a decision: to speak out, do nothing, or conceal your true feelings. What will you do? Will you give your team a glimpse of hope for a brighter tomorrow?

Chapter 17

COURAGEOUS CONVICTION: STANDING FIRM IN YOUR AUTHENTICITY

With an abundance of options and access to information, consumers are becoming more aware of what companies stand for and are demanding change. Global movements for progress and equality, from women's rights in the workplace to the eradication of gender and race discrimination, are the future most of us want to see.

More than ever before, consumers want to buy from brands that support their identities. As consumers become increasingly conscious of companies' true values and priorities, they will make informed decisions about where they spend their money. With the availability of mobile apps like Amazon, DoorDash, and Instacart, consumers now have more choices and purchasing power than ever before. Anything can be bought from anywhere, and you can have your desired items delivered right to your doorstep.

In other words, your customers are choosing to support businesses that align with their beliefs and values, while also avoiding those that do not share the same principles. Your customers' expectations are rising. An overwhelming majority of consumers (87%) claim they would buy a product from a company that takes a stance on a social issue they care about, and

55% say they would boycott or stop supporting a brand if it aligns with social issues they don't believe in.[161] If you are hesitant about being open and truthful about your thoughts on social issues, I understand. However, I believe that your objective is to uplift those who share your views, and by expressing those views, to bring positivity into people's lives and make them feel valued.

By avoiding controversy, you are choosing not to align yourself with certain beliefs and opinions, creating a divide between you and your customers. A recent example of this can be seen in Walgreens' decision not to distribute abortion pills in states where Republican officials threatened legal action, even in places where abortion is still legally available. By choosing to avoid potential legal issues, Walgreens has made it clear to their customers that they are not willing to stand up for freedom of choice when it comes to abortion access. In a statement to NPR, the pharmacy chain stated that they will continue to sell the drug in areas where it is both legal and feasible for them to do so.[162]

After announcing that they would not distribute the medication in 21 states, Walgreens faced backlash from both customers and political figures. People on social media called for a boycott of the company. Governor J. B. Pritzker of Illinois, where Walgreens is headquartered, held a virtual meeting with the top executives, including CEO Rosalind Brewer, to discuss the company's decision. Pritzker begged for Walgreens' reconsideration, pointing out concerns about Republican influence. As a result of the company's decision, the stock price for Walgreens suffered a sudden drop.[163]

The hashtag BoycottWalgreens went viral on Twitter, driven by advocates for abortion rights who were outraged by the company's position on the issue. Some consumers have vowed to never shop at Walgreens again, highlighting the fact that customers are paying attention to the stance businesses take on significant issues.

Regardless of your personal opinions, individuals are purchasing the logical and emotional advantages of your brand, as well as the tangible and intangible worth of your offerings. They are also considering how you fit into their own narrative—environmentally and politically.

BRAND INTEGRITY: ACTIONS SPEAK LOUDER

In the past, it was rare for companies to express their political views openly. However, nowadays, depending on the position you take, there may be repercussions, as Walgreens experienced. Despite these risks, many business owners and CEOs are speaking out on certain issues because they have the courage to stand up for what they believe in. For your brand to truly make a difference, sooner or later, you're going to have to be true to who you are. In today's world, consumers are looking for more than just empty promises—they want to see tangible results. It is vital for brands to not only talk about making a change but to also take action and make an impact. This requires a thorough understanding of your brand's target audience and the social issues that hold significance for them.

The crucial question is, how does your stance on matters align with the beliefs and values of your customers? And how are you going to make a point about something you really care about?

Big corporations such as Amazon, Microsoft, and Starbucks are funding travel expenses for their employees who need to seek abortions in states where it is no longer legal. Nike received backlash and faced potential boycotts for supporting Colin Kaepernick's stance against systemic racial and ethnic inequality. By kneeling during the national anthem, Kaepernick's demonstration was a clear and public call for a more just and fair society. Levi Strauss took a stance on gun control and backed related efforts.[164]

However, Bud Light faced backlash and saw a sharp decline in sales when they sent a promotional can to a popular influencer, Dylan Mulvaney, who is transgender. The can, which was personalized with Mulvaney's image, was part of an ad for their March Madness contest and was meant to celebrate the one-year anniversary of Mulvaney's transition. The collaboration gained widespread attention, leading to Anheuser-Busch's market value dropping by $5 billion as calls for a national boycott emerged. Additionally, bars and distributors across the country reported significant decreases in Bud Light sales.[165] Instead of standing behind their belief in diversity, equity, inclusion, and belonging, a belief that appears on their website as "we all feel we belong whatever our personal characteristics or social identities, such as race, nationality, gender identity, sexual orientation, age, abilities, socioeconomic status, religion and others,"[166] Anheuser-Busch CEO Michel Doukeris attempted to downplay the brand's partnership with influencer Mulvaney.[167] Bud Light should have remained true to their declared principles by standing behind Mulvaney instead of downplaying the collaboration. However, they caved to financial pressures and strayed from their stated convictions. This is the idea that "sooner or later, you're going to have to be true to who you are" in action—as the *New York Times* put it, "the company's attempt to backtrack drew further criticism, this time from liberals and members of the L.G.B.T.Q. community."[168]

Target, the retail giant, which has had a long history of standing up for LGBTQ+ rights,[169] faced retaliation as anti-gay customers disrupted displays of merchandise supporting the LGBTQ+ community. The Pride Collection from Target boasts over 2,000 products ranging from clothing and books to music and home furnishings. Its offerings include "gender fluid" mugs, "queer all year" calendars, and children's books with titles like *Bye Bye, Binary*; *Pride 1 2 3*; and *I'm Not a Girl: A Transgender Story*.[170] Sadly, in light of recent incidents involving harassment and threats toward their employees, Target has decided to remove certain items from their collections to guarantee the safety of their staff.

Following Bud Light's decline of sales due to their disconnect with the values of their customers, Target disclosed that the negative response to its LGBTQ+ merchandise during and leading up to Pride month had a significant impact on their sales. In response to this, Target's chief growth officer said, "The reaction is a signal for us to pause, adapt and learn so that our future approach to these moments balances celebration, inclusivity and broad-based appeal."[171] While Target remains steadfast in their principles, the pursuit of greater profits for their shareholders has led them to reevaluate their methods of reaching and engaging with a diverse audience. As more companies take a stand for their beliefs, they must consider the extent to which they are prepared to defend those beliefs. In an article for the *New York Times*, chair and CEO of Salesforce Marc Benioff emphasized the importance of considering society in addition to profits. He stated, "Yes, profits are important, but so is society. And if our quest for greater profits leaves our world worse off than before, all we will have taught our children is the power of greed."[172]

In a world where organizations are struggling to define their stance on social issues and movements, you must be unwavering in your convictions. While it's easy for companies to jump on the bandwagon and support causes that they don't truly believe in, just to appeal to their target audience, the truth will eventually come out. It's better to be honest about your beliefs and stand by them, rather than being fake and insincere. Supporting a cause without genuine conviction only dilutes the meaning of your brand and the cause itself. The fact is, if you truly believed in a cause or took a firm stance on a social issue, there wouldn't be any internal struggle or hesitation. Your marketing team would already be brainstorming ideas for how to promote your views and what content to share on your blog and social media. Your strong values would guide you. When something matters deeply to you, you will naturally feel compelled to fight for it. Your values and purpose should serve as your compass. People want to understand your beliefs and principles, so don't shy away from being authentic and genuine about them.

With consumers forcing businesses to take a stance on important social and political issues, organizations that are inauthentic will face scrutiny for their levels of genuineness and transparency. However, organizations that remain true to their identity and openly express their views will have a stronger ability to engage in these conversations compared to those who simply go through the motions because they feel obligated to.

In the first half of this book, you focused on defining your purpose and core values, using the infinite loop of connection to create a meaningful impact in your workplace, for your customers and for your community. You have created sustainable competitive advantages. Now it's time to lead your business with meaning by staying true to who you are in words and in actions. Take a stand for what you believe in and own it. This is your unique value. This is your gift to the world. Ultimately, your beliefs and values extend beyond your company and have an impact on the world around you. They live in the dreams and desires of those you seek to serve. Be brave enough to ignore everyone else.

As you moved into the latter half of the book, you learned how to apply a simple framework, working on strategy and planning with your team. Although this is not something that is shared publicly, the impact and value of this internal process can be seen through your specific actions and decisions influenced by your plan. Your strategic plan serves as a guide for carrying out your company's purpose and values. In contrast, the external elements of the strategic plan are how these values and meaning manifest in public-facing aspects of your company. If these do not align with your company's beliefs and goals, it could damage the work put into creating something meaningful. So, fully embrace and embody your purpose and values in everything you do.

When a business makes their purpose about inclusion, they firmly stand against exclusion. When you support Colin Kaepernick, you reject racial injustice and prejudice. When you believe in equality, you're against inequality. However, if your core values include sustainability, but your team won't recycle in the office, there is a disconnect between your words and actions. In situations like this, it's important to question who you truly are. Advocating for equality while maintaining unequal pay based on gender or race in similar positions creates a disconnect between your words and actions. This inconsistency raises questions about the authenticity of your beliefs and intentions.

When I was speaking with my son, Nicholas, who loves to debate social issues, he reminded me that making choices that align with your values is not always easy. He said, "Dad, I understand what you are saying, but your views are based on a Western perspective. Unethical business practices exist around the globe. What about your Apple iPhone?"

"What about it?" I asked.

"Are you going to stop using your iPhone because of Apple's problems in their supply chain, with a string of suicides in Shenzhen, China?"

"Hmmm, good question," I replied.

Nicholas was referring to the Foxconn City industrial park in Shenzhen that was hit with a string of suicides, all connected to the harsh working conditions and low wages. Similar incidents also occurred at other Foxconn-owned facilities throughout mainland China. These suicides were heavily covered by the media, leading to investigations into Foxconn's employment practices conducted by their major clients, including Apple and Hewlett-Packard.

In early 2010, Apple's spokesperson Steven Dowling addressed the string of suicides at Foxconn in a public statement, expressing the company's sadness and concern over the tragic events. He also mentioned that Apple had launched an independent investigation into the steps being taken by Foxconn and would continue to inspect all facilities where their products are manufactured. Although Foxconn was not specifically named, Apple acknowledged reports of poor treatment of workers and potential violations of labor laws and their own supplier regulations, including the use of child labor (as young as 14 years old).[173]

"And what about Tesla?" Nicholas inquired, and I could see where this was going.

My face began to twist into a grimace as I prepared to make my argument. As I was collecting my thoughts, Nicholas chimed in. "Tesla's battery supply chain is connected to human rights violations and exploitation of child labor in the mines of Congo."

"I understand your concern," I responded. "Tesla does not explicitly convey this message to their customers, and these are important social issues that must be taken into consideration."

I grabbed my phone from the coffee table and started searching for information on mining operations and lithium batteries. Nicholas had brought up a crucial point—one that I had overlooked—the challenges of globalization and ethical business practices. And I admitted this to him.

As the world strives for cleaner energy sources, the demand for materials used in solar panels, wind turbines, electric vehicles, and batteries increases. These six minerals—cobalt, copper, lithium, manganese, nickel, and zinc—are crucial components in renewable energy technologies. In looking into this further, I learned that the global mining company Glencore, which is a key Tesla supplier, has faced over 70 allegations of wrongdoing since 2010, including claims of corruption and unsafe labor practices. In fact, they have pleaded guilty to charges of foreign bribery and market manipulation and have agreed to pay a hefty $1.1 billion in fines.[174]

The mineral cobalt has gained a reputation as the blood diamond of batteries. However, it's crucial to acknowledge that the issues do not end there. Studies have revealed that clean-energy supply chains globally are plagued with reports of unlawful practices. For many years, organizations focused on human rights have been sounding the alarm about hazardous working conditions and the exploitation of child labor in mining operations.[175]

According to a Reuters article published in 2020, Tesla entered into an agreement with Glencore to acquire 25% of the mine's cobalt for their electric vehicle batteries.[176] In my perspective, this was a strategic decision to distance themselves from accusations of human rights violations within their supply chain.[177]

In the years that followed, the company conducted visits to cobalt mine sites in the Democratic Republic of Congo. During these visits, they addressed concerns raised by NGOs and academic studies regarding working conditions. As part of their supply chain due diligence efforts, the company removed 12 cobalt suppliers and 29 nickel suppliers after attempting to mitigate risks. However, Glencore does not seem to be one of the suppliers that was removed.[178]

THE ETHICAL EDGE

These are the kinds of complex issues that you need to navigate as a business owner and consumer. A company's dedication to ethical and social responsibility is becoming a decisive factor for customers. Over 60% of consumers in the United States consider a company's morals and genuine intentions before they make a purchase, according to research conducted by Accenture Strategy's Global Consumer Pulse.[179]

When it comes to upholding ethical standards in business, it's not just about treating customers well and maintaining a good reputation online. Every step of the supply chain presents potential for unethical actions. To address any challenges that may arise, having a code of ethics in place can establish the fundamental values and principles that guide your company.

This serves as a guiding light for both employees and customers in decision-making and sets clear boundaries for acceptable conduct within your business.

Creating a code of ethics for a business is no easy task. It requires careful consideration to ensure a positive and ethical work environment. According to the Deloitte report *Suggested Guidelines for Writing a Code of Ethics/Conduct*, "Companies that follow both the letter and the spirit of the law by taking a 'value-based' approach to ethics and compliance may have a distinct advantage in the marketplace."[180] Implementing a thoughtfully crafted code of ethics can aid in developing customer trust, improving employee satisfaction, and avoiding potential legal conflicts for your company. One crucial aspect to incorporate into the code is a clear set of the organization's core principles and moral standards. These serve as the foundation for the entire document, establishing the ethical and cultural framework for your company.[181]

After establishing your code of ethics, ensure that your suppliers and partners also adopt and agree to the code before you begin any partnership. It is important to include specific criteria for monitoring and enforcing the code as well.

As we consider our values and what matters to each of us, Apple and Tesla are just two examples of a much broader global problem. As companies grow, they must be more diligent as they face the challenges of foreign business practices—by working toward raising and improving ethical standards in their global supply chains, ensuring that they adhere to ethical practices. It's also worth noting that ethics go beyond supply chains. When companies engage in unethical practices, they betray all of our trust. Regrettably, there are businesses that prioritize profits over the safety, satisfaction, and well-being of their employees and customers.

A classic example of this behavior was the Volkswagen (VW) scandal, where it was revealed that VW had been cheating emissions tests by installing a "defeat" device in their vehicles. This software could detect when a vehicle was undergoing an emissions test and adjust its performance to minimize emissions levels. Even though VW was marketing themselves as environmentally friendly and promoting low-emissions features, these engines were emitting up to 40 times the legal limit for nitrogen oxide pollutants.[182]

The scandal, known as Dieselgate, proved to be the most expensive—over $30 billion in fines and damages—and the largest in the history of the automotive industry.[183]

After the scandal with their diesel engines, VW had no choice but to prioritize decarbonization as their corporate strategy. The negative connotations attached to diesel technology made it a risky option, leaving the company with limited alternatives. To restore its brand image and comply with stricter emissions regulations worldwide, embracing a transition to clean, electric-powered vehicles was the most viable solution.

After facing consequences, VW underwent a change in leadership and culture. The company moved away from a toxic environment, where profits were prioritized over ethics and failure was not tolerated, to a more cooperative and values-driven organization that could learn from its mistakes.

Since that time, VW has actively worked with policymakers to address climate change and support decarbonization in the automotive sector. This includes supporting a ban on new internal combustion engines in the EU by 2035 and collaborating with energy companies for clean-energy infrastructure and battery-cell production. In the U.S., VW defended California's greenhouse gas standards during the Trump administration and is currently standing against legal challenges to President Biden's policies.[184]

VW not only survived, but I believe they owe their continued existence to their decision to prioritize decarbonization and embrace a larger purpose beyond themselves. By making this cultural shift toward being driven by a greater cause, the company has secured its place in the world today. The VW scandal serves as a reminder that we hold the power to make decisions that prioritize making profits or doing what is right and just. Fortunately, there are businesses out there that prioritize ethical choices for the well-being of their employees and customers.

Chipotle Mexican Grill is recognized for their dedication to purchasing ethically raised meat.[185] In the American retail market, Costco Wholesale stands out as a major success story. They raised their base wage from $13 an hour to $14 an hour in 2018 and then again to $15 an hour in

2019.[186] This is significantly higher than the average retail worker's hourly pay of $7.25 to $9 at that time.[187] The key to Costco's success is their ability to attract top-notch employees, resulting in lower labor disputes, less employee turnover, and increased employee satisfaction.[188] H&M, a popular clothing retailer, prioritizes transparency in their supply chain. On their website, they consistently update a list of 98.5% of their suppliers' names and addresses, allowing anyone to verify if these suppliers meet the company's standards.[189] This not only holds H&M accountable for their suppliers' conduct but also demonstrates their commitment to responsible sourcing practices. In fact, H&M has set a goal to use only recycled or sustainably sourced materials by 2030, making them a leader in ethical fashion.

When I was building a business, we made a tough decision to reject a project worth $300,000 because the company requesting our services had a history of inhumane treatment toward animals. At first, I wasn't aware of this issue when our sales team was setting up demo equipment for testing at the company's facilities. One of our employees brought it to my attention with a passionate stance on animal rights. She pointed out that it didn't align with our company's values. I appreciated her honesty and brought it to the senior management team for discussion. We all agreed that we needed to take a stand, and turning down the sale became an easy choice. The company's actions were not in line with our beliefs and principles.

At many points in our lives, we come across situations that go against our personal values, both at work and in our personal lives. Recently, when my home internet service was down, I contacted Comcast for assistance. After troubleshooting remotely, the agent informed me that they would need to send a technician to our house. As I led the technician to our router, I noticed he appeared to be having a rough day. Concerned, I asked him if everything was all right. He then revealed to me that he had just come from a call where the homeowner had refused his service and even used a racial slur against him—a word that has caused pain for generations of African Americans. I was outraged by this despicable behavior and felt somewhat naive for not realizing that such blatant racism still exists in our community. "I am so sorry," I told him sincerely. "I had no idea that kind of racism continues to happen here." The technician, named Neal, sadly shared with me that he often faces racial discrimination while working in his customer-facing role.

When considering the issues that plague our society, it is evident that racial or ethnic discrimination is a pervasive problem that requires significant societal change. While many CEOs and companies are fighting against racial discrimination, where does Comcast stand on this issue? According to their website, Comcast made a $100 million pledge in June 2020 to further their ongoing dedication to diversity, equity, and inclusion. The company states that creating change must begin within its own organization—by promoting an inclusive culture and ensuring all employees feel valued, supported, and heard.[190]

I have to wonder, does Comcast truly practice what they preach when it comes to supporting and listening to their employees? I'm curious about how Neal responded when his boss questioned why the service hadn't been completed in our community. Does Comcast have the courage to follow through on their stated values of creating a more connected, fair, and ethical world? Have they taken any real action against the racist who remains nameless, or are they just going through the motions as a formality rather than genuinely standing up for the values they promote on the internet?

I'm not trying to impose my own ideals and morals onto you. Your individual principles and perspectives are important to me, and I find it valuable to acknowledge diverse viewpoints in discussions like this one. It's worth mentioning that there are organizations and associations that share your values and align with your beliefs, just as there are companies that fit into the story of who I strive to be. The point is, understanding what drives your customers comes down to tapping into their sense of identity, shared humanity, and core beliefs. There is no denying that consumer shopping habits are shifting in a dramatic way. It's our collective responsibility to make the right choices for our employees, customers, and communities. It's clear that the problems we are confronted with are growing increasingly intricate. When my son wonders who I choose to purchase from and why, it ultimately reflects my personal values and beliefs. Our individual choices may not align, but we must acknowledge that we are all connected by our shared humanity. Despite our differences, we share a common desire for peace, empathy, inclusivity, and mutual regard. By embracing our differences, we can collaborate toward a better and more harmonious world.

As you build your business, find like-minded individuals who share your passions, beliefs, and values. Support their growth and development and focus on building the trust of those you want to matter to. Spend your time and energy helping people become the best versions of themselves. Cherish the chance to make a positive impact on those who would miss you if you were gone.

In other words, make a choice and be the difference. Be unapologetically you. Many of us are tired of polished, artificial, and photoshopped forms of leadership. You have the power to foster trust, connection, and growth within yourself and your team by creating the future you want to see. As you take the next step in your journey, embrace authenticity. Do what matters to you, not what others expect. Don't let people's opinions limit who you are. You are not living their reality—you are leading yours. Be bold enough to lead your business on your own terms, because you are not here to fit in. You are here to make the people you serve feel seen, understood, heard, and valued. Place your flag in the sand. Make your promise your brand. Your flag isn't for everyone—it's for those who share similar perspectives, and it's these perspectives that make each of us who we are. Invite us into your story. If you make drill bits, don't just offer me a tool to create a hole in the wall. Instead, give me an old photograph on a newly installed shelf, cherished memories of sitting in my grandfather's lap in the backyard as he read a book and opened my mind to the wonders of the world.

AUTHENTIC ADVOCACY: BRANDING WITH PURPOSE

As you consider the future of your business, you can learn from the success of purpose-driven brands that recognize the significance of embodying a clear and meaningful ethos. This change in consumer perspective shows that it is possible to move beyond solely focusing on profit maximization and, instead, prioritize serving others with authentic values. As human beings, we all crave similar things—to feel cared for and understood. When individuals experience genuine care within their workplace, it naturally leads to increased motivation and dedication toward their companies. This, in turn, will positively affect how customers perceive your brand during interactions, leading to them feeling valued and heard. In the end, this is not only beneficial for customer relationships, but it's also good for business.

Showing genuine care and standing for what is meaningful can align your company with important causes and enable you to respond more authentically to both challenges and opportunities. By staying true to your beliefs, you will be better prepared and equipped to navigate today's business landscape.

While not all social and political issues may align with your company's brand and values, it is important to stand up for causes that truly resonate with you. The problem is, many companies struggle to uphold their values and beliefs. But if you have fully embraced the opportunity to make a positive impact on those you serve, then standing up against injustice and fighting for what you believe is right should come naturally. It's a risk worth taking because it aligns with your beliefs.

The downfall for brands often comes when they compromise their principles and values. Companies led by individuals lacking strong beliefs struggle when faced with social and political dilemmas. In such moments, they hesitate and are afraid to pick a side, fearful of losing potential customers if they take a stance. But when Nike made the decision to support and endorse Colin Kaepernick in his fight against racial injustice, they knew it would cause division among some of their consumers.[191] However, this did not stop them because standing up for what is right is at the core of Nike's beliefs. By taking a stand, Nike affirmed their commitment to diversity, equity, inclusion, and belonging. Of course, there was backlash on social media from those who opposed Nike's actions. Some believed it would be the downfall of the brand's reputation. But were those people correct? Absolutely not!

Look at it from a business standpoint. Did Nike permanently lose some customers? Without a doubt, there are individuals who will never purchase another pair of Nike shoes. But we must also take into account the substantial economic influence of marginalized communities, such as the LGBTQ+ and Black communities. According to Nielsen research, the Black population is projected to grow by 22% between 2020 and 2060, and by 2024, the Black community's buying power is estimated to reach $1.8 trillion.[192] It's safe to assume that many members of this community supported Nike's stance.

Target has been at the forefront of fighting for civil rights. After George Floyd's tragic murder in May 2020 by a Minneapolis police officer, the retailer—which has its headquarters in Minnesota—was committed to turning pain into purpose. Chair and CEO Brian Cornell released a statement expressing his team's sadness and frustration with the lack of progress in addressing issues facing Black Americans. But instead of simply issuing empty words like many other companies did, Target took swift action. They saved a job-training program in a low-income Black community from shutting down. They committed to investing $2 billion by 2025 to support Black-owned businesses across the country. They also donated $10 million to civil rights organizations and disaster relief efforts. Additionally, they launched a $700,000 awards program through the U.S. Conference of Mayors to recognize cities implementing initiatives for racial justice and police reform.[193]

The company has since made subsequent commitments to diversity, equity, and inclusion—efforts that Cornell says have played a significant role in the company's growth.[194] Target's strong convictions about doing what is right align with the values held by the people they serve, fueling their growth.

Although it may seem like larger companies have an upper hand when it comes to handling tough situations, it's crucial to acknowledge that all businesses strive to cater to the needs, expectations, and even unspoken desires of individuals who align with their beliefs. As leaders, we will undoubtedly encounter challenging problems, and as consumers, we will make our own choices based on what is morally just for each of us.

Some company leaders might simply choose to overlook their actions and focus solely on profit, but those who truly care about their impact and values take the time to introspect and ask themselves, "How can we improve?" and "What changes can we make to uphold our values?" For companies that don't prioritize empathy or fairness, issues like unfair pay and child labor in their supply chain are of little concern. They don't bother questioning how their suppliers operate. However, compassionate leaders strive to uncover any wrongdoing in their supply chain, finding solutions and addressing problems with transparency and determination. They lead by example, working with their teams to eliminate these abuses altogether.

Numerous companies have already cracked the code on this concept. Within this book, I have selected a handful to showcase. These enterprises have put in the effort and established ethical and equitable supply chains that support communities through just compensation and initiatives for improving living conditions in the regions where they work.

The path ahead presents numerous options. You can take a stand and fight for your beliefs with unwavering convictions, or you can stay on the sidelines and witness your customers flock to a company that stands up for its values and principles.

Which path will you choose?

ACKNOWLEDGMENTS

After I completed the second revision of this book, my father passed away. I had hoped he could hold a physical copy of it as a testament to everything he had instilled in me: love, support, hope, belief, values, compassion, and kindness. When I was growing up, my father was my biggest inspiration. He had an entrepreneurial spirit, and I have countless stories about him that I can tell. But for now, here is just one.

In my early 20s, I visited my dad, who lived in a secluded home on the Bay of Quinte. I shared my desire to become an entrepreneur, just like him. My dad saw this as an opportunity to share his insights with me. He asked me to walk with him along the shoreline, where he then paused to gaze out at the vast expanse of water and share a story with me. "Son," he began, "there are two types of men in this world—you're either a farmer or a fisherman. Which one will you choose to be?"

I gazed at my father with a questioning look, unsure of where his story was heading. I responded, "What are you trying to say, Dad?"

Turning to look at me, my father said, "Son, a farmer tends to his soil before sowing his seeds. He plants his crops at the right time and nurtures them with care. His seeds grow roots and become plants, maturing into harvests that support local economies. A farmer works hard to guide the life cycle of many growing seasons. And even then, he always makes sure to leave behind some seeds for future generations." He then turned to me warmly and said, "A fisherman, on the other hand, plans his days around going out on the water with his fishing pole. He spends his life hoping for that big catch, with some men spending their entire lives chasing after that elusive trophy fish. You must decide who you are—a farmer or a fisherman?"

I thought about his story for a moment and then declared, "A farmer!"

My dad smiled and replied, "Then it's time to start preparing your beds and testing the soil. If you want to start a business, consider how you can help others. Plant your ideas and tend to them with care."

We walked along the shore silently, without any further words of wisdom. Little did I know then how his story would shape my life and remain with me for all these years. Even now, I can close my eyes and still see the bay, still hear his voice fueling a young man's curiosity to be like his father.

After my father's passing, I reached out to a dear friend, Finn, who saw my father as his own. As I recounted the tale to Finn, he reminded me of something: "Your dad was undeniably a farmer, but he also lived on a farm with a river running through it. And now and then, during the season, your dad would go to the woodshed, grab his fishing rod and tackle box, and head down to the river. He'd cast his line and reel in a big fish from the shore."

A smile formed on my lips as I listened to Finn's voice through the phone. It was a small comfort, but in that moment, it brought me closer to my dad in a way nothing else could.

GRATEFUL FOR YOU

I am grateful you chose to buy a book on creating purpose and meaning in the workplace. It takes people like you, dedicated to making a positive impact, to lead us toward a better future. I am humbled that you chose to spend your time reading my words. I hope this book has given you some insight into finding fulfillment in your work and perhaps even sparked ideas on how you can shape a future that enhances the lives of others.

As I wrote this book, I couldn't help but think about the individuals who wake up daily to influence the world positively. They are the ones who motivate us, advocate for us, touch our hearts, and push us to become better versions of ourselves. Thank you.

I am forever grateful to my three superheroes, whose extraordinary abilities have allowed me to see this book through to publication. My wife, Jen, embodies empathy and compassion as an unwavering support system. Doug Humphreys possesses caring and thoughtfulness, while my (late) dad, Stewart Stanley, was recognized as a Hastings Hero for his exceptional ability to show kindness and empathy. This award was given to him at a long-term care facility months before he passed.

This book is a testament to their love, empathy, support, teamwork, friendship, and camaraderie.

I want to thank Seth Godin, Simon Sinek, Ozan Varol, Brené Brown, Adam Grant, Bernadette Jiwa, James Clear, Donald Miller, Bob Burg, John David Mann, Carol Dweck, Verne Harnish, Bob Cooper, and countless others who inspire and make a difference by sharing their ideas.

Collaborating with individuals who prioritize empathy and compassion is an honor—they are constantly motivating me with their creative thoughts and willingness to help others. To those I have yet to meet, thank you for sharing your perspectives and challenging my thinking. You make me a better person.

Special recognition goes to my mom, Betsey Stanley, and stepmom Karen Stanley, Russ Gentner, Dan Good, Finn Morch, Kip Kaplan, Rajiv Jagota, Mark Rienstra, Julie Broad, Yna Davis, Kate Duncan, Holly Akins, Peter Pantuso, Vicki Osman, Harriet Waterman, Maarten Groot, Scott Cosens, Jonathan Berzas, Kevin Wright, Colleen Cawley, Scott West, Wayne Johnson, Doug Robinson, Patricia Cowley, John Meier, and Brad McKee.

I would like to dedicate this book to Jen, whose love and unwavering support have been my constant source of strength. Your "not so gentle" reminders of gratitude hold a special significance for me that goes beyond words.

I am grateful to my children, Nicholas and Nasia, as well as my stepchildren, Grant and Sammie. As I wrote this book, I came to understand that they already value integrity and authenticity in those they interact with and support. They are not afraid to share their viewpoints and live their lives with courage. Gen Z's commitment to their beliefs and values serves as a reminder for us to live with our whole hearts. I hope this book serves as a reminder to continually grow, cultivate, and embrace your individual strengths with confidence by remaining true to who you are. Those who inspire hope in the next generation are the ones who will shape the future.

APPENDIX: SURVEYS

EMPLOYEE ENGAGEMENT SURVEY QUESTIONS

Although there are numerous online surveys available for measuring employee engagement, I suggest creating a custom survey for your organization to track progress over time. Keep the number of questions to a minimum—no more than 30—and tailor them to fit within one of six categories that best suit your needs.

Views on Leadership

1. How effective do you find the communication from leadership regarding company goals and strategies?
2. Do you feel leadership demonstrates a strong commitment to the company's values and purpose?
3. To what extent do you believe leadership promotes open and honest dialogue within the organization?
4. How well does leadership provide clear guidance and expectations for your role?
5. Do you feel leadership actively listens to and acts on employee feedback?

Focus and Direction

1. Do you know the company's strategic goals and objectives?
2. Do you feel your daily tasks align with the company's broader mission?
3. How well do you understand your department or team's specific goals and targets?
4. To what extent do you believe your work contributes to the company's success?
5. Are you confident in the company's direction to achieve its long-term vision?

Workplace Culture

1. How inclusive do you find the workplace environment regarding diversity and collaboration?
2. Do you feel teamwork and cooperation are encouraged and valued in your work environment?
3. Are you satisfied with the level of transparency in communication and decision-making within the organization?
4. How well does the company support a healthy work-life balance for its employees?
5. Do you believe that the company's culture reflects its stated core values?

Learning and Development

1. Are you provided with opportunities to enhance your skills and knowledge through training and development programs?
2. How well does the company support your career growth and advancement?
3. Are you satisfied with the feedback and guidance you receive for your professional development?
4. To what extent do you feel the company values ongoing learning and encourages continual improvement?
5. Do you believe the company offers resources to acquire new skills relevant to your role?

Recognition

1. How often do you receive recognition or feedback for your contributions and achievements?
2. Do you feel your efforts and hard work are acknowledged by your immediate supervisor or team leader?
3. Are you satisfied with the variety of employee-recognition programs and initiatives?
4. To what extent do you believe recognition plays a role in boosting employee morale and motivation?
5. Do you think the company's recognition efforts align with its core values and goals?

Job Satisfaction

1. How satisfied are you with your current job role and responsibilities?
2. Are you motivated to come to work each day, and do you find your tasks meaningful?
3. Do you feel you clearly understand your job performance expectations?
4. How satisfied are you with your autonomy and decision-making authority level in your role?
5. Are you comfortable with the work environment and the relationships you have with colleagues and supervisors?

Dividing the questions into yes/no or rating-scale formats, this survey provides a foundation for gauging employee engagement in your organization. Adapt the questions to reflect your company's culture and branding. The survey is designed to assess progress and inspire discussions about potential improvements at your strategy meeting.

Once the survey is completed, you can visually display the data for the strategy and planning team to review. After the semiannual leadership assessment survey, I will share some mathematical formulas to calculate the results.

SEMIANNUAL LEADERSHIP ALIGNMENT SURVEY

Effective communication and strong leadership are crucial for organizational alignment. When these elements are present, employees do not necessarily have to work in the same office from nine to five every day to maintain this alignment. If individuals understand your organization's purpose and how their work contributes to it, they will naturally be engaged and invested.

Below is a list of the top five survey questions for each of the six core areas of organizational alignment.

Leadership Alignment

1. Do you think that our leaders effectively convey and exemplify a strong dedication to the purpose and core values of our organization?
2. How well do you feel our leaders collaborate and make decisions that align with our purpose and strategic objectives?
3. Are you confident that our leadership team provides a clear vision of where the organization is heading and how it ties to our purpose?
4. To what extent do you perceive our leaders as role models for the behaviors we want to see in our purpose-driven culture?
5. Are you satisfied with our leadership's level of transparency and communication regarding aligning our activities with our purpose?

Strategy Alignment

1. Do you know how our organization's strategic objectives directly contribute to our overarching purpose?
2. Are our strategic decisions and initiatives aligned with our stated purpose and core values?
3. How well do you understand the link between your day-to-day tasks and the broader strategic direction of the company?
4. Are you confident that our strategy effectively addresses the challenges and opportunities that align with our purpose?
5. To what extent do you believe our organization's strategy reflects a commitment to achieving our purpose-driven mission?

Cultural Alignment

1. Are our organization's core values consistently upheld in daily operations and interactions?
2. How well do you think our culture encourages behaviors that align with our purpose and core values?
3. Are you satisfied with the efforts to integrate our purpose and values into our company culture?
4. Do you feel a strong sense of alignment between your values and the values promoted by our organization?
5. To what extent does our company culture promote inclusivity, respect, and collaboration, aligning with our purpose?

Operational Alignment

1. Are you confident that our operational processes and procedures reflect our organization's purpose and core values?
2. How well do you believe our day-to-day decisions align with the company's strategic goals and purpose?
3. Do you perceive that our operational activities effectively contribute to our purpose-driven mission?
4. Are you satisfied with the clarity and consistency of our communication about the alignment between operations and our purpose?
5. Do our operational practices demonstrate a commitment to achieving our purpose?

Employee Alignment

1. Do you understand how your role directly contributes to our organization's purpose and strategic objectives?
2. How well do you believe our organization communicates the link between individual contributions and our overarching purpose?
3. Are you motivated to deliver exceptional results, knowing that your work aligns with our purpose?
4. Do you feel empowered to make decisions that support our

purpose-driven mission in your daily tasks?

5. Do you feel a strong sense of personal alignment with our company's purpose and values?

Stakeholder Alignment

1. How well do you believe our organization communicates its purpose and core values to our customers and partners?

2. Are you satisfied with the level of alignment between our organization's purpose and the expectations of our stakeholders?

3. To what extent do you perceive our purpose guides our relationships with customers and partners?

4. Are you confident that our stakeholders view our organization as aligned with a meaningful and influential purpose?

5. How well do you think our organization integrates stakeholder feedback to improve alignment with our purpose?

Yes-no questions and ratings can be used to gauge if your organization is on the right track with its goals. You can include or remove questions to fit your brand image and company culture. The survey allows you to assess your progress every six months.

Here is a simplified version of those calculations.

1. **Average (Mean)**
   - Formula: Sum of all responses / Total number of responses
   - Explanation: Add up all the responses from the survey and then divide that total by the number of people who responded. This gives you the average, or mean, score.

2. **Percentage**
   - Formula: (Number of yes responses / Total number of responses) × 100
   - Explanation: Count how many people answered yes to a question and divide that by the total number of responses. Then multiply the result by 100 to get the percentage of yes responses.

3. **Scale Calculation**
   - Formula: (Sum of all individual ratings / Total possible ratings) × Maximum possible score
   - Explanation: Add up all the individual ratings given in the survey. Divide that by the total number of ratings that could have been given. Then multiply the result by the highest score possible to get a scaled score.

4. **Response Rate**
   - Formula: (Number of responses / Total number of survey invitations) × 100
   - Explanation: Count how many people responded to the survey and divide that by the total number of people invited. Then multiply by 100 to get the response rate percentage.

Using these employee engagement and leadership alignment formulas allows you to analyze the survey responses and transform them into meaningful data. While I personally prefer to use a radar chart for presenting leadership alignment data, there are many other methods available for sharing the results as well. Survey software solutions can create customizable charts and graphs for viewing the data. Be prepared to present and discuss these results at your strategic meeting.

As a friendly reminder, when you view the outcomes of your first survey, it's important to maintain a positive attitude even if certain scores for employee engagement and key alignment are lower than anticipated. Don't let it discourage you—instead, take advantage of this chance to discuss with your team how to enhance those specific areas.

Conducting the engagement survey once a year and the alignment survey twice a year allows for tracking progress and identifying any trends or inconsistencies in engagement and alignment scores. This information can then be used to develop strategy that you and your team can implement to improve overall organizational effectiveness.

ENDNOTES

1   Randy Pausch and Jeffrey Zaslow, The Last Lecture (New York: Hyperion, 2008), chap. 4.

2   Jim Harter, "U.S. Employee Engagement Needs a Rebound in 2023," Gallup, January 25, 2023, https://www.gallup.com/workplace/468233/employee-engagement-needs-rebound-2023.aspx.

3   Diana O'Brien and Andy Main, "Purpose Is Everything," Deloitte Insights, October 15, 2019, https://www2.deloitte.com/us/en/insights/topics/marketing-and-sales-operations/global-marketing-trends/2020/purpose-driven-companies.html.

4   SWNS, "Most Gen Z and Millennials base purchases on a brand's mission: poll," New York Post, August, 22, 2023, https://nypost.com/2023/08/22/most-gen-z-millennials-base-purchases-on-brands-mission-poll/.

5   Richard Branson (@richardbranson), Twitter post, March 27, 2014, 12:23 p.m., https://twitter.com/richardbranson/status/449220072176107520.

6   Fidelity Charitable, "Fidelity Charitable Study: 86% of Employees Want Employer's Values to Align with Their Own," NonProfit PRO, January 31, 2023, https://www.nonprofitpro.com/article/fidelity-charitable-study-86-employees-want-employers-values-align-with-own/#.

7   Robert S. Kaplan and David P. Norton, The Office of Strategy Management, Harvard Business Review, October 2005, https://hbr.org/2005/10/the-office-of-strategy-management.

8   U.S. Department of Commerce, "Business Formation Statistics, February 2024," news release no. CB24-42, March 12, 2024, https://www.census.gov/econ/bfs/pdf/bfs_current.pdf.

9   https://www.fundera.com/blog/what-percentage-of-small-businesses-fail

10 https://www.bcg.com/publications/2021/deep-tech-innovation

11 https://hbr.org/2013/06/when-ceos-talk-strategy-is-anyone-listening

12 "The Business Case For Purpose," https://assets.ey.com/content/dam/ey-sites/ey-com/en_gl/topics/digital/ey-the-business-case-for-purpose.pdf.

13 "Wells Fargo Survey: Small Businesses with Plans Have Brighter Future Outlook," Wells Fargo, April 29, 2015, https://newsroom.wf.com/English/news-releases/news-release-details/2015/Wells-Fargo-Survey-Small-Businesses-with-Plans-Have-Brighter-Future-Outlook/default.aspx.

14 Jimmie Butler, "90 Percent of Organizations Fail to Execute Their Strategies Successfully: A White Paper to Help You Avoid Being a Statistic," IntelliBridge, August 24, 2022, https://www.intellibridge.us/90-percent-of-organizations-fail-to-execute-their-strategies-successfully/.

15 Team Tony, "14 Reasons Why Businesses Fail: Learn More About Business Failure—and How to Avoid It," Tony Robbins, accessed March 12, 2024, https://www.tonyrobbins.com/career-business/why-do-businesses-fail/.

16 Diana O'Brien, Andy Main, Suzanne Kounkel, Anthony R. Stephan, "Purpose Is Everything: How Brands That Authentically Lead with Purpose Are Changing the Nature of Business Today," Deloitte Insights, October 16, 2019, https://www2.deloitte.com/us/en/insights/topics/marketing-and-sales-operations/global-marketing-trends/2020/purpose-driven-companies.html.

17 Simon Sinek, "How Great Leaders Inspire Action," filmed September 2009 at TEDxPuget Sound, TED video, 17:48, https://www.ted.com/talks/simon_sinek_how_great_leaders_inspire_action?language=en.

18 "The Golden Circle," Simon Sinek, accessed March 12, 2024, https://simonsinek.com/golden-circle/.

19 Dan Pontefract, "Salesforce CEO Marc Benioff Says The Business Of Business Is Improving The State Of The World," Forbes, January 7, 2017, https://www.forbes.com/sites/danpontefract/2017/01/07/salesforce-ceo-marc-benioff-says-the-business-of-business-is-improving-the-state-of-the-world/?sh=1590d8b07eb0.

20 Clayton M. Christensen, Scott Cook and Taddy Hall, "What Customers Want from Your Products," Working Knowledge, Harvard Business School, January 16, 2006, https://hbswk.hbs.edu/item/what-customers-want-from-your-products

21 Seth Godin, This Is Marketing: You Can't Be Seen Until You Learn to See (New York: Portfolio, 2018), 20–21.

22 "High Quality Clothing That Helps Kids Get to College," Story, Merit, accessed March 12, 2024, https://meritgoodness.com/pages/story.

23 "Social Impact," A Dozen Cousins, accessed March 12, 2024, https://adozencousins.com/pages/social-impact.

24 "About Us," About, Sightseer Coffee, accessed March 12, 2024, https://sightseercoffee.co/pages/about-us.

25 James Scott, "Sightseer Sets Their Sights on Sustainability," Austin Chronicle, October 13, 2023, https://www.austinchronicle.com/food/2023-10-13/sightseer-sets-their-sights-on-sustainability/.

26 "Our Mission and Impact," Impact, Helpsy, accessed March 12, 2024, https://www.helpsy.co/impact-report.

27 "We Stand for the Living World," Who We Are, Shades of Green Permaculture, accessed March 12, 2024, https://shadesofgreenpermaculture.com/who-we-are

28 "Live and Work from Anywhere," Careers at Airbnb, accessed March 12, 2024, https://careers.airbnb.com/

29 https://www.benjerry.com/values.

30 "Our Mission," Better World Books, accessed March 12, 2024, https://about.betterworldbooks.com/frequently-asked-questions/.

31 "Fuse by Cardinal Health," Cardinal Health, archived March 27, 2020, at the Wayback Machine, https://web.archive.org/web/20200327110653/https://www.cardinalhealth.com/en/about-us/who-we-are/fuse-by-cardinal-health.html.

32 "The Purpose of Our Company," Investor Relations, Coca-Cola Company, accessed March 12, 2024, https://investors.coca-colacompany.com/about/our-purpose.

33 "Our Mission," Kind, accessed March 12, 2024, https://www.kindsnacks.com/our-mission.html.

34 Yvon Chouinard, "Ownership," Patagonia, accessed March 12, 2024, https://www.patagonia.com/ownership/.

35 "About Us," Philips, accessed March 12, 2024, https://www.philips.com/a-w/about.html.

36 "Our Mission," Starbucks Stories and News, accessed March 12, 2024, https://stories.starbucks.com/mission/.

37 "Love Heals," Our Mission, Thistle Farms, accessed March 12, 2024, https://thistlefarms.org/pages/our-mission.

38 Jake Woolf, "Ryan Seacrest's Secret to Being the Hardest-Working Man in Hollywood," GQ, October 15, 2015, https://www.gq.com/story/ryan-seacrest-interview-american-idol-kardashian-knocked-up.

39 Fred Jacobs, "10 Reasons Why Ryan Seacrest Is Kicking Your Ass," Jacobs Media, January 6, 2016, https://jacobsmedia.com/10-reasons-why-ryan-seacrest-is-kicking-your-ass/.

40 "Cars and Automakers Database," Autoevolution, last updated March 12, 2024, https://www.autoevolution.com/cars/.

41 Vala Afshar, "What Is Customer Engagement? Key Findings from Global Research To Help Your Business Grow," Salesforce, accessed March 12, 2024, https://www.salesforce.com/resources/articles/customer-engagement/.

42 Alison J. Gray, "Worldviews," International Psychiatry: Bulletin of the Board of International Affairs of the Royal College of Psychiatrists 8, no. 3 (August 1, 2011), 58–60, https://www.ncbi.nlm.nih.gov/pmc/articles/PMC6735033/#.

43 "1984 Apple's Macintosh Commercial (HD)," Mac History, posted on February 1, 2012, YouTube video, 0:59, https://youtube.com/watch?v=VtvjbmoDx-I.

44 Matt Weinberger, "This Is Why Steve Jobs Got Fired from Apple— and How He Came Back to Save the Company," Business Insider, July 31, 2017, https://www.businessinsider.com/steve-jobs-apple-fired-returned-2017-7.

45 Steve Jobs, "Steve Jobs on Marketing and Values," PodiumVC, posted on September 13, 2018, YouTube video, 7:39, https://www.youtube.com/watch?v=4mvHgLy_YV8.

46 "Apple Steve Jobs Heres to the Crazy Ones," Nathan Hulls, posted on September 25, 2012, YouTube video, 1:01, https://www.youtube.com/watch?v=-z4NS2zdrZc.

47 Vanessa Page, "The Psychology Behind Why People Buy Luxury Goods," Investopedia, June 29, 2023, https://www.investopedia.com/articles/personal-finance/091115/psychology-behind-why-people-buy-luxury-goods.asp.

48 Guy Champniss, Hugh N. Wilson, and Emma K. Macdonald, "Why Your Customers' Social Identities Matter," Harvard Business Review, January–February 2015, https://hbr.org/2015/01/why-your-customers-social-identities-matter.

49 Gerardo A. Dada, "Buyer Psychology and Customer Value: Why People Buy Starbucks Coffee?," The Adaptive Marketer, September 1, 2014, https://theadaptivemarketer.com/2014/09/01/buyer-psychology-customer-value-people-buy-starbucks-coffee/#.

50 "Who Is Starbucks' Target Market? Customer Characteristics & Marketing Strategy Analysis," Start.io (blog), May 8, 2022, https://www.start.io/blog/starbucks-target-market-customer-characteristics-marketing-strategy/.

51 https://simonmainwaring.medium.com/how-lululemon-builds-community-to-create-an-iconic-brand-ff03d899a85f

52 https://www.deloittedigital.com/content/dam/deloittedigital/us/documents/offerings/offerings-20190521-exploring-the-value-of-emotion-driven-engagement-2.pdf

53 https://www.bbc.com/worklife/article/20220902-the-search-for-meaning-at-work

54 https://www.forbes.com/sites/allbusiness/2022/12/19/quiet-quitting-is-a-sign-of-a-deeper-problem-heres-what-it-means/

55 https://tech.co/news/what-is-coffee-badging-men#

56 https://www.oxfordreference.com/display/10.1093/oi/authority.20110803095606983

57 https://www.businessolver.com/workplace-empathy/

58 Businessolver's 2023 State of Workplace Empathy Report

59 https://www.gallup.com/workplace/393395/world-workplace-broken-fix.aspx

60 https://hbr.org/2022/03/the-great-resignation-didnt-start-with-the-pandemic

61 https://www.businessinsider.com/overachievers-leaning-back-hustle-culture-coasting-employees-work

62 https://www.tiktok.com/@alifeafterlayoff/video/7071415799247949099?lang=en

63 https://www.businessinsider.com/tiktok-coined-the-term-quiet-quitting-now-its-turned-against-it-2022-9

64 https://www.gallup.com/workplace/391922/employee-engagement-slump-continues.aspx

65 https://www.businessinsider.com/quiet-quitting-marginalized-backgrounds-minorities-diversity-2022-9

66 Gallup on State of the Global Workforce

67 https://www.gallup.com/workplace/398306/quiet-quitting-real.aspx

68 https://www.ey.com/en_gl/news/2023/09/ey-survey-finds-global-workers-feel-sense-of-belonging-at-their-workplaces-yet-most-are-uncomfortable-sharing-all-aspects-of-their-identities

69 https://hbr.org/2019/12/the-value-of-belonging-at-work

70 https://hbr.org/2018/11/9-out-of-10-people-are-willing-to-earn-less-money-to-do-more-meaningful-work

71 https://www.wespire.com/blog/15-insights-gen-z-purpose-and-future-of-work

72 https://www.forbes.com/sites/afdhelaziz/2020/03/07/the-power-of-purpose-the-business-case-for-purpose-all-the-data-you-were-looking-for-pt-2/

73 https://www.pwc.com/us/en/purpose-workplace-study.html

74 https://www.quantumworkplace.com/2020-employee-engagement-trends

75 https://www.workhuman.com/resources/reports-guides/unleashing-the-human-element-at-work-transforming-workplaces-through-recognition/

76 https://superman.fandom.com/wiki/Superman%27s_Powers_and_Abilities.

77 https://sproutsocial.com/insights/data/brands-creating-change/

78 https://www.porternovelli.com/findings/introducing-the-2021-porter-novelli-purpose-premium-index-ppi/

79 https://www.porternovelli.com/wp-content/uploads/2021/01/02_Porter-Novelli-Tracker-Wave-X-Employee-Perspectives-on-Responsible-Leadership-During-Crisis.pdf

80 https://everfi.com/blog/community-engagement/socially-responsible-companies/

81 https://twitter.com/TheSharkDaymond

82 https://www.linkedin.com/in/sarablakely27/

83 https://www.businessinsider.com/hobby-lobby-ceo-david-greens-obamacare-statement-2013-9

84 https://www.cnn.com/2021/06/10/business/climate-crisis-ceos-world-leaders/index.html

85 https://www.forbes.com/sites/afdhelaziz/2020/06/17/global-study-reveals-consumers-are-four-to-six-times-more-likely-to-purchase-protect-and-champion-purpose-driven-companies/?sh=67e839ab435f

86 https://www.pewresearch.org/science/2021/05/26/gen-z-millennials-stand-out-for-climate-change-activism-social-media-engagement-with-issue/#

87 https://www.hill70.ca/Accueil.aspx

88 https://www.burlingtoninvestors.com/static-files/619e04cf-2ce4-4760-bff7-685d51bf688b

89 https://www.successacademies.org/results/

90 https://www.drbronner.com/pages/about?6

91 https://www.lemonade.com/giveback-2022

92 https://pacificink.com/?shor=about-us

93 https://www.piperwai.com/pages/sustainability

94 https://janegoodall.ca/what-we-do/

95 https://www.bcorporation.net/en-us/certification/

96 https://www.thebodyshop.com/en-us/about-us/a/a00001

97 https://www.allbirds.com/pages/sustainable-practices

98 https://www.tentree.com/pages/about

99 https://www.cultivatingcapital.com/b-corp-certification-benefits/

100 https://www.radcliffe.harvard.edu/news-and-ideas/ruth-bader-ginsburg-tells-young-women-fight-for-the-things-you-care-about

101 Carl W. Buehner, Richard Evans' Quote Book, compiled by Richard L. Evans (Salt Lake City, UT: Publishers Press, 1971), 244.

102 Carmine Gallo, "The Maya Angelou Quote That Will Radically Improve Your Business," Forbes, May 31, 2014, https://www.forbes.com/sites/carminegallo/2014/05/31/the-maya-angelou-quote-that-will-radically-improve-your-business/?sh=62ea8065118b.

103 https://www.adcocksolutions.com/post/how-emotions-influence-purchasing-behaviour

104 https://hbr.org/2011/06/the-happiness-dividend

105 https://hbr.org/2022/07/motivating-people-starts-with-building-emotional-connections

106 HBR on The Happiness Dividend

107 https://hbr.org/2019/08/the-key-to-happy-customers-happy-employees

108 https://reviewed.usatoday.com/refrigerators/news/meet-the-fridge-that-orders-groceries-and-finds-recipes

109 https://www.smithsonianmag.com/smart-news/the-first-ai-lawyer-will-help-defendants-fight-speeding-tickets-180981508/

110 https://www.cbinsights.com/research/retail-apocalypse-timeline-infographic/

111 Robert Kaplan and David Norton, *The Balanced Scorecard: Translating Strategy into Action* (Boston: Harvard Business Review Press, 1996).

112 Steve Andriole, "Strategy Fails Because Companies Don't Do It. And Companies Don't Do It Because They Don't Know How. Until They Go Outside," Forbes, January 18, 2022, https://www.forbes.com/sites/steveandriole/2022/01/18/strategy-fails-because-companies-dont-do-it-and-companies-dont-do-it-because-they-dont-know-how-until-they-go-outside/.

113 Richard Rumelt, Good Strategy Bad Strategy: The Difference and Why It Matters (New York: Crown Business, 2011), loc. 70 of 312, Kindle.

114 https://consumerist.com/2013/04/09/ea-makes-worst-company-in-america-history-wins-title-for-second-year-in-a-row/

115 https://www.cnet.com/tech/gaming/how-electronic-arts-stopped-being-the-worst-company-in-america/

116 https://consumerist.com/2013/04/09/ea-makes-worst-company-in-america-history-wins-title-for-second-year-in-a-row/

117 https://www.linkedin.com/pulse/when-corporate-greed-takes-overshady-pricing-ea-pratik-vermun

118 https://www.forbes.com/sites/insertcoin/2013/04/09/ea-voted-worst-company-in-america-again/

119 https://www.forbes.com/sites/insertcoin/2013/03/07/ea-just-kidding-about-microtransactions-in-all-games/

120 https://www.forbes.com/lists/worlds-best-employers/

121 https://www.ea.com/commitments/social-impact

122 https://www.forbes.com/sites/petercohan/2019/12/02/best-buys-turnaround-began-in-2012-and-its-still-going-strong/

123 Burl Gilyard, "2018 Person of the Year: Hubert Joly," Twin Cities Business, December 1, 2018, https://tcbmag.com/2018-person-of-the-year-hubert-joly/.

124 https://www.fool.com/investing/general/2015/08/31/best-buys-turnaround-is-one-for-the-ages.aspx

125 https://justcapital.com/news/former-best-buy-ceo-hubert-joly-leading-for-next-era-of-capitalism/

126 https://www.hec.edu/en/news-room/steering-through-business-storm-leadership-lessons-best-buy-s-former-ceo-hubert-joly

127 https://corporate.bestbuy.com/social-impact/

128 https://en.wikipedia.org/wiki/List_of_largest_airlines_in_North_America

129 https://www.worldairlineawards.com/worlds-best-low-cost-airlines-2023/

130 https://www.southwest.com/food-and-beverage/

131 https://www.gray.com/insights/southwest-airlines-linking-strategy-to-excellence-by-abandoning-traditional-practices/

132 https://www.southwest.com/help/on-the-plane/our-airplanes

133 https://www.business.com/articles/southwest-airlines-great-customer-service/

134 https://www.jdpower.com/business/press-releases/2023-north-america-airline-satisfaction-study#

135 https://community.southwest.com/t5/Blog/Southwest-Named-on-Forbes-2023-Customer-Experience-All-Stars/ba-p/165571#

136 https://positivesharing.com/2006/07/why-the-customer-is-always-right-results-in-bad-customer-service/

137 https://www.southwest.com/assets/pdfs/communications/one-reports/Southwest-Airlines-2022-One-Report.pdf

138 https://www.southwest.com/citizenship/people/community-outreach/#

139 https://hbr.org/2019/09/put-purpose-at-the-core-of-your-strategy

140 https://www.forbes.com/sites/markmurphy/2022/10/30/smart-goals-5-shocking-reasons-why-they-might-be-dumb/

141 https://www.dukece.com/insights/optimal-number-strategic-goals-your-organization/

142 https://rogermartin.medium.com/strategy-vs-planning-complements-not-substitutes-ea08e56809d6

143 https://hbr.org/2022/07/the-best-leaders-arent-afraid-of-being-vulnerable

144 https://lsaglobal.com/insights/proprietary-methodology/lsa-3x-organizational-alignment-model/

145 https://www.brimstoneconsulting.com/blog/organizational-alignment/organizational-alignment-patagonia/

146 https://www.leadershipiq.com/blogs/leadershipiq/leadership-development-state

147 W. Chan Kim and Renée Mauborgne, Blue Ocean Strategy: How to Create Uncontested Market Space and Make the Competition Irrelevant, expanded ed. (Boston: Harvard Business Review Press, 2015), loc. 1312 of 3976, Kindle.

148 https://www.mckinsey.com/capabilities/strategy-and-corporate-finance/our-insights/getting-strategy-wrong-and-how-to-do-it-right-instead

149 https://jamesclear.com/goal-setting

150 https://hbr.org/2005/10/the-office-of-strategy-management

151 https://sloanreview.mit.edu/article/toxic-culture-is-driving-the-great-resignation/

152 https://www.forbes.com/sites/brentgleeson/2016/12/08/why-accountability-is-critical-for-achieving-winning-results/

153 https://www.surveymonkey.com/mp/net-promoter-score-calculation/

154 Brené Brown, The Gifts of Imperfection: Let Go of Who You Think You're Supposed to Be and Embrace Who You Are (Center City, MN: Hazelden Publishing, 2010), 67.

155 Betsy Reed, "Ben & Jerry's Lose Bid to Block Sale of Ice-Cream in Israeli West Bank Settlements," Guardian (US), August 22, 2022, https://www.theguardian.com/us-news/2022/aug/22/ben-jerrys-lose-israeli-settlements-palestinian.

Sarah Butler, "Ben & Jerry's Criticises Deal That Will Resume Sales in Occupied Territories," Guardian (US), June 30, 2022, https://www.theguardian.com/world/2022/jun/30/ben-jerrys-criticises-deal-that-will-resume-sales-in-occupied-territories.

156 https://variety.com/2022/film/news/bob-chapek-disney-lgbtq-unrest-1235202205/

157 https://www.npr.org/2022/03/08/1085130633/disney-response-florida-bill-dont-say-gay

158 https://www.youtube.com/watch?v=UYaY2Kb_PKI&t=33s

159 https://www.theguardian.com/world/2019/jan/15/gillette-metoo-ad-on-toxic-masculinity-cuts-deep-with-mens-rights-activists#

160 https://hbr.org/1982/01/can-a-corporation-have-a-conscience#

161 https://conecomm.com/2017-csr-study/

162 https://www.npr.org/2023/03/04/1161143595/walgreens-abortion-pill-mifepristone-republican-threat-legal-action#

163 https://www.nytimes.com/2023/03/07/business/walgreens-abortion-pill.html

164 https://www.cbsnews.com/news/companies-weigh-in-political-social-issues-heres-why-disney-bud-light-target/

165 https://www.cbsnews.com/news/bud-light-dylan-mulvaney-transgender-anheuser-busch/

166 "An Inclusive Future. An Empowered Future. An Equitable Future," ABInBev, accessed March 7, 2024, https://www.ab-inbev.com/who-we-are/diversity-equity-inclusion/.

167 https://www.foxbusiness.com/markets/ceo-distances-anheuser-busch-bud-light-dylan-mulvaney-controversy-not-formal-campaign

168 https://www.nytimes.com/2023/06/14/business/bud-light-lgbtq-backlash.html

169 https://www.advocate.com/transgender/2016/5/12/target-ceo-says-company-wont-back-down-trans-bathroom-policy

170 https://www.reuters.com/business/retail-consumer/target-remove-some-lbgtq-merchandise-after-facing-customer-backlash-2023-05-23/

171 https://www.npr.org/2023/08/16/1194176045/target-sales-lgbtq-pride-bud-light

172 https://www.nytimes.com/2019/10/14/opinion/benioff-salesforce-capitalism.html

173 William Foreman (26 May 2010). "Tech: Apple Supplier Foxconn Suffers 10th Death This Year, Asks Workers To Sign Anti-Suicide Pledge". Huffington Post, accessed 20 March 2024, https://www.huffpost.com/entry/foxconn-suffers-10th-deat_n_588524.

174 https://www.theverge.com/2023/6/15/23760915/tesla-supplier-glencore-human-rights-abuse-allegations-battery-minerals-mining-energy

175 https://www.theverge.com/2022/2/15/22933022/cobalt-mining-ev-electriv-vehicle-working-conditions-congo

176 https://www.reuters.com/article/us-tesla-congo-breakingviews/breakingviews-tesla-kills-three-birds-with-one-congolese-stone-idUSKBN23O1JX/

177 https://www.tesla.com/ns_videos/2021-tesla-impact-report.pdf

178 https://www.tesla.com/ns_videos/2022-tesla-impact-report-highlights.pdf

179 https://www.accenture.com/gb-en/insights/strategy/brand-purpose?c=strat_competitiveagilnovalue_10437228&n=mrl_1118

180 https://www2.deloitte.com/content/dam/Deloitte/in/Documents/risk/Board%20of%20Directors/in-gc-suggested-guidelines-for-writing-a-code-of-conduct-noexp.pdf

181 https://www.caseiq.com/resources/6-essential-things-to-include-in-your-companys-code-of-ethics/

182 https://www.nytimes.com/interactive/2015/business/international/vw-diesel-emissions-scandal-explained.html

183 https://www.nbcnews.com/business/autos/judge-approves-largest-fine-u-s-history-volkswagen-n749406

184 https://www.forbes.com/sites/georgkell/2022/12/05/from-emissions-cheater-to-climate-leader-vws-journey-from-dieselgate-to-embracing-e-mobility/

185 https://marketmadhouse.com/is-chipotle-mexican-grill-the-future-of-fast-food/

186 https://fortune.com/2019/03/08/costco-increases-minimum-wage/

187 https://www.job-applications.com/retail-jobs/retail-salaries

188 https://www.caseiq.com/resources/employee-relations-best-practices-costco/

189 https://www.tradeready.ca/2015/trade-takeaways/innovation-traceability-creating-accountability-in-retail-supply-chain/

190 https://corporate.comcast.com/impact/diversity-equity-inclusion/our-progress

191 https://abcnews.go.com/Business/nike-sales-booming-kaepernick-ad-invalidating-critics/story?id=59957137

192 https://www.forbes.com/sites/jennmcmillen/2023/03/11/black-brands-at-retail-how-target-ulta-amazon-and-others-rate/

193 https://www.bloomberg.com/news/features/2021-08-25/how-target-tgt-police-surveilled-black-neighbors-in-inner-cities

194 https://finance.yahoo.com/news/target-ceo-dei-fueled-much-221502055.html

Made in United States
Orlando, FL
26 March 2025

59871152R00173